THE SOCIAL AP RAI

Related titles from The Macmillan Press

Dasgupta and Pearce: COST–BENEFIT ANALYSIS
Ng: WELFARE ECONOMICS
Pearce: COST–BENEFIT ANALYSIS
Price: WELFARE ECONOMICS IN THEORY AND PRACTICE

THE SOCIAL APPRAISAL OF PROJECTS

A Text in Cost–Benefit Analysis

D. W. PEARCE

Professor of Political Economy
University of Aberdeen

C. A. NASH

British Rail Lecturer in Rail Transport
University of Leeds

M

First published 1981 by
THE MACMILLAN PRESS LTD
London and Basingstoke
Associated companies in Delhi Dublin
Hong Kong Johannesburg Lagos Melbourne
New York Singapore and Tokyo

ISBN 0 333 19303 2 (hard cover)
0 333 19304 0 (paper cover)

Typeset in Great Britain by
PINTAIL STUDIOS LTD
Ringwood, Hampshire

Printed in Hong Kong

For Sue and Claire

Contents

Preface

This book arises from a decision, some years ago, to produce a second edition of one of the authors' texts on cost—benefit analysis (D. W. Pearce, *Cost—Benefit Analysis* (London: Macmillan, 1971)). As always seems to be the case in academic life, various other work projects interfered in the process of finding time to keep up with the literature, let alone finding time for the process of writing. Partly out of a sense of promise to Macmillan, the publishers, who had waited patiently and with reasonable good humour for the planned second edition, and partly because the ideas in the earlier volume needed expanding and revising in the light of more experience in teaching and implementing cost—benefit analysis, it was decided to enlist the aid of a co-author. The current authors of this volume had worked together extensively and it seemed natural to renew the partnership for this text. Even then, one of us, the original author, failed repeatedly to keep promises for deadlines so that, at one stage, Chris Nash's chapters were complete while David Pearce had completed none. Happily, time was found and this new volume is the result.

In virtually all respects the current text replaces the earlier one. Some readers may, however, still find the simplicity and 'overview' status of the earlier volume appealing. What we have done here is to substitute a far more rigorous and, we hope, better considered product. Some chapters may appear 'mathematical' but, with minor exceptions, they are in our view readily comprehensible to the average undergraduate with a little effort. They are also thought to be essential for an understanding of the theoretical underpinnings and problems of cost—benefit analysis (CBA). The text is not a substitute for one other of the co-author's texts (David Pearce and Ajit Dasgupta, *Cost—Benefit Analysis: Theory and Practice* (London: Macmillan, 1972)). That book contains some material we have not duplicated or built upon here, notably the chapters on the relationship between cost—benefit and the social welfare function literature emanating from Kenneth Arrow's famous 'impossibility theorem'.

Since 1972 various texts have appeared on cost—benefit. Ed Mishan's major excursion into welfare theory in *Cost—Benefit Analysis* (London: Allen & Unwin, 1971; revised edition 1975) deserves a special mention for its comprehensiveness. We are not at one with Mishan on the very underlying philosophy of cost—benefit and the two texts therefore need comparison rather than substitution in this one respect at least. We would also draw attention to Robert Sugden and Alan Williams's recent text, *The Principles of Practical Cost—Benefit Analysis* (Oxford: Oxford University Press, 1978). This is an excellent guide to the salient problems of cost—benefit, and the approach is one which proceeds from private financial analysis to social cost—benefit appraisal. This is not, however, one we personally favour. In this text we plunge immediately into the welfare aspects of CBA. Nor would we espouse to the same degree as Sugden and Williams the use of 'decision-makers'' valuations (i.e. prices posited by actual decision-makers, rather than prices derived from individual valuations). But one of the messages of our book is that there *are* differing views of CBA, its value-basis and the degree to which it can (or should) be varied in its application. By and large, our view is that there is no unique method for carrying out cost—benefit studies. Rather, there are many methods, all equally consistent within their own value structures. We hope we make this clear in the early part of the book.

Finally, we have 'extended' ourselves into CBA as it might be applied in less-developed countries. Here we have less expertise to offer and we have largely synthesised and contrasted other work. We felt it necessary to add this chapter, however, because the continued exposition of rules applicable only to developed countries clearly imparts a bias which is unrealistic.

We do therefore think there is a degree of product differentiation in what we have written, and hope readers agree.

We are deeply indebted to Winnie Sinclair (Aberdeen) for her patient and highly efficient typing of David Pearce's chapters and to Claire Nash and Diane Petch for performing the same dedicated service for Chris Nash's chapters. Sue Pearce checked the entire text in an attempt to avoid the authors' hopeless failings in this discipline. We would like to thank a succession of editors of Macmillan, Shaie Selzer, Nick Brealey and Gerard Dummett, for their patience beyond all reason. Undoubtedly, someone, somewhere bears responsibility for the errors in the text. Some, sadly, are our own and we apologise in advance for our failings.

D. W. P.
C. N.

1 Introduction

In 1936 the United States Flood Control Act came into being. This Act might, apart from its laudable aims anyway, have faded into comparative insignificance had it not enunciated a simple but persuasive principle that flood-control projects should be deemed desirable if 'the benefits *to whomsoever they may accrue*, are in excess of the estimated costs' (our emphasis). What this Act did was to introduce, almost inadvertently, the discipline of welfare economics into the practical world of public decision-making. For, whatever its merits and demerits at that time, welfare economics did not recognise limitations to the definition of whose gains and losses from the implementation of some project should count. The way was therefore opened for the assessment of projects first, on the basis of calculating their net benefit and second, in the context of the entire *social* assessment of that net benefit. The combined effect could be construed as being a synthesis of utility maximisation for producers and consumers alike, in contrast with financial appraisal, which looked only at the interests of producers. The principle was an important point of departure as far as the appraisal of public projects was concerned.

While the 1936 Act initiated the idea of cost–benefit analysis (CBA) it would be naïve to think that all projects, even in the limited area of flood control, were subsequently assessed on this basis. Political, random, *ad hoc* criteria continued to be used. Indeed, not until 1950 did the U.S. Federal Inter-Agency River Basin Committee authorise the publication of the so-called *Green Book* (the full title was *Proposed Practices for Economic Analysis of River Basin Projects*), which attempted to lay down clearer guidance on the use of cost–benefit techniques, and only then in the light of a substantial debate since 1936 on the nature of welfare economics. In 1952 the Bureau of the Budget in the United States issued its *Circular A–47*, which also added to the formalisation of the assessment rules, although those rules tended still to be couched in terms of gains and losses to the national product, whereas CBA was to secure its status from attempts to value in money terms gains and losses which had no cash-flow counterpart.

These early attempts to formalise CBA are also interesting in so far as they reflected a belief, still widespread in academic and other circles, that the discipline could in fact be reduced to a set of rules with universal application. Economists still tend to operate with a set of cost–benefit techniques which derive from the formulations produced in the 1960s in which the emphasis was on the principles of allocative efficiency. In the 1970s due regard was paid, in theory and practice, to the fact that social objectives other than pure allocation are both legitimate and in use. One of the messages of this book is that CBA rests on value judgements and that disputes over value judgements are not capable of resolution through some logical process. As such, different structures of CBA can be built up on the basis of different sets of value judgements, all equally 'legitimate'. Debating which approach to CBA is 'correct' is therefore fruitless in the purely logical sense: as long as the practice is consistent with the underlying value judgements (each of which must be consistent with the others used) then that approach is as 'valid' as any other. That does *not* mean that the different approaches should not be compared or discussed; differing value judgements will have differing 'appeal', and one man's CBA may not be to another's liking. But it does mean that we should not be surprised, or perturbed, to find a given project being subjected to studies based on differing value foundations. The answers may be quite different, with one approach indicating potential acceptance of a project and another indicating potential rejection. That may not be aesthetically very pleasing, but it creates no insuperable problem for decision-makers. Quite simply, as long as the value judgements are clearly stated, they can be presented for their persuasive appeal in the same way as one might present different values of any parameter in the technical CBA because of a dispute over the value of that parameter. Chapter 2 elaborates on this thesis, but it is important to present it in outline at the outset.

One of the interesting features of the history of CBA is that it secured its most significant development and advance at a time when the welfare economics on which it was based had come under increasing critical scrutiny. In the 1930s it had been recognised that the Pareto 'unanimity' principle – whereby a policy could be judged socially beneficial if and only if it increased the welfare of at least one individual and left no single individual with reduced welfare – was empty in terms of its application to real-life problems. Quite simply, it is hard to imagine a policy which does not harm someone, even if it benefits others. The restrictiveness of the principle is even more obvious when it is remembered that CBA works with costs and benefits over time so that beneficiaries and losers are not just those comprising the affected parties in the immediate time-period. The 'solution' to the problem was found in the Kaldor–Hicks compensation approaches (Hicks, 1939; Kaldor, 1939). All that the compensation principle says is that a policy is to be judged socially beneficial if the gainers secure sufficient by way of benefits such that they can compensate the losers and still have some net gain left over. If the compensation is exact the losers are automatically translated into the category of persons who neither gain nor lose; they must therefore be indifferent to the policy. But the gainers still have net benefits after the compensation is paid; hence they still prefer the policy in question. The Pareto principle is thus restored and a project fulfilling this criterion would be judged one that generates a Pareto improvement if compensation were actually paid.

The perplexities of the Kaldor–Hicks test are many, and the detailed discussion in Chapter 3 shows what the problems are. Suffice it to say that in the eyes of many economists in the 1950s the problems were held to be so severe, despite some heroic efforts to resuscitate the principle and augment it, that welfare economics was truly dead as a discipline with practical application. There was suspicion that the compensation tests reintroduced the concept of comparing one person's welfare with another's (the so-called problem of 'interpersonal comparisons of utility'); there was the problem that the compensation test could work in reverse — gainers could compensate losers to move to a new situation only to find that, because relative prices had changed in the transition, losers might be able to compensate gainers to move back to the original situation (the 'Scitovsky paradox'); and there was the problem that the compensation tests did not require *actual* transfers of money from gainers to losers, merely hypothetical ones. In respect of the last problem, it seemed legitimate to ask whether 'society', construed as no more than the sum of the individuals comprising it, could meaningfully be said to be 'better off' if the losers still actually lost.

To these criticisms were added a whole host of others on the underlying economic assumptions required for the principles of the compensation test to be put into practice — for example the presumption that prices were everywhere equated to marginal costs of production. Thus, while writers such as Little (1951, 1957) sought to criticise but revive welfare economics, others such as Graaff (1957) declared its demise. The historical oddity is that this academic debate was taking place at exactly the same time that CBA, the practical 'arm', as it were, of welfare economics, was gaining in strength. How did this apparent paradox arise? It may be for future historians of economic thought to consider in more detail, but a general explanation can be offered. Project evaluation had to have *some* economic calculus. The alternative to CBA was, in the decades we are considering — the 1950s and 1960s — a pure financial appraisal. But the context of CBA was one of growing public expenditure and increasing domination of economies by public or quasi-public sectors (road-building, water resource projects, anti-pollution expenditure, and so on). While financial appraisal was often technically applicable, in many cases the 'product' of the project was not a saleable item. Roads did not carry tolls, irrigation projects did not attract charges, and cleaning up pollution did not have a counterpart market in 'pollution benefits'. Quite simply, mechanisms had to be found for appraising ventures that tended to take place in contexts outside markets. Only CBA held out any promise of success, even if too much was certainly claimed for it in its halcyon days. Not surprisingly then, CBA was seized upon as *the* approach to public projects. And of course, once it was applied to public projects and was seen to subsume financial appraisal within its wider framework, so the obverse step could be taken of socially appraising purely private ventures.

What happened next perhaps requires more historical perspective than is possible at the time of writing. By and large however, the problems of actually *applying* the principles of CBA were found to be far more complex and extensive than the early guidebooks to CBA had suggested. Indeed, it is more than a casual observation to suggest that those who most fervently advocated CBA were often those who never practised it. Frequently, the problem was a matter of data and information: these simply did not exist on a scale sufficient for a robust CBA to be carried out. Quite often, however, it was a matter of lack of methodology for evaluating the very costs and benefits that CBA held out most promise for: the 'intangible' items such as aesthetic damage, loss of wildlife, recreational benefits, loss of life, human suffering and so on. Not that all these items lacked one or more methodologies (indeed, they all have their strong advocates still); it was simply that, as the 1970s consciousness about 'non-material' costs and benefits grew, there was increasing disillusionment with approaches that often seemed to require heroic assumptions for them to be applied at all. There was also a more 'political' criticism. When evaluations of, say, environmental costs took place they often seemed to be trivial in comparison with the material benefits obtained from the projects: this was true of road appraisal and airport construction, for example. Yet the political climate suggested a different relative valuation — the environment should have figured more, not less, prominently. In short, CBA seemed to be out of step with political pressures and changing values; yet CBA should have reflected those changing values, proceeding as it does on the basis of eliciting values through simulation of wants and desires in 'shadow' markets. This apparent inconsistency was enough to cause a major shift in attitude towards its worth.

What emerged then was a proliferation of 'alternative' techniques, ranging from disaggregated CBAs, in which aggregation was permitted only for *some* costs and benefits, the others being regarded as non-additive, to virtually physical statements of impact in which matrices of effects were presented to the decision-maker for judgemental assessment. Apart from planning balance-sheets and environmental impact statements, there emerged also goals and achievement matrices as well as other multiple criteria techniques, all varying in degrees of complexity and rationality.

That, in broadest outline, is the current state of play. CBA, for many, is discredited on both the theoretical grounds advanced against it in the 1950s and the empirical grounds that emerged from the attempts to apply it in the 1960s and 1970s. For others the alternatives fare no better and, indeed, could be markedly worse. For those who occupy the middle ground, CBA is best replaced by cost-effectiveness analysis whereby the 'hard' and aggregatable data on costs can be compared to some index or indices of outcome measured in non-money units. The decision to accept or reject then becomes one of leaving a decision-maker to opt for some level of effectiveness judged desirable on some ground or other, but with reference to the resource cost of achieving it.

Just how far CBA *can* succeed is for the reader to judge in the light of this and other works on the subject. There is certainly an argument for suggesting that the pendulum has swung too far against CBA. First, it is far from evident that other techniques are any more successful. Second, the discipline of CBA (or a similar formal technique) at least forces the process of evaluation to *list* all gains and losses and to weigh up their relative values. This may seem a small virtue. But in a world where decisions are made more often than not on irrational assessments, it could remain the single most important attribute of any calculus designed to assist the decision-making process.[1]

2 The Rationale of Cost–Benefit Analysis

2.1 Introduction

A little reflection should indicate that no individual would be rational if he did not weigh up the advantages and disadvantages of a particular action. To whom those advantages accrue is something he will also wish to consider. A *selfish rationalist* would consider the net gains to himself or herself. The *pure altruist* would consider the net gains to those he or she cares for and might well totally disregard personal gain or loss. If, then, we substitute 'benefit' for gain or advantage, and 'cost' for loss or disadvantage we can immediately establish an elementary but useful proposition. This is that CBA merely formalises a common-sense concept of rationality. Note that this does not mean we are virtually obliged to approve of what CBA indicates as far as a proposal is concerned, because (*a*) the detailed structure of CBA will be seen to embody other characteristics which might not be morally appealing and (*b*), in any event, we might not personally approve of the use of a calculus based on the rationality of a whole series of self-seeking individuals. Rationality and moral appeal are not the same thing. All we have pointed out is that, viewed from the individual's standpoint, the cost–benefit approach has the characteristics of individual rationality. Moreover, the costs and benefits recorded are not affected by whether the individual is wholly self-seeking or wholly altruistic.

But the essence of CBA is that it is not confined to decisions that affect one individual. It relates to social decisions about matters which affect a group of individuals – perhaps a locality, a region, a state or the whole nation. Does the characteristic of rationality remain if we extend it to the social context? The basic argument underlying CBA is that this rationality does remain. That is, if we leave a whole group of individuals to carry out their own 'personal' CBAs in respect of a given policy then we can simply aggregate the results to secure a social evaluation. Of course we must know what it is we are aggregating. As we shall see, it is not a set political votes, and for very good reasons. What is being aggregated is a set of money valuations – all positive valuations would indicate that the persons expressing them reckon that the project has net benefits for them; all negative valuations would reflect net costs to the persons expressing them. Just how these money values are formed is discussed in Chapter 3.

To analyse the idea of 'collective rationality' a little further we should now be able to see that adding up 'money votes' in this way effectively allows for two types of 'balance of advantage'. First, each individual will have carried his or her own CBA for themselves. Second, once these individual valuations are recorded, some will show net benefits and some will show net costs. The essence of the collective rationality argument is that it is legitimate to aggregate the individual money votes in such a way that the difference between the votes in favour and the votes against defines the concept of *net social benefit*.

The schema below illustrates what we mean. Individuals 1 to 5 are shown as having various (arbitrary) benefits and costs arising from an individual project. Reading across the rows we see that the net benefits for each individual can be calculated: some are positive, some negative. These calculations for each individual are therefore the equivalent of the 'personal cost benefit' calculations we spoke of above. The 'social' calculation is achieved by summing the net benefit *column* where we see that this gives an overall net benefit of one unit.

Two observations are in order. The first is trivial and it is simply that we could have secured the net social benefit figure by adding the column sum for personal benefits and subtracting from it the column sum for personal costs. The second point is that three of the personal net benefit totals are negative and two positive. If therefore we treated each individual as a single voting unit, three would vote against the project and two in favour, and a simple majority voting system would lead to a *rejection* of the project. But using money values has led to the result that society appears 'better off' by accepting the project. While they need not be inconsistent, 'political' and 'economic' voting systems may well come up with quite different answers.

We look a little more closely at this phenomenon shortly. For the moment we need to understand what the rationale is for this situation. Essentially what is being argued is that if individuals 2 and 3 paid out 12 units of their 13 units net gain to individuals 1, 4 and 5 they would still have 1 unit left over between them, while individuals 1, 4 and 5 would have zero net gains — they would be no worse off than they were before. What is being illustrated here is the *principle of compensation* (the Kaldor–Hicks compensation test). This is dealt with analytically in Chapter 3. For the moment we need to observe only that it is the cornerstone of CBA.

INDIVIDUAL	BENEFITS	COSTS	B – C
1	10	11	−1
2	10	7	+3
3	12	2	+10
4	7	10	−3
5	6	14	−8
	TOTAL	TOTAL	TOTAL
	45	44	+1

2.2   Political Votes and Economic Votes

The very simple example in the previous section illustrates the distinction between the kind of 'one-man-one-vote' principle we are used to in democratic societies, and the kind of vote which actually gets recorded in a cost–benefit study. This difference arises because we have used money values in the CBA whereas in a political voting procedure (of the kind we have hypothesised) the net benefit column would record only a 'plus' or 'minus', indicating a yes or no vote. That is, political voting would involve each of the *numbers* in the final column being unity. They would differ only according to their sign, with, in our example, individuals 1, 4 and 5 recording negative signs ('no' votes) and 2 and 3 positive signs ('yes' votes). The difference comes about because the use of money values permits some expression of the *intensity of preference* in the vote: it enables the individual to say how deeply he wants or does not want the project or good in question. Even if we mark our ballot paper with 'definitely yes' or 'most certainly yes', or 'yes, but only just' it will however still be recorded only as a yes vote.

The fact that economic voting allows for some measure of intensity of preference is just one reason why many economists prefer it to the use of the ballot box as far as the allocation of economic goods and inputs is concerned anyway. The other reasons are even more persuasive. First, political systems, other than in very well defined referenda, involve voting not for issues so much as for individuals to represent the constituent's views. Exactly what the Member of Parliament or Congressman will do when elected is not always clear from the manifesto at election time, and, indeed, there are all too many examples of free votes in which the representative most distinctly does not represent the views of his constituents, and of other issues where manifesto promises are not kept, are forgotten and so on. Market or economic voting is far more faithful to the voters' intentions: by definition if the voter doesn't want it, he doesn't buy it.

Second, even if referenda were desirable they cannot be held every day of the week on every economic decision that has to be made. We might well want to have some sort of public inquiry about fairly discrete issues like new power stations or major roads, but life would be unliveable if everything were subject to special referenda. Quite when the market should give way to some political process is a complex issue. For our purposes it is only necessary to note that all issues cannot be subject to a political process and that the existence of markets effectively acts as a kind of highly developed vote-sensing device. It is largely for this reason that markets are so attractive as a subject of study. *But* this does not mean that we should replace political decisions by market decisions. All that is being argued is that CBA, in embodying the economic voting concept rather than the political voting concept, can provide extra information for the political process. In the view of some it can actually remove the need for political decision altogether. In the view of others the two are so incompatible that CBA should not be allowed to impinge on political decisions, a view we discuss later.

Third, political voting is very much an affair influenced by personalities and, often, purely irrational factors. Voters may often be voting for one issue in a manifesto with no chance to record a 'no' vote for other aspects of a manifesto. With economic voting individual items can be separated out and 'voted' on separately.

Fourth, failure to vote in an election simply results in the outcome being determined by those who decide to vote. The existence of governments brought into being by a minority vote of the whole eligible voting population is not at all uncommon. But in the market a failure to vote is a vote *against* the project: it will show up in a benefit figure lower than it would otherwise be. Besides 'voice' (an expression of a want), the economic system permits 'exit' (the non-expression of a want which is equivalent to a vote against).

Now it would be wrong to exaggerate these differences. Some intensity of preference can be conveyed via the political system by special pleading, lobbying, the facilitating of 'deals' between politicians, sheer persistence, demonstrations and so on. The absence of the 'politicisation' of issues dealt with in the market-place may not always be a good thing – perhaps we should all vote on whether or not a new drug is to be introduced to the market rather than let its introduction be determined by individuals' demand. Market votes are also open to influence from the 'hidden persuaders' of advertising, and so on. None the less, the general theme is correct. Economic votes have attributes not possessed by political votes, so that there is value in finding out what an economic calculus such as CBA would indicate. *How* the findings of that calculus should be integrated into the decision-making system is a matter we discuss shortly, but one cannot secure a sensible discussion without understanding this fundamental distinction between political and economic votes.

As it happens there is a problem with the procedure we have used for aggregating the votes of individuals to secure a 'social vote'. In essence this problem is that while individuals may all behave in the rational manner we have described, collecting their votes together and securing a net overall result may offend some other principles of rationality that seem equally appealing. We leave this issue to an appendix to this chapter so as not to interrupt the general flow of argument.

2.3   Value Judgements and CBA

Extensive confusion surrounds the issue of exactly what value judgements are involved in CBA. The first task is to establish what is meant by a 'value judgement'. We define it as any proposition which, on analysis, can be reduced to the form '*X* is good' or '*X* is bad'. This is simplistic, but will be found to be a valuable general guide. Quite how one further analyses such statements is the subject of extensive debate in moral philosophy. For example, '*X* is good' might simply mean 'I like *X*'. Or it might mean 'I like *X* and you should like it too'. For our purposes this debate is not of central importance and, in any event, we cannot do justice to the sophistication of the philosophical debate. The central point about a value judgement is that it is not verifiable or falsifiable in the way in which an empirical statement is. That is, we do not have recourse to observation of the facts in order to establish whether they are true or false statements. Indeed, one can ask whether it makes much sense to say that the statement 'X is good' is capable of possessing the characteristic of truth or falsehood. Of course, if 'X is good' *means* 'I like X' then there is an obvious sense in which the statement is verifiable since I must presumably know what I like, and 'I like X' would then be true as long as I said it and was not lying at the time. But the general point about empirical verification stands. Indeed it is this distinction that is used to distinguish so-called 'positive economics' (economics dealing with statements which can be verified by reference to facts) from 'normative economics' (economics dealing with how things ought to be) of which welfare economics, and hence CBA, are the main constituents.

Note that the non-verifiability of value judgements is no reason, as many economists have wrongly assumed in the past, for rejecting normative economics as a 'proper' area of study. To see this we must consider exactly what economics is about as a subject. It is about making the 'best' use of scarce resources. But that definition means nothing unless we know by what yardstick 'best' is to be measured. The presumption underlying neoclassical economics is that to have more goods and services (including all things that contribute to well-being) is a 'good thing'. The best allocation of resources is therefore the one that maximises the flow of goods and services in any time-period for a given resource constraint. But any other yardstick could be used — the best allocation could be held to be one which maximises the availability of just one of the contributing factors to human welfare, let us say environmental quality. Or it could be one which yields the most stable form of society measured in some fashion (a low crime rate or whatever). No matter how the yardstick is determined, to make the 'best' use of resources is to imply some value judgement about what the desirable end of economic activity is. We can therefore quite legitimately argue that the meaning of economics itself is 'value-laden' — there must be a value judgement of some sort underlying economics. Value judgements are not therefore something to be *avoided* as if it is somehow ascientific to be involved with them. They are unavoidable. What does matter is that they should be made explicit. The reason why this is important is that, as we have seen, value judgements are not verifiable in the manner we are used to for 'positive' statements. In a prescriptive discipline such as CBA, it may therefore be the case that the result of the CBA will be quite different when a different set of value judgements is used. Whether one set is to be preferred to another is something we discuss shortly, but what we are saying here is that a CBA will be sensitive to the value judgements underlying it. It is therefore important to know what value judgements are being used, what alternatives one might use and exactly how sensitive the result will be to the different value judgements.

Now we are in a position to discuss what value judgements tend to underlie CBA *as conventionally practised*. The previous section indicated that what CBA deals with are economic votes — expressions of money values. Since these are expressed in the market-place (or, as we shall see, in 'surrogate' markets where no market-place actually exists) they reflect individuals' *willingness to pay* (WTP). Willingness to pay for benefits is a familiar concept. Willingness to pay for costs is nonsensical: one would be bearing the costs and paying for them again. What *is* meaningful, however, is the idea of being willing to pay to *avoid* costs that would otherwise be incurred, or being prepared to accept compensation for costs actually suffered. Quite how these concepts are formulated in CBA is dealt with in Chapter 3. For the moment we can see that economic votes will reflect two things: (i) an underlying political vote for or against the project or event in question, and (ii) the power of the individual to pay or be paid. The second aspect demonstrates that economic votes are dependent upon the individual's ability to pay, i.e. upon his income and wealth. This is most obvious if we think of willingness to pay, but not quite so obvious if we think of compensation. By and large one might not expect requirements for compensation to be linked to income but rather to the actual magnitude of the loss involved. However, if we measure that magnitude in terms of the sum of money necessary to restore the individual to his original level of welfare, this will in general be correlated with his income (see Chapter 3).

This simple analysis is all we need to establish the two value judgements underlying 'conventional' CBA. These are

(i) that individual preferences should count;

(ii) that individual preferences should be weighted by some 'intensity' factor which will be correlated with the individual's income.

Both propositions are reducible to the form 'X is good' and therefore meet our simple test for a value judgement. (i) becomes 'a decision which reflects individuals' preferences is a good decision' (or some such formulation) and (ii) becomes 'a voting system in which those with higher incomes have more say than those with lower incomes is a good thing'.

Formulated in this way we can see the difficulties faced by the normative economist. Not all of us would agree that individual preferences should count. Some would argue that many decisions need to be made 'on behalf' of people since they are not always good judges of what is best for society. We do not, for example, generally accept the idea of referenda on capital punishment, speed limits or the safety of new drugs. The second judgement would cause even more problems. As stated it would offend egalitarians, for example. On the other hand, some would argue that the distribution of income reflects differing productivities of individuals and hence differing contributions to the nation's output. If so, perhaps it is 'right' that higher income individuals should have more say. The arguments are endless and will ultimately not be resolved in any sense akin to empirical verification. But that simply reflects the fact that we are dealing with value judgements, not factual statements.

Clearly, however, a change in statement (ii) will quite possibly change the outcome of our CBA. For what it says is that the *prevailing income distribution* should be used when evaluating projects. This is clearly a value judgement. It is therefore open to us to vary it and ask what would happen if we evaluated the project *as if* the income distribution were different. Just how this can be done is shown in Chapter 3. What this discussion demonstrates is that *some judgement about a desirable income distribution is implicit in any CBA*. It is necessary to emphasise this point because there is a widespread and quite false view that any attempt to value costs and benefits on the basis of an income distribution *other than the prevailing one* is tantamount to the analyst 'imposing' his own value judgements on the analysis. But unless the prevailing distribution is somehow sacrosanct, the person offering this criticism has already made a judgement himself about the desirable income distribution — it is the prevailing one at the time of the analysis. There can therefore be no question of an *extra* value judgement being introduced or 'imposed': it is simply a different value judgement replacing proposition (ii) above.

One argument that may be used to justify proposition (ii) — i.e. the use of the prevailing income distribution — is that it commands wide assent. What is being said here can be broken down into two parts. First, that consensus is the criterion we should use for selecting value judgements. Second, that consensus would dictate the use of the prevailing income distribution. The first part of the argument is appealing. After all, decisions have to be made and we cannot leave any decision-making procedure in a limbo. A decision based on the idea of consensus is democratically appealing and, indeed, we could argue that democracy is the general philosophy underlying proposition (i). But even if we do accept this view the second part of the argument by no means follows. For it is unclear how a consensus on income distribution could ever be obtained. We could argue that governments are elected or rejected by the electorate on the basis of what income distribution they offer. But all the evidence suggests that it is remarkably difficult to change the distribution of income over anything other than very long time-periods. Moreover, policies designed to make such changes can have extensive time-lags and may not even achieve their purpose. There is therefore no manner in which we can discern what income distribution it is that is being 'voted for'. And even if we could, those votes may oscillate over time and hence over the lifetime of the project. There is a very real danger then that what the argument reduces to is a justification for adopting the *status quo* income distribution simply because it is the *status quo*. 'What is' becomes 'what should be'.

The way round the problem is to make value judgements explicit and then show how the outcome of a CBA varies with different value judgements. In this way the analyst does not impose value judgements but he does highlight the fact that they must be used. Of course there may be a problem in selecting which value judgements should be used to illustrate this sensitivity. Arguments may exist for and against using proposition (i) for any particular item. But there is little doubt that the most significant area of controversy is over proposition (ii), that individual preferences should be weighted by an 'intensity' factor (see p. 10).

2.4 Criticisms of 'Conventional' CBA

The previous sections have established the *value basis* of CBA. We noted in particular that (i) two and only two value judgements were called for in establishing this value basis; (ii) that the nature of the second judgement — concerning the distributional weighting to be attached to costs and benefits — could be varied without offending any principle of logic or alleged observation about political consensus on income distribution; and (iii) that adopting a second value judgement which did not imply that the prevailing income distribution was, in some way, sacrosanct, effectively defined the distinction between 'conventional' CBA (where the prevailing distribution is used) from 'non-conventional' CBA (where the sensitivity to alternative distributions is indicated). Note that the analyst may wish to advocate some specific distributional objective — if so he or she may simply present the CBA in a form which incorporates the distributional weights they wish to use. We cannot declare such an approach illegitimate — it is, after all, exactly what the conventional analyst does when he calls for agreement on the use of the existing distribution (for such a plea see Harberger, 1971). In our own view, however, failure to operate the kind of 'value-sensitivity' approach we advocate will only obscure the manner in which the results have been obtained and, eventually, bring suspicion and possible discredit on the practice. Of course, in Machiavellian terms, this capacity to obscure the underlying value premises will be seen by some as a distinct advantage of CBA.

In recent years various criticisms have been advanced against CBA. Most of these have centred on the various problems of securing information, on the 'immorality' of valuing unique assets such as human life, and on the ease of manipulation for political purposes, as noted above. But there have been other, more systematic, attacks aimed at the underlying philosophy of CBA. We briefly overview these to see just how far the structure of CBA, as outlined in this book, is weakened.

2.4.1 THE 'LIBERAL' ATTACK

One major attack has come from the so-called 'liberal' school of thought in economics. Exactly what it is that constitutes liberalism would seem to vary according to which author one reads. But essential to the philosophy is the preservation of 'negative freedoms' — the right not to be coerced into doing something against one's will. The argument then proceeds that the underlying value judgements of CBA are at variance with this fundamental principle of liberalism. If liberalism is appealing, then CBA cannot be embraced; and vice versa.

Two statements of the 'liberal' critique can be selected. The first is by Sen (1970). Note that what is being criticised, or argued to be incompatible, is Paretian welfare economics and liberalism. Since we have argued that an extended Paretian welfare economics defines the underlying value basis for

CBA, we may take it then that the 'liberal' critiques are also critiques of CBA.

Sen produces an 'impossibility' theorem which purports to show that 'liberal' values and Paretian-choice rules are inconsistent. Simplified considerably the theorem proceeds as follows. Let there be two individuals 1 and 2 and let their preferences be shown as below where *a*, *b*, and *c* are the alternatives facing them and where the notation *P* denotes 'is preferred to'. Following Sen we let the options relate to a book of which individual 1 disapproves. The options are then

a. 1 reads the book, 2 does not.
b. 2 reads the book, 1 does not.
c. neither reads it.

Since 1 is a prude he would rather no one read the book but, failing that, he would prefer to read the book himself than have anyone else read it. So his rankings are:

Individual 1
cPa
aPb

Now 2 would prefer most of all for 1 to read the book: he gets some satisfaction from making the prudish individual read it. But if he cannot manage this he will prefer to read it himself rather than have no-one read it. So the sequence for 2 is:

Individual 2
aPb
bPc

Now we introduce some liberalism whereby both individuals are allowed to choose for themselves what they read. Since we have *bPc* for individual 2, and *cPa* for individual 1, the sequence now goes *bPc*, *cPa*. Yet *both* individuals prefer *a* to *b* so that a *Pareto* ruling would declare *aPb*. The sequence *bPc*, *cPa* and *aPb* is, however, 'cyclical'. Each option is preferred to each other option such that a social choice cannot be determined. We thus have an 'impossibility' theorem which has been brought about by permitting liberalism in choice.

The basic problem with Sen's approach, as various critics have pointed out (Peacock and Rowley, 1972; Peacock and Rowley, 1975) is that, while he does not discuss the precise nature of a 'liberal' it does not accord with what one might regard as the popular conception of such a person, nor for that matter to the kind of individual characterised by the traditions of liberal philosophy. Essentially, liberalism is concerned with the absence of coercion – the non-sanctioning of social decisions that result from individuals making choices they would not have made voluntarily.

Thus, Peacock and Rowley (1972, 1975) have launched a rather different attack on Paretian welfare economics, namely that the sets of value judgements underlying Paretian welfare economics and the value judgements underlying

liberal welfare economics are in fact incompatible. Since we have already
deduced the two principles underlying Paretian welfare economics, and hence
CBA, it is therefore necessary to see why Peacock and Rowley (henceforth PR)
consider those value judgements to be such that they are incompatible with
liberal judgements. PR define the Paretian value judgements as:

  (i) concern should be with the welfare of all members of society;

 (ii) the individual is the best judge of his/her own welfare;

 (iii) If any change improves the welfare of any one individual without
       reducing the welfare of any other individual in society, then 'society' is
       deemed to be better off.

On proposition (iii) PR note: 'This value assumption, which denies the possibility
of making interpersonal welfare comparisons, is frequently referred to as *the*
Paretian value judgement, so profound is its impact upon Paretian welfare
economics.' (Peacock and Rowley, 1975, p. 9.)

Now on the face of it, there is indeed some incompatibility between the
three propositions above and the two that we derived in Section 2.3. If we
cannot agree on the value judgements underlying Paretian welfare economics
there may be little point in investigating how, if at all, a liberal welfare
economics would differ.

There is little difficulty in fact, since propositions (i) and (ii) in the PR
statement are formally reducible to our first value judgement. Quite simply, to
say that 'individual preferences should count' is to say no more than the PR
propositions (i) and (ii) combined (although the PR statement serves to remind
us that we may be called upon to define 'society' rather more carefully). Note
that PR proposition (ii) is in fact not a value judgement at all, and we have
already discussed why this is so in Section 2.3. This leaves us with proposition
(iii), and this is problematic. In the first place it is not a value judgement at all,
but rather a rule of aggregation. It simply says that given a set of stated
preferences we need some rule for translating these into a social ordering and
one such rule is that stated in proposition (iii). We have already noted how
sterile that proposition is, anyway, since there is virtually no policy that
improves the welfare of some without harming the welfare of others. Moreover,
when once extended by the use of the Kaldor–Hicks compensation principle,
it is quite unclear if the welfare economics underlying CBA does indeed eschew
interpersonal welfare comparisons. For the moment however it is sufficient to
note that PR interpret proposition (iii) as denying the possibility of welfare
comparisons. But proposition (iii) is not a value judgement, even if it were true.
It is a statement about the world, a statement to the effect that it is not possible
to compare directly the utility of one individual with that of another. If we
apply our simple test for value judgements it is not possible to reduce such a
statement to the form required for it to be a value judgement. To be fair, PR
refer to proposition (iii) as a 'value assumption' which may merely be an

unfortunate use of language. In any event, it is not a value judgement and can therefore be deleted from any list of such judgements relevant to welfare economics. This does not deny that proposition (iii) may well be a proposition defining *what we mean* by a social improvement. But that is not a value judgement and nor is it binding — indeed we have seen that CBA uses that rule in a rather different way, namely by engaging in intensity of preference comparison through the Kaldor–Hicks compensation test.

Finally, note that having reduced PR's propositions (i) and (ii) to our first value judgement and having eliminated proposition (iii), we can now introduce our own second value judgement about the weighting of preferences for intensity of preference, a statement omitted altogether in the PR formulation.

If, then, the PR judgements can be suitably reformulated to make them compatible with our own, how precisely does their own set of 'liberal' value judgements differ? Our proposition (i) remains, although it is 'endorsed only with strict reservations' (Peacock and Rowley, 1975, p. 83). Their main reservation is that no Pareto improvements will be endorsed if it results from expressions of preferences which do not value freedom as highly as a 'liberal' values it. An extra value judgement is indeed being added here, to the effect that there are 'higher-order' levels of morality which override the basic value judgement about the importance of individualistic preferences. It now becomes important to establish how those preferences are formed. If they are formed through *coercion* then they will not count as highly as others, if at all. PR elaborate on their meaning of 'freedom' and the interested reader is referred to their book (Peacock and Rowley, 1975) for a discussion. For our purposes we may simply list them as freedom of conscience, freedom of religion, freedom *not* to conform, academic freedom, and the various 'political' and economic freedoms such as freedom of work and choice, and so on. Self-evidently, these freedoms conflict with each other, so that coercion becomes necessary. Your freedom not to work is an infringement on me if I have to pay extra taxes to help you survive: it is virtually impossible to find a 'right to freedom' that does not infringe on that of someone else, and this is the classical 'liberal dilemma'. Moreover, since all individuals are not created equal, there has to be a right to protection and hence to coercion.

Finally, in what could of course be an extensive philosophical discussion, let us note perhaps the most important fact in the 'liberal' restatement. This is that the various 'freedoms', once they are in turn ranked to ensure that the problem of internal conflict is overcome, can often be positively related to the possession of income and wealth. The 'freedom' to choose, let us say, private education is non-existent if one cannot afford the school fees. Unless therefore there is some sanctity in the prevailing income distribution, the value judgement which states that 'freedom' is more important than other rights, duties and preferences (strictly, this is a meta-ethical statement: one which uses a value judgement to rank value judgements) cannot be divorced from that income distribution chosen as being 'desirable'. Either 'liberals' endorse the existing distribution or they endorse some other. Whichever is the case the allocation of 'freedoms' within the economy will vary. And if it varies one can then legitimately ask how sacrosanct 'freedom' is, if it varies with straightforward economic conditions. That is, one would expect the liberalist concept of 'freedom' to be some form of absolute, not dependent upon other value judgements underlying a given welfare economics. But that is not so and hence the PR reformulation leaves as many questions unanswered as it provides moral appeal.

For the sake of summary we can restate the various value judgements of the two philosophies:

Paretian system	*'Liberal' system*
(1) Individual preferences shall count	(1) Individual preferences shall count, subject to:
	(2) No 'coerced' preference shall count
(2) The prevailing income distribution is good	(3) The prevailing income distribution is good
Comment	*Comment*
(3) All income distributions are legitimate for weighting preferences since (2) is a weighting system. The choice of a weighting system *other than* (2) is *not* an extra value judgement.	(4) 'Coercion' is the absence of a 'freedom' and 'freedom' is therefore of higher moral value than other goods. None the less, many 'freedoms' are functionally related to income levels so that the distribution of the good 'freedom' is itself a function of the distribution of income. To this extent 'freedom' is not a liberal absolute, but is subsumed under proposition (3).

2.4.2   THE POLITICAL SCIENCE ATTACK

Section 2.3 indicated some of the most important ways in which the economic votes underlying CBA differ from political votes, where the latter are construed simply in one-man-one-vote terms. Many political scientists have objected to the use of CBA, or perhaps it would be more accurate to say its 'over-use', on the grounds that it already embodies a political philosophy which need in no way coincide with that embraced by those who make decisions. Indeed, some would argue further that CBA has been designed to *replace* political decision-making with a 'mechanistic calculus'. Whether CBA simply assists with the process of decision-making or whether it replaces it, it is evident that at least the prospect of incompatible political philosophies exists, while at another extreme there is the prospect of a specific philosophy actually being used to make decisions without that philosophy having received any sanction from the electorate.

While the above statement is an amalgam of a number of different criticisms it reflects some of the attacks on CBA made by writers such as Wildavsky (1966) and Self (1972). In addition to the 'displacement' and 'incompatibility' arguments these writers tend to stress also their belief that CBA cannot embrace the wider considerations which the political system can deal with. Quite what these wider implications are is never too clear however. Many of these attacks have been based on the view that CBA is an allocative calculus only – that it has nothing to say about distributional impacts. But we have already seen why this is false: projects can contribute to national prestige, foster an innovative image, impinge on civil liberties or whatever. What is not clear then, is quite why CBA is thought to be incompatible with considerations of this kind, since no analyst should engage in CBA as if it ever could *or should* embrace all implications in a quantitative net. There is, after all, nothing wrong in quantifying the quantifiable and leaving the qualitative factors in list form for consideration by the decision-maker. What appears to have happened is that CBA has been seen by these critics as a substitute for decision-making by political means, and this is not what is intended.

Apart from this misdirection, it is also unclear quite what is meant by the 'political process' in these critiques. Sometimes they refer to the planning process whereby local planners decide on projects by using 'planning guidelines'. The difficulty here is that it is very far from clear what these 'planning guidelines' are and whether or not they fit the very simple requirement for rationality stated at the outset of this chapter, namely a balancing of advantages with disadvantages. For others, decisions should be reached by political argument between those who favour the project and those who do not. The use of lobbies and pressure groups will, it is argued, enable intensity of preference to be reflected. There is no great difficulty in accommodating such demands however since no one is suggesting that CBA precludes this kind of political activity. Yet, if this activity is not precluded and CBA is not designed to substitute for it, what then is the point of CBA? The political process will ultimately decide anyway. There is something to this argument, but it is somewhat defeatist and cynical. What it is really saying is that no matter what quantitative exercise one carries out, and no matter how carefully one might delineate costs and benefits, even when they cannot be quantified, the exercise will be ignored in favour of some other procedure the rationality of which cannot be defined. Williams (1971) in an elegant defence of CBA has stressed the uses of rigorous analysis and the importance of continuing to apply economic techniques in a world in which 'political decision-making' all too often means *ad hoc*, arbitrary and occasionally quite irrational decision-making. To this end, small virtue though it may seem, even a CBA *framework* represents an extensive advance on how the decision would be made otherwise.

2.4.3   THE RADICAL CRITIQUE

Since CBA is based on neoclassical welfare economics it will come as no surprise
to find that orthodox Marxists and 'neo' Marxist economists find little attraction
in this aspect of normative economics. Indeed, Hunt and Schwartz have defined
CBA as the 'highest stage' in the development of conventional economics, of
which they disapprove (Hunt and Schwartz, 1972). In large part therefore, CBA
stands or falls for these critics by the extent to which it embraces neoclassical
economic concepts. This it clearly does, when prices which emerge in
unregulated markets are taken as appropriate expressions of individual values.
It is of interest, however, that similar techniques have evolved for use in
conjunction with central planning in East European economies.

But there are two other aspects of the radical critique that are relevant here.
The first, briefly enunciated by Hunt (1968), is that CBA, although based on
welfare economics, has proceeded as if all the criticisms of welfare economics
simply did not exist. These relate to such issues as Scitovsky reversal tests,
second-best theorems, the absence of risk and uncertainty, the identity of
preferences with what is desirable, Arrow's theorem and so on. We have already
noted the force of such views — CBA did indeed evolve at exactly the same
time that other writers seem to have been nailing down the coffin of welfare
economics very tightly. Some of the listed criticisms seem inconsistent however.
One could legitimately argue that it is CBA and project appraisal in general that
have done more to bring risk and uncertainty into economics than any other
considerations. Moreover, exactly how far one considers that the existence of
market imperfections invalidates the technique depends on how far one
considers that appropriate shadow-pricing techniques are available.

The second criticism most often aired by radicals is that CBA ignores income
distribution, or, rather that it assumes that the prevailing distribution is
optimal. We have already considered this issue at length and have shown that
this criticism is quite justified as a complaint against 'conventional' CBA. But
we have also shown that such a criticism is not applicable if, as we argue, CBA
can and should be modified to indicate the outcomes as they would be with
differing value judgements about income distribution.

2.4.4   THE 'MANAGEMENT SCIENCE' APPROACH

One school of thought has argued not that CBA itself is undesirable — indeed
members of this school tend to be its ardent advocates — but that the basic
value judgement about individual preferences counting should be subject to
more question. In essence what is being said is that the dichotomy between
CBA and political decision-making (which we noted in Section 2.3 and in
subsection 2.4.2 above) would be largely removed if decision-makers themselves
provided the valuations for costs and benefits. The analyst is then essentially a
management consultant — he seeks the client's valuations and feeds them into
the evaluation formula. Advocates of this view vary in the extent to which they

would go. First, there are those who point to the fact that it is often impossible to secure money estimates of individuals' preferences. If so, the decision-maker must substitute. We have little quarrel with this, provided of course we are satisfied that strenuous (but not unreal) efforts have been made to secure individual preference revelations. Second, there are those who afford the first stated role to the decision-maker and add that the exercise of securing 'implicit-values' should also be carried out. That is, besides seeking the client's valuation for the items that cannot be valued by reference to individuals, the exercise should look at past decisions and see what valuations were implied in similar contexts. Suppose, for example, the issue is one of valuing lives saved and we are not satisfied that any of the methods suggested for measuring 'willingness to pay' is sound. Then we can look for projects where lives saved were the benefit, but where there was also a cost. If the decision was made in favour of spending the money the lives were worth at least the cost of saving them. If the decision was not to spend the money, then the lives saved were being valued at less than the money spent. One way or the other one can secure minimum or maximum 'implicit' valuations. What one does with these valuations then depends. For consistency they might be borrowed for use in the study under consideration. Or they might first be 'fed' to the decision-maker, who can then reappraise the implied valuations in the light of the figures that seem to emerge (remember he or she will not necessarily have gone through an overt valuation process the first time). This 'feedback' technique is indeed valuable, not only for consistency over time (valuations may justifiably change over time) but more so for consistency in valuations across projects at any one given time.

So, implicit valuations may be sought as a guide for the decision-maker, as a kind of service rendered by the analyst for the client so that the client may impose some kind of consistency test on himself.

Others would go further and argue that, even where individual valuations are available, they should not be used, but should instead be replaced by values sought directly from the decision-maker. After all, the decision-maker is the person elected to make the decision, the process of securing individuals' valuations is possibly complex and surrounded by uncertainty and so on. In this way instead of individual valuations we would secure 'postulated prices'. And there need be nothing to say that this procedure should not apply to the numerical value of the discount rate as much as to the price of a specific benefit.

There are problems with this view. Two main ones can be cited. First, 'the decision-maker' is a nebulous concept referring not necessarily to politicians, but often to one or more paid civil servants who, outside of regimes such as those in the United States, are not elected. They are permanent and do not, in general, vary even with a change of government. It is unclear then what the rationale is for elevating their valuations above those of individuals. Second, there is a basic philosophical problem in that the 'postulated prices' approach rejects not only the first of the CBA value judgements but probably both. The

rejection of the second is of no great moment, as we have seen, since *some*
weighting has to be found. The rejection of the first could however be held to
be morally unappealing and, in any event, generates a problem of its own.
This is that the cost estimates will still tend to be based on market valuations
that in turn approximate opportunity cost that in turn reflects individuals'
valuations of the forgone alternative. On the cost side, then, we are accepting
individuals' preferences as being relevant, but rejecting them when referring to
benefits. Arguably there is no clear reason why this proliferation of value
judgements should occur.

On the other hand, there are many contexts in which individuals are content,
and indeed may positively desire, to leave the valuations of benefits (or costs) to
others. First, the individual may feel simply inadequately informed or find the
issues too complex to make a decision. Provided there is 'trust' between the
individual and the decision-making machine delegation of the valuation process
may be entirely acceptable. Second, individuals may think there is adequate
information but may be unclear about the consequences of any specific action.
Again, 'experts' may have to decide. Third, many individuals do not want the
burden of decision-making, arguing that they have elected representatives to
make those decisions for them. Those representatives in turn must be guided by
those who are, one hopes, responsible to them.

All in all then, one's view of the management-science approach depends on
how far one finds these arguments appealing.

2.5   Conclusions

The underlying rationale of CBA has been spelled out in this chapter. We have
seen that 'votes for and against' are recorded in a particular way and that this
procedure makes some allowance for the intensity of preference of the voter,
whereas political systems tend not to. This said, there is an aggregation problem
in that individual preferences based on a simple concept of rationality may not
themselves be capable of being combined to form an expression of social net
benefit without offending other reasonable rules for collective rationality.
However, pursuing this line of reasoning it was observed that CBA rested on
specific value judgements — far fewer than are normally listed in works on the
subject — and that no defence could be made for the conceptual distinction
between allocative and distributional aspects of CBA. A distributional
judgement is made whether the analyst wishes to make it or not.

We then considered the objections to CBA as a philosophy, and saw that the
attacks have come from both radicals and conservatives (the latter being the
group that dubs itself 'liberal'). How far the radical attack is accommodated
depends on one's entire view of the neoclassical economics' structure. How far
the 'liberals' are correct depends on the strength of their view that 'freedoms'
are goods which must themselves be ranked in order of merit and on the extent

to which those 'freedoms' can be seen as being independent of income distribution. We argued in this chapter that they could not be.

APPENDIX

Arrow's Impossibility Theorem

The general result of Arrow's theorem is that individual preferences cannot be aggregated in such a way that a consistent *social* ordering of alternatives can be obtained without offending principles which seem 'reasonable'. The proof is as follows (for details see Arrow, 1963).

1 Social choice should have the same set of relationships as individual choice, i.e. transitivity, reflexiveness, etc.
2 Condition 1 — the Free Triple Condition.
   Given any three alternatives, no matter what the individual orderings of these alternatives are, the social welfare function must give rise to a (connected and transitive) social ordering. In effect this means that the aggregation rule represented by the social welfare function must apply to all logically possible sets of individual orderings and not just to a selected few.
3 Condition 2 — Non-negative Association.
   If one alternative social state rises or remains still in the ordering of every individual without any other change in those orderings we shall expect it to rise, or at least not to fall, in the social ordering.
      This condition is referred to as the condition of Non-negative Association between individual orderings and the social ordering. It is in essence an expression of the basic value judgement that individual preferences should count.
4 Condition 3 — Independence of Irrelevant Alternatives.
   The social ordering of a set of alternatives should depend only on the orderings by individuals over this set and not on the existence or ordering of alternatives outside this set.
      Thus, the social ranking among states in any set depends only on the individual rankings of states over the elements of that set. Hence, if one alternative is deleted from the set, the choice between the rest is not affected thereby. At the same time the social ordering depends only on individual orderings and not, for example, on their intensities of preference.
5 Condition 4 — Non-imposition.
   It must always be the case that society can express a preference between a

pair of alternatives if those alternatives have preferences stated for them by the individual members of society. Quite simply, we can 'remove' certain preference relationships from the social ordering.

6   Condition 5 — Non-dictatorship.

The social welfare function must not be dictatorial, i.e. social orderings should not be determined solely by the preferences of a particular individual member of society.

In other words, there should be no individual such that, whenever he strictly prefers x to y, society strictly prefers x to y, no matter what other individuals' preferences are.

Arrow's theorem then states that no social ordering can exist which simultaneously satisfies Conditions 1—5 above. For further discussion see Dasgupta and Pearce (1972, ch. 3).

3 The Welfare Foundations of Cost–Benefit Analysis

3.1 Social Appraisal in a World of Identical Consumers

The basic requirement needed to judge projects in accordance with the individual preferences of consumers as outlined in Chapter 2, is a measure of the strength of consumers' preferences for the benefits of the project at hand relative to the benefits that those resources could have yielded in their next best use. This comparison is clearly facilitated if the various benefits and opportunity costs in question are expressed in terms of a common 'measuring-rod', and the presence of market prices, appearing to express values in terms of just such a common unit, made existing market values the obvious choice of unit for early cost–benefit appraisals. The circumstances in which the use of unadjusted market prices to value costs and benefits was found to be consistent with the value judgements underlying the appraisal came to be appreciated only much later.

Consider first an economy in which all consumers have identical tastes, given by the ordinal utility function $U = U(X_1 \ldots X_n)$, identical incomes (Y), and face identical fixed prices for goods ($P_1 \ldots P_n$). If consumers are able freely to allocate their money incomes between all goods and services then, subject to the usual assumptions of rationality and perfect knowledge, they will maximise the following expression:

$$Z = U(X_1 \ldots X_n) - \lambda[Y - \Sigma P_i X_i]. \tag{3.1}$$

First-order conditions for a maximum are

$$\frac{\partial Z}{\partial X_i} = \frac{\partial U_i}{\partial X_i} - \lambda P_i = 0 \qquad \text{for all } i. \tag{3.2}$$

Or

$$\frac{\partial U_i}{\partial X_i} \bigg/ \frac{\partial U_j}{\partial X_j} = \frac{P_i}{P_j} \qquad \text{for all } i, j. \tag{3.3}$$

This is the well-known condition that the consumer equates his marginal rate of substitution between each pair of goods with the price ratio.

Suppose now that a project yields increased production of certain goods (i to k) at the expense of diverting resources from production of goods (l to n). Assuming that these changes in output are also distributed equally among all consumers (and ignoring for the moment the problem that prices will change as well), we may test whether the consumers are more or less content with the new situation by simply examining the sign of $\sum_i P_i \, dX_i$. For, substituting in from the first-order conditions above,

$$\sum_i P_i \, dX_i = \frac{1}{\lambda} \sum_i \frac{\partial U_i}{\partial X_i} \, dX_i. \qquad (3.4)$$

If this is positive, the value of U is increased. In other words, under the assumptions stated, relative prices provide a perfect measure of the relative benefit of changes in output in terms of consumer preferences.

Note, however, that to compute this measure we had to know not only the additional amounts of goods (i to k) produced by the project, but also the amounts of goods (l to n) forgone by the diversion of resources. It is highly unlikely that this could ever be predicted for a particular project. What is usually known are the amounts of inputs of factors of production and inter-mediate goods required, and their market prices. Is the total value of inputs any guide to the value of the output forgone?

Let F_{ji} represent the amount of factor (or intermediate good) j devoted to the production of final good i. We are concerned to measure $\sum_{i=1}^{n} P_i \, dX_i$. Now dX_i may be written

$$\sum_j \frac{\partial X_i}{\partial F_{ji}} \, dF_{ji}$$

(in words, the change in output of i is equal to the sum of the changes in inputs devoted to i multiplied by the marginal product of each input). Thus

$$\sum_{i=1}^{n} P_i \, dX_i = \sum_{i=1}^{n} \sum_j P_i \frac{\partial X_i}{\partial F_{ji}} \, dF_{ji}. \qquad (3.5)$$

It is now clear that the market value of the inputs diverted from other uses will equal the value of the outputs forgone if

$$P_i \frac{\partial X_i}{\partial F_{ji}}$$

(the value of the marginal product of input j in production of output i) is equal to the market price of input j (W_j). For we may then write

$$\sum_{i=1}^{n} P_i \, dX_i = \sum_{i=1}^{n} \sum_j W_j \, dF_{ji}. \qquad (3.6)$$

Our measure of net benefit may then be rewritten

$$\sum_{i=1}^{n} P_i \, dX_i = \sum_{i=1}^{k} P_i \, dX_i + \sum_{i=l}^{n} \sum_j W_j \, dF_{ji} \qquad (3.7)$$

(in words, the benefits of the project are measured by the market value of the outputs produced less the market value of the inputs diverted from other uses for implementation of the project).

The conditions necessary for the market value of outputs to represent their relative value in terms of consumer preferences were not particularly stringent. Nothing needed to be said about the state of competition or production planning within the production sector of the economy. Unfortunately the same does not hold for the conditions necessary for the market prices of inputs to represent the opportunity cost of outputs forgone. It is well known that the condition that the price of inputs equals the value of their marginal product will be satisfied in a perfectly competitive economy, but is likely to be infringed by the presence of monopoly power or external effects in *either* the final output market *or* the input market. For instance, a profit-maximising monopolist will raise the price of his product above the marginal cost of producing it (i.e. $P_i > W_j [dX_i/dF_{ji}]$). Similarly, a monopsony buyer of labour will be able to lower its price below the value of its marginal product to the same effect. It is possible that government intervention — in the form of taxes or controls — may offset such effects, or indeed that the required condition may be achieved in a centrally planned economy. All that is required is that, for whatever reason, the condition that the prices of all factors and intermediate goods equal the value of their marginal products should hold. Unfortunately neither competition nor government planning are often this perfect in practice. What to do when these conditions do break down is the subject of succeeding chapters, but in this chapter, our concern is with the initial assumption that all consumers are identical in terms of tastes and income.

Suppose that first we relax only the assumption of identical incomes. If all consumers have identical tastes, and face identical prices, then clearly a ranking of individuals in terms of money incomes will also represent a ranking in terms of real incomes. As long as all goods are consumed to some degree by all income groups, market prices will still reflect relative marginal valuations for each individual taken separately. Thus one might still compute $\sum_i P_i \, dX_i$ for each individual as a test of whether he has gained or lost from the project in question. In the unlikely event of all consumers experiencing exactly the same change in their levels of consumption of all goods, then — given that all individuals face identical market prices — the result will be the same for every individual, and there is no problem of distribution of effects. This result is unlikely, however, as the changes in consumption of various goods will usually differ according to the income of the consumer in question. Some income groups will not consume certain goods at all, as for example Rolls-Royces. Consequently, it is quite possible for a project to lead to a positive value of $\sum_i P_i \, dX_i$ for some consumers, and to a negative value for others. We cannot then judge the project as good or bad without making a value judgement about its distributive effects.

3.2   Cardinal Utility and Cost—Benefit Analysis

One way out of this dilemma, often to be found explicitly or implicitly in the literature, is the adoption of a 'Benthamite' objective function that maximises the sum of individual (cardinal) utilities, (i.e. $SW = \sum_h U_h$ where the subscript h denotes the individual to whom the utility function applies), and the assumption that the marginal utility of money income (λ) is identical for all individuals. In this case, we may simply sum equation (3.4) above across all individuals to obtain the social worth of a project, i.e.

$$dSW = \sum_h \sum_i \frac{\partial U_{ih}}{\partial X_{ih}} \cdot dX_{ih} = \lambda \sum_h \sum_i P_i \, dX_{ih} = \lambda \sum P_i \, dX_i \qquad (3.8)$$

where the h subscript denotes the individual to whom the utility function and quantity X_i apply. In other words, the procedure of simply valuing changes in output at market prices is again justified. However, there are serious problems with this approach.

First, in appealing to a particular objective function as a basis for our procedure, we are going above and beyond individual preferences as a basis for our system of social valuation, unless it should be the case that all individuals are in agreement on the welfare function to be used. In the absence of such unanimity, it is impossible to base the choice of an objective function on individual preferences alone. Some rule to determine how individual preferences are to be aggregated has to be imposed from outside. Thus any claim that cost—benefit analysis provides unique answers, given only the value judgement that individual preferences are to decide the issue, will have to be forgone (see Chapter 2).

Second, the assumption that the marginal utility of money income (λ) is identical for all individuals is untenable. If incomes differ while tastes are identical, this assumption clearly does not hold. For it to hold when incomes and tastes both differ would require money income to be distributed in such a way that it yielded the greatest aggregate utility to all consumers. In other words, one requires the assumption that the distribution of income is optimal in terms of the objective function at hand. But there is no good reason why such optimality should come about by chance; and if it is deemed to be the result of government action, then that government must not only have found a way of measuring each individual's (cardinal) utility function but also possess the instruments to achieve the necessary redistribution to the full.

If it is desired to adopt this objective function, it would seem essential to find a way of measuring variations in the marginal utility of income across individuals in order to convert measures of costs and benefits at market prices into measures of the change in utility of the individuals affected. Attempts have been made to estimate the elasticity of the marginal utility of income (β) with respect to money income. Given the value of β, one could measure the change in social welfare as

$$\mathrm{dSW} = \sum_h \sum_i \frac{\partial U_{ih}}{\partial X_{ih}} \, \mathrm{d}X_{ih} = \sum_h \sum_i \lambda_h P_i \, \mathrm{d}X_{ih}. \qquad (3.9)$$

Treating λ_j (the marginal utility of money income for the jth individual) as the numéraire, one may write

$$\mathrm{dSW} = \sum_h \sum_i \frac{\lambda_h}{\lambda_j} P_i \, \mathrm{d}X_{ih}. \qquad (3.10)$$

But if λ_h is related to income (Y_h) by the constant elasticity function $\lambda_h = \alpha Y_h^\beta$ then

$$\frac{\lambda_h}{\lambda_j} = \left(\frac{Y_h}{Y_j}\right)^\beta. \qquad (3.11)$$

Thus

$$\mathrm{dSW} = \sum_h \sum_i \left(\frac{Y_h}{Y_j}\right)^\beta P_i \, \mathrm{d}X_{ih}. \qquad (3.12)$$

(In words, one first finds the net benefit to each income group and then weights it by the ratio of its income to that of the reference group, raised to the power of the elasticity of the marginal utility of income.)

One study which attempted to measure β (Theil and Brooks, 1970) found a value of approximately -2. However, such studies require the extreme assumption that the utility function is additively separable and unique; empirically, the absolute value of β will be arbitrary if monotonic transformations of the utility function are equally admissible. (See Appendix.) (They also require maintaining the assumption of identical tastes within the set of consumers of differing incomes across which the function is estimated.) Thus most economists remain unshaken in their belief in the impossibility of measuring differences in the marginal utility of income across individuals. As a consequence, this approach to the treatment of distributive effects appears inoperable.

3.3   Compensation Tests

The foundations of a totally different approach to social appraisal of projects which purports to be able to deal with situations in which both tastes and incomes differ are based on the Hicks–Kaldor compensation test (Hicks, 1939; Kaldor, 1939). Under this test, if the beneficiaries from a project remain on a higher indifference curve after paying sufficient compensation to return the losers to the indifference curve they would be on in the absence of the project, the project is deemed desirable. Now of course, if the full compensation is actually paid, implementation of the project brings about a Pareto improvement in welfare (i.e. it makes some people better off without making anyone worse off). Seen as an isolated event then, implementation of the project would clearly be desirable under these circumstances as long as the Paretian value judgements are accepted. This would not be the case however, if compensation were not paid and the move were only a *potential* Pareto improvement in welfare. In practice full compensation is not paid, especially since, when one is choosing between projects as is most usually the case in project appraisal, this would have to include compensation for benefits forgone as a result of non-implementation of alternatives, as well as for any actual worsening in the position of certain individuals. And, even if the practical problems in assessing and awarding such compensation could be overcome, one cannot say whether it is desirable that compensation be paid or not, in the absence of specific value judgements as to which of the two distributions of income is superior. Nor can one say that a project which passes the compensation test is necessarily superior to one which does not; the latter may be so attractive on distributive grounds as to be judged superior to the former. As a way of avoiding the need to make distributional judgements in appraising projects, the pure Pareto approach is then of little use.

But what can be said in favour of the potential Pareto improvement in welfare as a criterion? The main justification for its adoption seems to be as follows. Let us suppose that the two objectives of efficiency and equity may be examined separately, and that project selection is to take place solely with respect to the efficiency objective. An efficient situation is one in which it is impossible to make anyone better off without making someone else worse off: therefore a situation cannot be efficient if any project yielding a potential Pareto improvement in welfare is left undone. Applying the compensation test consistently throughout the economy will ensure that we always reach a position of Paerto optimality. While ensuring in this way that we reach some position on the welfare frontier, we may use taxation and income supplementation as policy instruments to move along the frontier to our chosen distribution of income (Musgrave, 1969).

This argument may sound attractive enough. Unfortunately even if the presumptions on which it is based were true, it still does not avoid the need to make distributional judgements in the social appraisal of projects. For choice of projects will still be influenced by the distribution of income that is regarded as optimal. Consider an economy comprising two persons X and Y. In Figure 3.1, schedule I illustrates the alternative combinations of ordinal utility open to the two consumers if a particular project is implemented. Schedule II illustrates the possibilities if it is not. There is no reason why the two schedules should not cross one or more times (Samuelson, 1950). For instance, suppose that the project in question will establish a plant for the production of luxury goods for domestic consumption. If the optimal distribution is regarded as existing at a point such as A' or B' (where income is very unequally distributed) then it is likely that implementation of the project will pass the compensation test. The

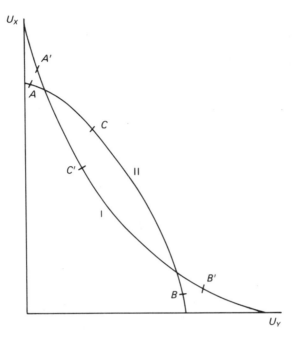

FIGURE 3.1

existence of one very wealthy consumer will ensure that he is willing to pay
sufficient compensation to the less-well-off consumer to compensate him for
diverting resources into the production of the luxury good in question. Thus
schedule I will pass north-east of schedule II in the diagram at these
distributions. Consequently, if we are starting from a point such as *A* or *B* on
schedule II, after implementing the project we may attain a position such as *A'*
or *B'* on schedule I. A move from *A* to *A'* or from *B* to *B'* raises the utility level
of both consumers, and therefore implementation of the project must pass the
compensation test. Suppose now, that the optimal income distribution is more
egalitarian, as it is at points *C* and *C'*. Here, neither consumer is sufficiently
wealthy to wish to spend a lot of money on the luxury good, and its introduction
(a move from *C* to *C'*) fails the compensation test. For there is no way, after
implementing the project, of reaching a point north-east of point *C* — one
consumer will always remain worse off as a result of its implementation. Only if
the two schedules happened not to intersect could we say whether implementation of the project passed the compensation test without reference to the
distribution of income.

   The appropriate procedure for applying the compensation test in circumstances in which the current distribution of income is non-optimal but is to be

rectified by fiscal means, is then as follows:

(i) Make the value judgement about what distribution of income is deemed desirable.

(ii) Estimate the outcome of the compensation test assuming that distribution of income to have been reached. A simple procedure to approximate this result is to assume that the cost or benefit in question is subject to a constant income elasticity (β). Thus the observed valuation of the ith income group (B_i) will be given by the formula

$$B_i = \alpha Y_i^\beta$$

where Y_i is the ith group's income level.

If the desired income level for this group is Y_i', then the appropriate adjusted cost or benefit measure (B_i') is given by

$$B_i' = B_i \left(\frac{Y_i'}{Y_i}\right)^\beta. \tag{3.13}$$

Only if $Y_i' = Y_i$ — that is, the current income level of the group is deemed optimal — will the unadjusted measure be valid.

But the above approach makes an assumption which is often unwarranted. It assumes that it will be possible to redistribute income between groups on the basis of money incomes and a limited set of personal circumstances. Whenever projects harm or aid specific groups in terms of location or taste, it is unlikely to be possible to achieve such a redistribution through the tax system. (Local property taxes might make this easier, but they would need to be far more flexible, equitable and therefore complicated than the current United Kingdom rating system.) In any event, tax rates are determined with respect to a host of political and macro-economic considerations, as well as to their possible effects on incentives. That they provide an alternative and superior method of influencing the distribution of income to that of project selection is not necessarily the case.

Suppose we accept that the project we are evaluating will have distributive consequences, and that these will not be compensated for by fiscal action. It is in these circumstances that the Scitovsky paradox may arise (Scitovsky, 1941): that is, implementation of the project may involve shifting from a point such as *A* or *B* in Figure 3.1 to a point such as *C'*. In this case, at the initial distribution of income, implementation of the project satisfies the compensation test, for it will be possible to move from *A* or *B* on schedule II to a point such as *A'* or *B'* on schedule I, at which both consumers are better off. However implementation of the project itself shifts the income distribution to *C'*, from which a move to abandon the project and move to a point such as *C* will in itself satisfy the compensation test.

TABLE 3.1

Project	A	B	C	D
Satisfied compensation test	√	√	√	X
Scitovsky paradox does not arise	√	√	√	X
Distributive effects favourable	√	√	X	√

Even if this problem does not arise, we can no longer justify projects in terms of potential Pareto improvements when in practice these cannot take place. One way out of this dilemma is to argue for a three-part criterion, in which a project is justified only if it satisfies the compensation test, does not lead to a Scitovsky paradox situation, and improves the distribution of income (Little, 1957). Unfortunately, such a criterion is of limited use in practical decision-taking. Typically, project evaluators find themselves ranking projects which are mutually exclusive, if not for technical reasons then simply because of the presence of a budget constraint. Now suppose one is evaluating projects A, B, C and D, and that the findings with respect to the Little criterion are as in Table 3.1. It appears that either project A or B is justified under the three-part criterion. However, project C or D may be preferred; project C because it offers such great net benefits that these outweigh its harmful distributive effects, or project D because its beneficial effects on distribution are sufficient to outweigh all else. Even if projects C and D are rejected, one still has to compare projects A and B. The move from one to the other measured in terms of incremental costs and benefits may satisfy the three-part criterion, but if it does not, we shall likewise be unable to rank these two projects. The likelihood of being unable to rank projects under the Little criterion severely restricts its practical usefulness; in many cases, there will be no alternative but to adopt a distributive weighting system, explicitly to trade off the costs and benefits to different groups of society against each other.

3.4   Distributive Weighting Systems

We have already introduced one set of adjustments, or weights, to be applied to costs and benefits when the existing distribution of income is non-optimal and redistribution is to be achieved by other (e.g. fiscal) means unrelated to project appraisal. In the situation where this redistribution of income is inappropriate because an optimal distribution of income cannot be achieved by these other means, one is forced back to trading off costs and benefits to different groups against each other. This implies converting money measures of costs and benefits into a measure of the social utility of the effects. The approach, then, has much in common with our earlier discussion of cardinal utility measurement of costs and benefits. This time, however, one is not relying on measurement of the marginal utility of money to derive the weights; instead the weights will simply be based on the preferences of the decision-taker regarding distribution. For instance, if the weights are assumed to be linear, one may measure net social benefit (NSB) as follows:

$$\text{NSB} = \sum_i \alpha_i (B_i - C_i) \tag{3.14}$$

where α_i is the distributive weight attached to costs and benefits accruing to the ith income group.

The weights, α_i, could take any form according to the value judgements on which they are based. One such value judgement is that they should seek to give equal weight to the preferences of all consumers. It has been suggested that this might be achieved by making the weights equal to the ratio of the mean income in the economy to the current income of the consumer concerned (Foster, 1966), i.e.

$$B_i' = B_i \left(\frac{\bar{Y}}{Y_i} \right) \tag{3.15}$$

where $\bar{Y}$ is the mean income level of the community.

The effect of this is to adjust cost and benefit figures to the value the recipient would place on them if he had the mean income but still devoted the same proportion of his income to each good. Benefits with an income elasticity of demand greater than one will continue to be more highly valued by the rich than by the poor even after adjustment, and vice versa for income-inelastic benefits. Thus the method can only be said to give equal weight to the preferences of each income group if it is used to evaluate a full range of costs and benefits whose income elasticity of demand in aggregate equals one. Where it is being used to evaluate a small number of projects, it may be preferable to take variations in income-elasticity of demand into account and adjust by the formula

$$B_i' = B_i \left(\frac{\bar{Y}}{Y_i} \right)^\beta . \tag{3.16}$$

This is equivalent to evaluating projects as though income were equally distributed, and as such is a special case of the formula given in the previous section (Nash, Pearce and Stanley, 1975).

However, in the circumstances we are currently discussing, it is not clear why we should wish to evaluate projects as though the distribution of income were equal, even if we viewed an egalitarian distribution of income as optimal. While in the previous section we assumed that an egalitarian distribution of income was attainable, we are now dealing with a situation in which there are constraints preventing an optimal distribution of income from being attained. In this case, we may well wish to use project selection itself as a positive way of redistributing income, rather than as merely offsetting the extra weight given to the preferences

TABLE 3.2   Variation of Weight Attached to Costs and Benefits with Income and Value of γ

Income Level	Value of γ			
	1	2	3	4
$\frac{1}{4}\bar{Y}$	4	16	64	256
$\frac{1}{2}\bar{Y}$	2	4	8	16
$\bar{Y}$	1	1	1	1
$2\bar{Y}$	0.5	0.25	0.125	0.0625

of the better-off by the use of market value. The result is to introduce a further set of weights based purely on a notion of equity; that is to say, determined solely by value judgement (Atkinson, 1973). These weights may be based solely on the income level of the recipient of the cost or benefit, or they may take into account other factors. For instance, extra weight may be given to those who suffer from a particularly bad environment or from physical or mental disability, while reduced or zero weight may be given to the preferences of those committing serious crimes. Once again, the weights could take any form, but the simplest to manipulate may well be of a constant elasticity form

$$W_i = \left(\frac{\bar{Y}}{Y_i}\right)^{\gamma}. \tag{3.17}$$

For in this case, our final adjusted measure simply becomes B_i''

$$B_i'' = B_i'\left(\frac{\bar{Y}}{Y_i}\right)^{\gamma} = B_i\left(\frac{\bar{Y}}{Y_i}\right)^{\gamma+\beta}. \tag{3.18}$$

For instance, the weight given to measures of costs and benefits of different income groups which had already been adjusted to give B_i' would vary with the value of (γ) chosen as shown in Table 3.2.

It is worth noting that even if one did believe one could measure how the marginal utility of money varied with income in a unique, cardinal fashion, one might well still want to apply equity weights of this kind. That is, one might wish to place more weight on an extra unit of utility going to a poor man than on one going to someone already having a high level of utility. In this case, one would take formula (3.12) above and apply an additional weighting system in exactly the same way as in equation (3.18).

3.5   For and Against the Use of Weighting Systems

In the previous sections, a strong case has been put forward for the adoption of a distributive weighting system in the social appraisal of projects. Yet this approach remains controversial, and has been severely criticised in the literature

(Harberger, 1971; Mishan, 1974). It is necessary, therefore, to examine the validity of these criticisms.

In the first place, it is sometimes argued that distributional factors may be ignored in project appraisal, since the effects on distribution of the choices made are likely to be small (Harberger, op. cit.). No evidence for this assertion has been presented, while good evidence exists to the contrary, at least for certain sectors of the economy (Dalvi and Nash, 1977). It is hard to see how a method of project selection which attaches higher weights to the preferences of consumers the higher their incomes, could fail to have different results for both allocation and distribution from one which treated all consumers equally or which gave greatest weight to the preferences of the poor.

Second, weighting systems have been denounced as 'arbitrary', as removing the independence of the economic evaluation of projects, and as introducing considerations other than purely economic ones into the evaluation (Mishan, 1974). Now we have shown above that such weighting systems need not be arbitrary; each can be derived from a particular set of value judgements and assumptions regarding the existing distribution, the changes that are feasible and the changes that are desirable. Moreover, a decision to adopt no weighting system is itself equivalent to adopting a particular value judgement, namely, that the existing distribution of income is optimal. In other words, there is no such thing as a 'purely economic' appraisal; in any appraisal, one has to introduce some value judgement about distribution.

Third, it is argued that use of weighting systems will prevent the same method being used in all projects, and thus prevent ready comparability between projects. Furthermore, the fact that different results may be obtained for the same project at different dates simply because the weights have changed will bring cost—benefit into disrepute. Now consistency between projects is essential where evaluations are taking place on behalf of the same agency, and that agency will have to achieve this by laying down the distributional rules of the game. Consistency in weighting systems between agencies, however, is only desirable if the relevant decision-makers share the same value judgements. In other words, it is consistency between the methods used and the value judgements underlying them that is important. Comparability between projects can be preserved, however, if results are presented in a disaggregated fashion to show who gains and who loses (e.g. by an extension of Lichfield's planning balance sheet approach; Lichfield, 1968). For then, the effect on project selection of changing the weights may readily be perceived. This also may help to overcome the objection that if weighting systems are built in to the evaluation process, the weights will be determined by an unrepresentative bureaucrat, and will fail to become the object of public and political debate.

Perhaps the strongest arguments put forward by the critics of weighting systems relate to the difficulty in obtaining the appropriate information on both the distribution of costs and benefits and the determination of the weights themselves. It is to these problems that we now turn.

3.6   Some Practical Difficulties with Distributive Weighting Systems

We concluded in the above sections that only if the current distribution of income is regarded as optimal can the use of unadjusted market values in the social appraisal of projects be justified. In all other cases, some form of adjustment according to the income of the recipient will be required. However it should be appreciated that practical difficulties exist in implementing these adjustments.

In the first place, as presented, it is required that costs and benefits be traced to the income group of their ultimate recipient. This is not necessarily the same as that of their direct recipient, since subsequent price changes may pass the benefits or costs on to other hands. For instance, measures which improve the environment or mobility of tenants in a particular area may raise property prices and rents, passing some or all of the net benefit on to landlords. Establishing the real income group of the ultimate recipient will almost certainly require a considerable degree of averaging; one hurdle to be crossed here is the adjustment of household income to allow for differences in household structure, so that households with different numbers of adult and child members are grouped together if they achieve approximately the same living standard. A further difficulty is that the cost of living may vary by location or occupation.

The task may be simplified if one is dealing with a decision which simply affects the prices faced by all consumers (or a substantial identifiable group of them). In this case, for each good whose price is affected, one may identify the 'distributional characteristic' (Feldstein, 1972; Boadway, 1976). The distributional characteristic of a good (d_j) is simply the weighted average of the marginal social utility of income to all consumers (α_i) where the weights are the consumers' share of consumption of the good in question (θ_{ij}/θ_j), and is given by

$$d_j = \sum_i \alpha_i \left(\frac{\theta_{ij}}{\theta_j} \right). \tag{3.19}$$

A change in the price of the good in question may now simply be multiplied by d_j to give the appropriate distributive weighting to the costs or benefits it brings about, i.e.

$$\text{NSB} = \sum_j d_j Q_j \, \mathrm{d}P_j. \tag{3.20}$$

Unfortunately, this approach does require the distributive weights to be made explicit *ex ante*, and it is to this problem, which has attracted the most academic work, that we now turn. Now as long as one is performing the evaluation on one's own behalf, the determination of the weights is simply a matter for introspection and personal soul-searching. On the other hand when an economist is undertaking an appraisal for a third party (a government body or some other agency), he is in the position of a management consultant being asked to assist the body in question to achieve its objectives. If he is to do this effectively, he must know its views on the distributional issue.

Amongst the ways that have been suggested for finding these out are:

(i) *An analysis of the progressivity of the income tax schedule (Krutilla and Eckstein, 1958).* For instance, suppose that tax rates are set in such a way as to equalise the marginal burden of taxation across income groups. This would imply that if two income groups faced marginal tax rates of t_1 and t_2 respectively, then the social value of t_1 to group 1 would equal the social value of t_2 to group 2. The weights would be in the proportion $w_1/w_2 = t_2/t_1$. For instance, twice the weight would be given to those effects on someone facing a marginal tax rate of 25 per cent that was given to those effects on someone facing a marginal tax rate of 50 per cent. However, income tax is not the only fiscal measure which affects distribution of income; strictly, it should be the marginal effect of all taxes and income supplementation that is used in estimating weights.

Unfortunately, considerations other than that of equity enter into the determination of tax and income supplementation rates. If this were not the case, achievement of an optimal distribution of income would be much simpler, and the major reason for requiring distributional weights at all would vanish. For instance, the effect on incentives has to be borne in mind (although doubt has been raised about its importance; see Brown and Dawson, 1969): current macro-economic considerations (particularly with respect to incomes policy and inflation) may influence decisions, and administrative simplicity is an important factor, often leading to common marginal tax rates over wide sectors of the population for whom this would not otherwise be desired.

(ii) *An analysis of the distributional effects of past government decisions.* Weisbrod (1968) has suggested that we might determine the set of weights which correctly classifies past projects so that $\sum_i w_i(B_i - C_i) > 0$ for projects which were selected and $\sum_i w_i(B_i - C_i) < 0$ for projects which were rejected. (Although he used an example in which the number of income groups was equal to the number of projects examined, and therefore a range of weights which explained these decisions exactly could be found, given an adequate sample size a more formal statistical technique such as discriminant analysis may be applied to select the weights which come nearest to a correct classification of projects into selected and not selected groups.)

Interesting as this approach is, there are still objections to its practical use. First, for it to be valid, one must assume past government decision-taking was able to take income distribution systematically into account without an explicit weighting system (if so, we may wonder with Musgrave (1969) whether politicians really need the assistance of cost–benefit analysts in order to take correct distributional decisions!). Second, to have any confidence that the results had not occurred by chance or due to the influence of some third unquantified factor, we require a much bigger sample of cases. Third, even if one derived a reliable set of past weights, these may not apply at the present time. Either the ethical views of the government or the existing distribution of income may have changed in the interim, and one would require reassurance on this point.

On the other hand, the approach may be illuminating in revealing to the public (and to the government itself!) the implicit weightings involved in the decisions in question, and any inconsistencies or changes in weights between decisions. In the absence of any clearcut system of determining weights, there is a very real danger that the weights used implicitly will fluctuate from project to project, so that the government's redistributive objectives are not achieved in the most efficient way possible. Weisbrod's approach, while not offering an unequivocal way of stating what the weights should be, does at least offer a prospect of keeping such random and unintentional fluctuations in weights in check.

Ultimately, then, the derivation of weighting systems remains a major problem, although the approach of Weisbrod looks the most encouraging. If the relevant political figure could be prevailed upon to give an unequivocal statement of his distributional views, the problem would be easily solved, but it is in the nature of politics that no such clear statement will be forthcoming (indeed, if it were, it might lead to a weighting system which attached particular weight to socio-economic groups known to be floating voters, and to voters in marginal constituencies!). In the absence of such clarification, and in any case in the interest of open government, probably the best an economist can do is to explore the consequences of a variety of plausible weighting systems, as a form of 'value sensitivity analysis'.

3.7 Conclusions

We have outlined three different welfare economics bases on which the social appraisal of projects may rest. First, we may see it as an attempt to compute the aggregate utility to society of the project. This approach founders on the lack of any scientific method of making interpersonal utility comparisons. Second, we may see it as an application of the compensation test, to discover whether the project yields a potential Pareto improvement in welfare. Unfortunately, whether or not a project passed the compensation test was shown to depend on the distribution of income. Thus even if one adopted the philosophy that distributive issues could be resolved through fiscal policy, leaving project selection to be determined solely in terms of allocative efficiency, one would still have to decide what distribution of income to assume in evaluating projects. Only if the existing distribution of income were regarded as optimal would the use of unadjusted market measures of costs and benefits be appropriate.

But there exist political, administrative and macro-economic constraints on the use of taxation and income supplementation to redistribute income; in any case, such measures may themselves incur costs by introducing distortions in resource allocation. Thus there may be a case for using project selection directly to redistribute income by the use of 'equity' weights. The third basis for social appraisal of projects sees it then as an attempt to maximise a weighted sum of net benefits, where the weights are derived purely on ethical grounds.

Although many difficulties in the use of weighting systems have been discussed above, particularly with respect to information requirements, failure to use any weighting system in itself implies making the value judgement that the existing distribution of income is optimal. If, and only if we are happy with such a value judgement, we may reasonably use unweighted market valuations to measure costs and benefits. If not, we have to concern ourselves with one of the weighting systems outlined above.

APPENDIX

The Non-constancy of the Elasticity of the Marginal Utility of Income with Respect to Monotonic Transformations of the Utility Function

Suppose that an individual possesses a utility function $U = X_1^2 + X_2^2$. His maximisation problem is then

$$\text{Max } Z = X_1^2 + X_2^2 - \lambda[Y - P_1 X_1 - P_2 X_2].$$

First-order conditions are:

$$\frac{\partial Z}{\partial X_1} = 2X_1 - \lambda P_1 = 0 \tag{A3.1}$$

$$\frac{\partial Z}{\partial X_2} = 2X_2 - \lambda P_2 = 0 \tag{A3.2}$$

$$\frac{\partial Z}{d\lambda} = Y - P_1 X_1 - P_2 X_2 = 0 \tag{A3.3}$$

From (A3.1) and (A3.2)

$$-X_1 = \frac{P_1 X_2}{P_2}.$$

From (A3.3)

$$X_2 = \frac{Y - P_1 X_1}{P_2}$$

$$\therefore \quad X_1 = \frac{P_1 Y}{P_2} - \frac{P_1^2 X_1}{P_2}.$$

Solving for X_1

$$X_1 = \frac{P_1 Y}{P_1^2 + P_2}.$$

Similarly

$$X_2 = \frac{P_2 Y}{P_2^2 + P_1}.$$

From (A3.1)

$$\lambda = \frac{2 X_1}{P_1} = \frac{2Y}{P_1^2 + P_2}.$$

Consequently the elasticity of λ with respect to

$$Y \left(\frac{d\lambda}{dY} \cdot \frac{Y}{\lambda} \right) = 1.$$

A second individual possesses the utility function $U = (X_1^2 + X_2^2)^2$. He seeks to maximise

$$Z = (X_1^2 + X_2^2)^2 - \lambda[Y - P_1 X_1 - P_2 X_2].$$

First-order conditions are:

$$\frac{dZ}{dX_1} = 4(X_1^2 + X_2^2)X_1 - \lambda P_1 = 0 \tag{A3.4}$$

$$\frac{dZ}{dX_2} = 4(X_1^2 + X_2^2)X_2 - \lambda P_2 = 0 \tag{A3.5}$$

$$\frac{dZ}{d\lambda} = Y - P_1 X_1 - P_2 X_2 = 0 \tag{A3.6}$$

From (A3.4) and (A3.5)

$$X_1 = \frac{P_1 X_2}{P_2}.$$

Hence from (A3.6) we again obtain

$$X_1 = \frac{P_1 Y}{P_1^2 + P_2} \qquad \text{and similarly } X_2 = \frac{P_2 Y}{P_2^2 + P_1}.$$

However, this time from (A3.4)

$$\lambda = \frac{4}{P_1}(X_1^2 + X_2^2)X_1 = \frac{4}{P_1}\left[\frac{P_1^2}{(P_1^2 + P_2)^2} + \frac{P_2^2}{(P_2^2 + P_1)^2}\right]\frac{P_1 Y^3}{P_1^2 + P_2}.$$

Hence the elasticity of λ with respect to Y will be 3.

While this utility function yields identical demand curves to the previous one, the elasticity of the marginal utility of income with respect to the level of income is 3 as opposed to 1. Empirically, however, there is no way of telling which form is generating the stipulated demand curves.

4 Investment Criteria in the Public Sector

4.1 Introduction

We have established that the principle of CBA is to weigh up the advantages and disadvantages, the costs and benefits, of any project. Ideally, these costs and benefits are expressed in money terms. The total costs are then the whole set of different costs, and similarly for benefits. Each individual cost and benefit item, i, will have a quantity, q_i^c, and q_i^b, and a price (preferably a shadow price) p_i^c, and p_i^b. In any one year, then, costs will be given by

$$C_t = \Sigma q_{i,t}^c \cdot p_{i,t}^c \qquad (4.1)$$

and benefits by

$$B_t = \Sigma q_{i,t}^b \cdot p_{i,t}^b \qquad (4.2)$$

where t is the time period (year) in question.

In turn, these costs and benefits will be distributed through time. We could simply add up the costs and benefits up to some time period, T, after which they either do not occur or, for one reason or another, we cease to worry about them. The time period T is called the *time horizon*. It is most frequently set by the economic life of the investment in question. This may differ from its physical life — i.e. the time at which it literally wears out — because other factors, such as technological change, render the investment obsolescent. The economic life will therefore be shorter than the physical life. As we shall see, however, T might also be determined by other factors of a purely practical nature.

If we were to add up the costs and benefits we could obtain an expression for *net benefits* which would simply be

$$N(B) = \sum_{t=0}^{t=T} [B_t - C_t] \qquad (4.3)$$

where B_t and C_t are defined by equations (4.1) and (4.2). But equation (4.3) neglects an important factor. If we adopt the basic value judgement that individual preferences ought to count, we are logically obliged to incorporate in our formula the fact that individuals may prefer present consumption to future consumption. That is, offered a unit of benefit now rather than later, in a hypothetical context in which they can be certain the benefit will exist and that they will exist to receive it regardless of when it occurs, the expectation is that they will still prefer to have the benefit now. They *discount the future*. They are said to have 'time preference' and the *rate* at which they discount the future is called the 'marginal time-preference rate' (MTPR). The word 'marginal' simply reminds us that individuals are considering small changes in their levels of consumption of goods and services, namely the changes brought about by the investment in question. Quite how these individual time-preference rates are determined is something we consider in Chapter 9, where we also need to consider how they might be aggregated to form a '*social* time-preference rate' (STPR).

Note, that we have not categorically stated that individuals *do* discount the future. Negative time preference rates are not illogical. Indeed, in recent years, inflation rates have often been so high as to outweigh any monetary interest rate, thus giving rise to negative real rates on return on savings. Moreover, the individual's time-preference rate is likely to depend not just on his or her current income but also on expected lifetime earnings. In this respect, expectations of a fall in future income could lead to a willingness to surrender more than £1 now for £1 in the future. However, with these important caveats in mind, we proceed on the assumption that individuals' discount rates are positive.

The relevance of the existence of time preference is that it means we cannot treat each unit of benefit or cost as being of equal value *regardless of when it occurs*. Since preferences count, we must somehow 'downgrade' or 'discount' £1 of benefit in the future compared to £1 now. The same principle applies to costs. The easiest way of seeing how this is done, conventionally, is to think of the benefits and costs as financial flows. As we know, in CBA the benefits and costs need not be financial flows but streams of, say, aesthetic benefits or painful experiences. Provided that individuals are able to translate these into money terms we lose nothing by thinking in financial terms only. Now, one reason for preferring £1 now rather than next year arises if positive real interest rates exist. By taking the £1 now it can be turned into £1 + £1 · r or £$(1 + r)$ next year, where r is the interest rate expressed in decimal terms (e.g. 7 per cent = 0.07). The choice is not therefore really one between £1 now and £1 next year, but £1 now and £$(1 + r)$ next year.

Between what sums would the individual be indifferent over the two years? The answer is that he would be indifferent between £1 next year and £$1/(1 + r)$ now. To see this, simply take the latter sum now, lend it out at the rate of interest r for one year and it will be equal in year 1 to

$$\left[\frac{£1}{1 + r}\right]^{(1+r)} = £1.$$

In exactly the same way, the individual will be indifferent between £1 in *two* years' time and the sum £$1/(1 + r)^2$ now. To see this, again consider what would happen if he took the latter sum now and lent it at the interest rate r for *two* years. It would grow to

$$\left[\frac{£1}{(1+r)^2}\right]^{(1+r)(1+r)} = £1.$$

In general terms, £1 of benefit in any year t must be discounted at $(1 + r)^t$. The same is true for costs.

We can now return to equation (4.3). Its expansion should now be fairly obvious. In full it would be written

$$N(B) = (B_0 - C_0)\left[\frac{1}{(1+r)^0}\right] + (B_1 - C_1)\left[\frac{1}{(1+r)^1}\right]$$

$$+ (B_2 - C_2)\left[\frac{1}{(1+r)^2}\right] + \cdots + (B_T - C_T)\left[\frac{1}{(1+r)^T}\right].$$

This unwieldy expression is more simply written as

$$N(B) = \sum_{t=0}^{t=T} (B_t - C_t)\frac{1}{(1+r)^t} \tag{4.4}$$

or

$$N(B) = \sum_{t=0}^{t=T} (B_t - C_t) \cdot d_t \tag{4.5}$$

where

$$d_t = \frac{1}{(1+r)^t}. \tag{4.6}$$

The expression d_t is the *discount factor* and it is seen to be determined by the time period t and the interest rate r. Instead of the term 'interest rate', which, as we shall see, may relate to many different rates of interest ruling at any one time in the economy, we shall use the term *discount rate*. Exactly how the discount rate r is determined is the subject of Chapter 9. We shall also have more to say about the discount factor in this chapter. For the moment, note that the expression for net benefits in equation (4.5) differs from that in equation (4.3) by the expression for the discount factor. What we have done is to express future benefits and costs in terms of how they would be viewed *from the standpoint of the present*. We did this by applying indifference analysis to units of benefit or cost of equal nominal value (£1). Instead of net benefits, therefore, we now need to speak of 'net benefits as viewed from a present standpoint'. For this unwieldy expression we substitute the widely used one of *net present value* (NPV). Very simply then

$$NPV(B) = GPV(B) - GPV(C). \tag{4.7}$$

That is, the net present value of benefits (or the 'present value of net benefits') is equal to the (gross) present value of benefits minus the (gross) present value of costs. In using the term 'net present value' the 'net' refers to the difference between benefits and costs.

4.2   Net Present Value and Depreciation

The net present value formulae in equations (4.4) and (4.5) were seen to permit a single-valued estimate of the 'worth' of the project in question, regardless of the way costs and benefits are distributed through time. For example, the formulae will work for a sequence in which capital costs are incurred in year 0, no costs and benefits are incurred for, say, 30 years, and then costs and benefits accrue in year 31. Forestry would be a good example of such a sequence of costs and benefits, with the planting costs occurring early on, with some fairly small costs and benefits from thinning of plantations after every five years or so, and with the main benefit coming when the mature tree is actually felled and sold for timber and/or pulp. A power station might exhibit a sequence of capital costs for, say, ten years, a few years with operating costs as the station reaches its full output and then perhaps 25 years of operating costs and the benefits of electricity output. At the end of its 'economic life' we will have a 'decommissioning' cost — i.e. the cost of dismantling and, if it is a nuclear power station, decontaminating for radioactive components. The formula for NPV can accommodate any of these sequences. As we shall see later, one other method of expressing the worth of a project, through its 'rate of return', presents some difficulties for sequences such as that outlined for forestry investment.

It is worth looking at one issue that causes some confusion to students of CBA. The preceding chapters have described the kinds of costs and benefits that would appear in a CBA study, and how each would, ideally, be valued in money terms. But one item that many people expect to find in a CBA is absent, namely *depreciation costs*. Accountants are used to thinking of depreciation as a real cost, simply because a firm must 'write down' the value of its capital assets in order to make some provision for the replacement of those assets at the end of their 'life'. However, these accounting costs are not, to the economist, real costs. The easiest way of seeing this is that there is no obvious corresponding opportunity cost involved, for opportunity cost relates to the value of the assets in their next best use. For machinery this value may actually be zero if the machinery is highly specialised in use, or it may be a relatively small sum if it has some scrap value. Since CBA operates with the concept of opportunity cost, depreciation allowances are simply not relevant.

But does this mean that the use of NPV approaches does not allow the investing agency to recoup the value of its investment? The answer is that it *does* make such an allowance. We can use an example to illustrate how this happens, and the example will also tell us a little more about the *meaning* of NPV. Consider the cash flow in Table 4.1. We take a very simple example in

TABLE 4.1

Years		0	1	2	3
Cash flows		−100	+50	+50	+50
Discount factors at 10 per cent			0.9091	0.8264	0.7513
Discounted values		−100	+45.5	+41.3	+37.6
GPV = 124.4	NPV = 124.4 − 100 = 24.4				

which the economic life of the project is three years. The capital cost is 100 units. In years 1–3 a cash flow of 50 units is obtained. The second row shows the discount *factor* as given by the formula in equation (4.6). For convenience we have *r* equal to 10 per cent (i.e. 0.1 in decimal terms). The third row shows the discounted values. The NPV is seen to be 24.4 units. Now, what this figure means is that if the investing agency had invested 124.4 units at 10 per cent it would have secured the same cash flow. To put it another way, the agency saves 24.4 units compared to what it would have to invest to get the cash flow of 50 units in each of the three years.

To prove this consider Table 4.2. This shows an investment of 124.4 units. At the end of year 0 we add interest at 10 per cent which is what the investing agency regards as its marginal rate of return on investment. At the end of year 1 we take out a cash flow of 50 units, compute a new balance for year 2 at the end of which we add 10 per cent interest, and so on. What Table 4.2 shows is that at the end of three years, the agency has withdrawn cash flows of 50 units per annum, has recouped its initial investment and is left with a balance of zero. In short, the investment in Table 4.2 requires 124.4 units of initial outlay to secure the same cash flow as the investment of 100 units in Table 4.1.

TABLE 4.2

Investment in year 0	124.4
Interest at 10 per cent for year 1 on capital	+12.4
Balance at end of year 1	136.8
Withdrawal at end of year 1	−50.0
Balance at beginning of year 2	86.8
Interest at 10 per cent for year 2	+ 8.7
Balance at end of year 2	95.5
Withdrawal at end of year 2	−50.0
Balance at beginning of year 3	45.5
Interest at 10 per cent for year 3	+ 4.5
Balance at end of year 3	50.0
Withdrawal at end of year 3	−50.0
Balance at beginning of year 4	zero

Two features of interest are apparent. First, the meaning of the NPV in Table 4.1 can be construed as 'the value now of the surplus that the agency can make over and above what it would make by investing at its marginal rate of interest'; and second, the discounting procedure automatically allows for the recoupment of the initial sum. Hence the cost stream in any CBA must *not* include depreciation allowances.

4.3   Net Present Value and Project Acceptance

Three contexts arise within which the NPV criterion may be used. These are:

(i)   *Accept–Reject*. Here the agency must decide whether a given project is to be accepted or not.

(ii)   *Ranking*. Here the agency may have a series of investments all with positive NPVs. How do they rank them?

(iii)   *Mutual Exclusion*. Here the agency may have to decide between two projects simply because undertaking one means that the other cannot be undertaken.

Taking the three contexts in turn we can see how the NPV rule is applied.

4.3.1   ACCEPT–REJECT

Faced with a single project, the NPV rule dictates that it should be accepted if the NPV exceeds zero and rejected if it is less than zero. If, by chance, NPV equals zero, the agency would be indifferent between undertaking the project or not.

4.3.2   RANKING

Clearly, if the agency has unlimited funds it should adopt every project it can find with an NPV greater than zero. For in this way it would secure higher net benefits than if it used its unlimited funds in any other way – this, as we saw, is the meaning of a positive NPV. (Note that we are charging the agency with the responsibility of maximising net *social* benefits: a public utility will typically not do this unless specifically required to do so by government.) However, the context of unlimited funds rarely applies either to single agencies, firms or governments. The context is nearly always one of 'rationing'. The most obvious constraint is money capital: the agency will simply have a fixed investment budget to work with. What should it do in these circumstances? It clearly needs to *rank* projects in order of desirability and work down the list until the budget is exhausted. But what it should *not* do is to rank by NPVs. This may seem surprising at first sight, but a simple example will demonstrate why such a ranking will not give the right answer. Table 4.3 shows four projects and the GPVs of their cost and benefit flows. Consider projects *X*, *Y* and *Z only* for the

TABLE 4.3

Project	GPV(C)	GPV(B)	NPV	$\dfrac{GPV(B)}{GPV(C)}$
X	100	200	100	2.0
Y	50	110	60	2.2
Z	50	120	70	2.4
Z'	55	120	65	2.18

moment. If a capital constraint of 100 units exists then an NPV ranking would give the sequence X, Z, Y and only project X would be undertaken. The net benefits would be 100 units. However, casual inspection shows that both Y and Z could be chosen, the capital constraint would be honoured, but net benefits of 130 units would be achieved. Ranking by NPV gives the wrong answer, since choosing the two apparently lower ranked projects maximises the overall NPV that can be achieved for a given capital constraint. The final column suggests a better way to rank projects, namely by the *ratios* of the GPVs of benefits and costs. More familiarly, this is known as ranking by *benefit–cost ratios*.

Even this rule does not always work. Suppose project Z were replaced by Z'. Of the three projects X, Y, Z', only one would now be possible within the budget constraint, and the highest benefits would be obtained by choosing project X, even though it has the lowest benefit–cost ratio.

Moreover, the rule advanced here operates for a capital constraint effective in the initial year. It may well be that constraints exist in future years and/or there may be constraints to other inputs, such as labour. The presence of such problems requires the use of programming techniques to find the correct ranking, and the matter is not pursued further here. See a text such as Weingartner (1963) for further detail.

4.3.3   MUTUALLY EXCLUSIVE PROJECTS

Where the choice is between projects, the general rule is to select the project offering the highest NPV. This general rule does however require that the proper context be established. Two particular observations should be made. First, strict 'exclusivity' implies that *either* project X *or* project Y be undertaken, or neither. In many cases, however, there may be a variable degree of exclusivity such that a total commitment to X does preclude any commitment to Y, but where some combination of X and Y may none the less be possible. If that is so, it is essential to consider any possible combinations of the projects and compute their NPVs. These 'combined' projects should then be treated as if they were extra projects. Exclusivity still applies — that is, one may only be able to undertake X *or* Y *or* some combination, say, $\frac{1}{2}X + \frac{1}{2}Y$. But the rule of selecting the highest NPV remains.

The second aspect is that in the presence of capital rationing it is necessary to 'normalise' projects so that they are comparable. If X costs 100 units and yields an NPV of 90, and Y costs 40 units and yields an NPV of 35, we should not immediately assume that X is preferable simply because it has the higher NPV. Rather we should consider project Y and observe that it costs much less than X. The question should then be asked as to what return can be obtained from the difference of 60 units. The NPV of some further project, not exclusive with Y and costing 60 units, may be 70 units, in which case the choice is between X with an NPV of 90 and Y *plus* an extra project with an overall NPV of $35 + 70 = 105$ units.

4.4   The Internal Rate of Return

The calculation of NPV requires the use of some social rate of discount r. This is assumed to be derived independently and the methods by which it might be calculated are discussed in Chapter 9. An alternative approach to investment appraisal is to calculate the *internal rate of return* (IRR) and compare it directly to the social rate of discount. The internal rate of return is in fact another name for Keynes' 'marginal efficiency of capital'. It is calculated by setting the discounted value of the net benefit stream equal to the initial capital outlay and solving the resulting equation for the value of the discount rate. That is, an equation of the form

$$\sum_{t=1}^{t=T} (B_t - C_t) \cdot \frac{1}{(1+r)^t} = C_0 \qquad (4.8)$$

is solved for the value of r, where C_0 is the initial capital outlay. By simple rearrangement it will be obvious that equation (4.8) could also be stated as

$$\sum_{t=0}^{t=T} B_t \cdot \frac{1}{(1+r)^t} = \sum_{t=0}^{t=T} C_t \cdot \frac{1}{(1+r)^t} \qquad (4.9)$$

so that it makes no difference if we equate the present value of the *net* benefit stream with the initial capital outlay, or if we equate the entire gross benefit stream with the entire gross cost stream: the result is the same.

The approach to calculating the IRR thus uses equation (4.8) or (4.9) in which the values of C, B and T are known but r is assumed unknown. The equations are solved to determine r. No simple mechanism exists for calculating such solutions, whereas with the NPV approach discount tables can be found which facilitate comparatively easy calculation. One fairly simple approach is to guess at the likely solution and then go through the process of computing the two present values, for costs and benefits. If the present value of benefits exceeds the present value of costs after this first guess, then the rate is too low and should be raised, and so on in an 'iterative' fashion until the IRR is approximated. Algorithms which converge more rapidly are readily available for the solution of such problems by computer.

The rule for accepting a project then becomes, accept if r^* is greater than r, where r^* is the IRR (or the 'yield' or 'solution rate') and r is the predetermined discount rate. If r^* is below r then the project is rejected.

As far as *ranking* is concerned, we saw that the NPV rule had to be modified to reflect benefit—cost ratios if there was capital rationing present. In general, IRR cannot be relied upon to give the same rankings as either NPV or benefit—cost ratios for the reasons discussed below. Because of this, many practitioners of CBA feel that the NPV approach is safest. We can briefly outline the problems that arise with IRR calculations.[1]

4.4.1 THE MULTIPLE-ROOTS PROBLEM

In computing the IRR it is quite possible to obtain more than one solution rate. The reason for this is simple, once it is realised that the IRR is the solution to a polynomial equation. If the polynomial is of degree n, there will be n roots, i.e. n solution rates. Clearly, if a project's IRR has two solutions, say 10 per cent and 15 per cent, and the social discount rate is 12 per cent, there appears to be no clearcut criterion for acceptance or rejection. This objection is considered by many to preclude the use of IRR as a decision rule.

The only roots of the polynomial equation which are of interest are those with positive and real values.[2] Thus, although an IRR of -2 per cent is conceivable, it has no relevant economic meaning and can be ignored. Imaginary numbers (such as $\sqrt{-2}$) are without significance and can similarly be ignored. The number of positive roots can be found by Descartes' 'Rule of Signs'. If the decision formula is expressed as an equation in i, the IRR, the positive roots can be indicated. Thus, in the simple two-period case we have

$$\frac{B_1}{1+i} + \frac{B_2}{(1+i)^2} = K$$

or

$$-K \cdot i^2 + (B_1 - 2K)i + (K + B_1 + B_2) = 0$$

so that the sequence of signs before the terms in i is $-$, $+$. There is only *one change* of sign, so there is one positive root. If the equation were of a higher order, the same rule would apply. The sequence $-$, $-$, $+$, $+$, for example, still has only one change and hence one positive root. The sequence $-$, $+$, $-$, however, has two changes and hence two positive roots. This last sequence is perhaps the one most common to public investment projects. The initial expenditure ($-$) is followed by positive returns ($+$) and then by negative returns ($-$) as the project ages, possibly costing money to dismantle and scrap.

This sequence is illustrated in Figure 4.1 below.

The proposed modifications to the IRR rule to allow for multiple-roots are numerous. It has been suggested that the project be terminated at point T in Figure 4.1 — i.e. the second change of sign is not permitted, and a unique rate is

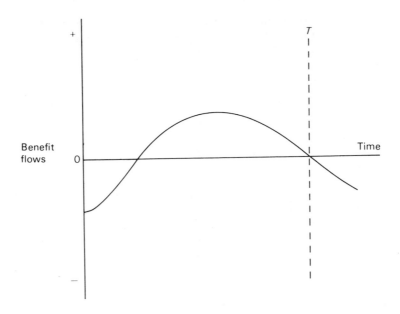

FIGURE 4.1

preserved. In addition, such a procedure seems to be common sense because there is little point in carrying on with a project that yields negative returns. The problem here is that the negative returns usually reflect costs of closure, and removal or dismantling costs which cannot be avoided.

Others have suggested rules by which 'valid' IRRs can be distinguished from 'invalid' ones. In the $-$, $+$, $-$ case a useful rule is to observe the two roots resulting from this particular benefit flow, call them i_1 and i_2 and formulate the following rules ($i_2 > i_1$):

(*a*) if $i_1 < e < i_2$, accept the project;

(*b*) if $e < i_1$,   reject the project;

(*c*) if $e > i_2$,   reject the project;

where e is the social rate of discount in our case. Notice that this rule permits — case (*a*) — the lower internal rates of return to be *less* than the social discount rate, so long as the higher rate exceeds the social rate. This rule is correct and reflects the fact that between i_1 and i_2 the NPV is positive (see Figure 4.2), but unfortunately has application only to the $-$, $+$, $-$ flow indicated; it cannot be generalised beyond this. It is possible to develop further rules, but these increase in complexity and do not embrace all possible cases. Thus, while the multiple-roots problem is not perhaps as serious as some commentators would suggest, it remains a slightly awkward obstacle to the confident use of the internal rate of return rule.

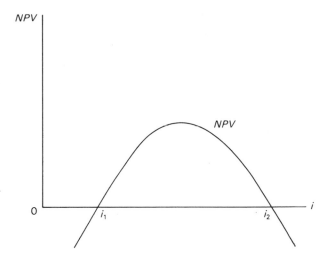

FIGURE 4.2

4.4.2   SENSITIVITY TO ECONOMIC LIFE

Where projects with different economic lives are being compared, the IRR approach may overstate the desirability of a short-life project. Thus, £1 invested now has an IRR of 100 per cent if it cumulates to £2 at the end of the year. Compare this to a £10 investment which cumulates to £15: i.e. an IRR of 50 per cent. The IRR rule would rank the former project above the latter, yet at a 10 per cent rate of discount the NPVs are respectively 0.8182 and 3.6364.

4.4.3   SENSITIVITY TO TIME-PHASING OF COSTS AND BENEFITS

Frequently projects may not yield benefits for many years (dams, nuclear power stations) – they have long 'gestation' periods. Suppose we have two projects A and B, of which the latter only gives returns after a longer gestation period, so that its NPV is more sensitive to the rate of discount. It is perfectly possible for their NPVs to vary with r as shown below in Figure 4.3.

At the appropriate rate of discount, $NPV(B) > NPV(A)$ (if the outlays are the same, clearly this is also true of the benefit–cost ratios). Yet the internal rate of return on A exceeds that on B. The problem here is essentially the same as that in subsection 4.4.2 above: IRR will give high ranking to projects which 'bunch' the benefits into the early part of their economic lives relative to other projects.

4.4.4   MUTUAL EXCLUSIVITY

The IRR is further complicated when used to compare mutually exclusive projects. It is not necessarily the case that the best project is the one with the

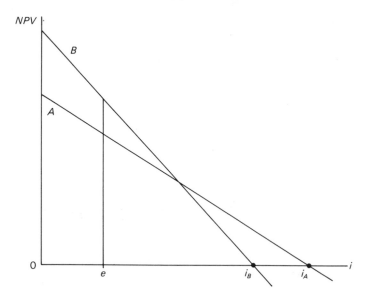

FIGURE 4.3

highest IRR. Consider the two projects in Table 4.4 X and Y, each with a life of ten years.

On the IRR rule, X is preferred to Y, but on the NPV rule, Y is preferred to X. The IRR rule is misleading here since it discriminates against Y because of the size of its capital outlay. To avoid this problem it is necessary to calculate the rate of return on the hypothetical project '$Y - X$' — i.e. on the difference between the capital outlays. Since the IRR on '$Y - X$' is in excess of the subjective rate of 8 per cent used in the example, the larger project is to be preferred to the former.

Thus the mutually exclusive context requires a two-part rule to the effect that a project Y be accepted if and only if

$$i_Y > r$$

and

$$i_{(Y-X)} > r$$

TABLE 4.4

Project	Cost	Benefits (p.a.)	IRR %	NPV at 8%
X	1	0.2	15	0.34
Y	2	0.36	12	0.42
'$Y - X$'	1	0.16	9	—

where i is the IRR and r the predetermined rate. The rule is usually described as the 'incremental yield' approach, or Fisher's 'rate of return over cost'.

It is generally possible to devise ways, such as the 'incremental yield' approach, to overcome these problems with IRR. But the effort is unneccesary, since NPV will give the correct answer with far less effort.

4.5 Discount Factors and Time

It has been argued that a formal decision rule in CBA should be formulated in terms of net present values. Where the net present value (NPV) exceeds zero, the project under scrutiny is *potentially* worthwhile. Whether it deserves to be undertaken depends on its ranking *vis-à-vis* other projects with positive NPVs. The NPV formula has been presented as if the discount factor can always be formulated as

$$d_t = \frac{1}{(1 + r)^t} \qquad (4.10)$$

or, in continuous form,

$$d_t = e^{-rt}. \qquad (4.11)$$

These are necessarily the formulae that emerge if one accepts the view that the process of discounting derives its rationale from the very existence of alternative uses of funds, the opportunity cost argument. Thus, £1 now becomes £$(1 + r)$ in one year's time if there exists a rate of compound interest of r per cent that could be earned. In two years' time the sum would be $(1 + r)$ invested at r per cent for a further year – i.e. $(1 + r)^2$. And so on. Inverting the procedure, the present value of £1 two years hence is £$1/(1 + r)^2$. This simple argument, based on the opportunity cost argument and the existence of compound interest, is sufficient to justify the discount factor equations (4.10) and (4.11) given above (although there is no reason why r should necessarily be constant over time).

If, however, we consider the alternative view, that individuals' preferences with respect to the future *alone* should determine the discount factor, it is quite possible that the expression for d_t would look different. Consider Figure 4.4, which shows time on the horizontal axis and the discount factor on the vertical axis.

The present is shown by the origin. The discount *factor* is then unity, which is the same thing as saying that the discount *rate* is zero for the immediate period. Benefits and costs that occur immediately are not discounted. This is intuitively logical. However, the *rate* at which the future is discounted could follow any path. Several are shown in Figure 4.4. The curve A is in fact the curve that would be traced out by the formula in equations (4.10) and (4.11). It will be seen that it does not coincide with the horizontal axis at the arbitrarily chosen time horizon T. This is simply because unless T is very large, the

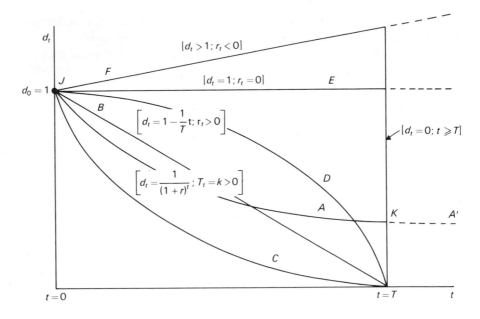

FIGURE 4.4

equation for d_t given by (4.10) and (4.11) would not in fact converge on the axis (technically, it only does so at t = infinity). Note that, the higher the discount rate r, the closer will path A be to the horizontal axis at T.

Another possibility, in keeping with the idea that the time horizon is chosen in such a way that benefits and costs *beyond it* have a discount *factor* of zero (a discount *rate* of infinity), is given by curve D. Or the straight line B might describe the discount path. It too obeys the requirements that the discount factor should be unity at the start and zero at the end of the period of investment. Other paths, such as C also have this property. Path E is included for further interest: it is in fact the path that would be traced out if d_t was equal to unity at all values of t up to T. This would correspond to a discount rate of zero, often thought to be the rate that would correspond to 'genuine altruism'. In fact of course, 'genuine altruism' might be construed as requiring extreme sacrifices for the future in terms of current benefits forgone. There is nothing illogical, then, in suggesting that an altruistic discount factor path would appear something like F in Figure 4.4. Nor is it difficult to show that such a path implies a *negative* discount rate.

Suppose we consider period 1. Then a curve like F implies

$$d_1 > d_0 = 1.$$

Therefore

$$\frac{1}{(1 + r)} > 1.$$

By simple arrangement,

$$1 > (1 + r)$$

and hence

$$r < 0.$$

It seems correct to argue that any formula for d_t must give a value of $d_0 = 1$. But should the value of d_T be zero? By choosing T as the 'cut-off' point we are implicitly saying that benefits and costs beyond T are valued at zero. This must mean either that they are not there at all, or that, if they are there, the discount rate effectively 'jumps' to infinity at $T + 1$: we simply do not care what happens after period T. The choice of the time horizon T is seen to be of potential importance. The use of equations (4.10) and (4.11) effectively means that, for a finite time horizon, we are ignoring all costs and benefits after period T. This is tantamount to saying that the equation is not quite complete — we should strictly add the additional statement that benefits and costs after T are to be discounted at infinity and are therefore deemed to be zero.

This may all seem rather pedantic. For, in practice, the use of a positive discount rate of 5 or 10 per cent will tend to render the computation of benefits and costs after a certain period not worthwhile. The additional net present values will be so small that they are unlikely to affect any choice rule we care to adopt. To illustrate, £1 in 50 years' time would have a NPV of £0.0085 at a discount rate of 10 per cent. At 5 per cent its NPV would be £0.0872. However, suppose that the costs or benefits are small but stretch a long way beyond year 50, perhaps to year 1,000 or year 24,400? Then it may well matter that we have chosen a time horizon of T where T is perhaps 30 or 50 years hence. In terms of Figure 4.4, the 'tail' of curve A, shown as 'A', would show the discount factors to be applied to all costs and benefits beyond year 50 if we chose to use the discount rate applicable to path A up to year 50. If we compute the value of the net benefits beyond year 50 we shall have

$$\text{NPV} = \sum_{t=51}^{T=24,400} (B_t - C_t) \cdot d_t. \tag{4.12}$$

If, then, we 're-set' the time horizon at 24,400 years, the value yielded by equation (4.12) could well be significant enough to affect the size of the NPV of the net benefits from years 0–50. And just to demonstrate that very large values of T are not at all unrealistic we may be reminded that the radioactive half-life of plutonium-239, one of the products of nuclear-fuel reprocessing, is in fact 24,400 years, which is why we chose that particular number.

So, for perhaps the vast majority of investments the choice of T may not matter much as long as we make a brief check to see if the distribution of costs and benefits through time is likely to have a long 'tail', as in the plutonium example. For some investments it may be necessary to incorporate very long time horizons. The immediate problem in doing so is that the uncertainty surrounding the values of costs and benefits tends to increase with time. We address ourselves to this matter in Chapter 5. Note that the choice of path E in Figure 4.4 strictly entails that we set the time horizon at a very high value of t, indeed at infinity, *unless* we wish to adopt the 'two-stage' rule formulated above whereby we use one discount factor up to the time horizon and a zero discount factor (infinite discount rate) thereafter. Path F raises exactly the same problem, but with the additional paradox that by arbitrarily setting the time horizon at T, we are infinitely discounting *increasing* net present values of each £1 after year 50. Whether or not such a path can be feasibly chosen we consider in Chapter 9.

4.6   Optimal Time-phasing of Investment

The choices considered so far have related to *which projects* one should choose. A special case of mutual exclusion arises, however, when we ask *when* should a project be implemented? For the investment could be made in year 0, 1, 2 or whenever *unless* there is some reason why demand must be met and that demand dictates a specific year. We consider this problem shortly. For the moment consider the case where flexible timing is permitted.

In many cases this aspect of investment planning is ignored, timing being a matter of arbitrary rules. It can be shown, however, that the net present value of a project can sometimes be increased by delaying implementation of the project, and even that projects which are judged not worthwhile now can be worthwhile later on. This illustrates the dangers of looking at the project from a 'static' rather than from a 'dynamic' viewpoint.

Suppose a project is initially considered for construction in year 0, and that it has a capital cost of C which is the same whether it is built in year 0, 1, 2 or whenever. Assume too that it has a 'life' of n years. No other costs are associated with the project. If the project is postponed by one year, there will be a saving of interest on C. Essentially, the present value in year 0 of the capital outlay in year 1 will be $C/1 + r$, and

$$\text{savings in capital cost} = C - \frac{C}{1+r} = \frac{rC}{1+r}$$

where r is the rate which can be earned on capital. On the benefit side, however, there will be a *loss* of benefits in year 1 equal to $B_1/(1+r)$ (assuming r is applied to both benefits and costs). On the other hand, the project will still last n years, so that there will be a *gain* in year $n+1$ of $B_{n+1}/(1+r)^{n+1}$. The overall net gains from postponement are therefore

$$\left[\frac{rC}{1+r} + \frac{B_{n+1}}{(1+r)^{n+1}} \right] - \left[\frac{B_1}{1+r} \right]. \tag{4.13}$$

This calculation can be repeated for each possible length of delay. The year for which the gains from postponement are greatest is the 'optimal' year for implementing the project. Or, in other words, the optimal year will be that in which the net benefits of the project are maximised.

Equation (4.13) shows the net benefits (or costs) of postponement for *one* year. Arguably, the second expression, the discounted benefit for year $n + 1$ will be small. If we ignore it, we see that the net gain consists of the discounted value of the interest saved minus the discounted value of the first year's benefit. That is, postponement for *one* year makes sense if

$$\frac{B_1}{1 + r} < \frac{rC}{1 + r}$$

or

$$B_1 < rC. \tag{4.14}$$

This condition is more usually expressed as $(B_1/C) < r$, and is known as the 'first-year rate of return' condition. It should be noted however, that its validity is confined to issues of timing. It is always necessary to check that a project which passes the first-year rate of return criterion also satisfies the NPV criterion for the whole of its life. If postponement for one year is worthwhile, one may re-apply the first-year rate of return criterion for the new starting date, and so on until a positive first-year rate of return is found. The year in which it occurs is the optimal starting date for the project. For further discussion, see Marglin (1963).

But there is another factor weighing in favour of postponement and which receives little attention in CBA. This is the benefit gained from the extra information generated by delay. For example, for transport projects the delay may result in better traffic forecasts which, if they show a downwards revision, could justify postponement and hence save capital outlays. If the forecasts are revised upwards they may add to the costs incurred through extra congestion but may facilitate a better planning of future capacity. The desirability of retaining this sort of flexibility will be discussed in Chapter 5 on risk and uncertainty.

How does the discount rate affect the picture? For our simple one-period postponement it would raise the benefit side in the inequality in equation (4.14). In other words it will tend to make postponement more likely. Other factors may outweigh this, however, if the size of the project is variable. We can show this more formally by looking at one of the standard (but none the less very simple) problems in the 'optimal time-phasing' of investments — the case where demand has, for one reason or another, to be met.

For this example we use an equation relating capital cost to the investment's physical capacity. This equation is a generalised form of one that tends to be found in engineering literature and it takes the form

$$C = aV^b$$

where C is the capital cost, V the physical capacity, and a, b constants, b being generally known as the 'economy of scale factor'. Now consider Figure 4.5. This shows a *linear* increasing demand for the product in question. We assume demand must be met, so that installed capacity of V meets demand for a period of t years. Note that the plant has excess capacity up to point B when it is necessary to introduce a second plant to take the situation to C, and so on. We wish to know the value of t — i.e. the optimal time-phasing of investment.

Concentrating on capital costs only we see that the *total* discounted costs at A are made up of the initial capital cost at A (C_A) and the *total* costs at B (which include all *subsequent* investment costs as well) discounted back to A. We may write this as

$$TC_A = C_A + TC_B \cdot e^{-rt}.$$

Since we assume demand increases at a rate D for ever, the series is infinite and we have $TC_A = TC_B$. We also have

$$C_A = aV^b.$$

Substituting gives

$$TC_A = aV^b + TC_A \cdot e^{-rt}$$

or

$$TC_A = \frac{aV^b}{1 - e^{-rt}}.$$

From Figure 4.5 it can be seen that

$$V = t \cdot D$$

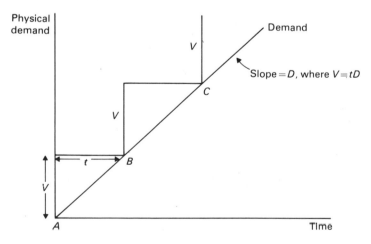

FIGURE 4.5

so that we can write

$$TC_A = \frac{a(tD)^b}{1 - e^{-rt}} \ .$$

Taking logarithms of both sides of the equation and differentiating gives the result

$$b = \frac{rt}{e^{rt} - 1}$$

which tells us that the optimal phasing is determined by the 'economy of scale' factor (as we would expect) *and* the discount rate *r*. For any *given* value of *b*, the picture will be as in Figure 4.6. The higher the discount rate the shorter is the time between investments. Note that, throughout, the problem has been stated in terms of minimising the discounted value of capital costs.

The example of a linear increasing demand function where that demand must be met could be extended to geometrically increasing demand functions, 'logistic' demand functions and so on. Moreover, we could relax the requirement that demand has always to be met. All of this would however take us well beyond the level of this text.

For our purpose it suffices to observe that (i) the investment agency should be equally concerned with *when* to invest as with the choice of investments; (ii) that there are costs and benefits of postponement and the CBA framework

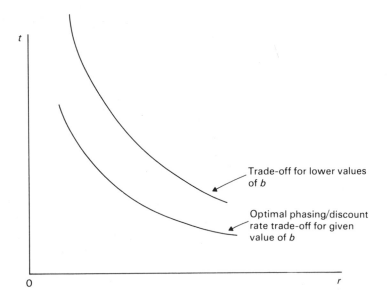

FIGURE 4.6

is the proper context in which to evaluate the postponement decision; (iii) that where repeated investment is required, economies of scale will affect the optimal phasing of investment; and (iv) the discount rate will similarly affect time-phasing decisions.

4.7   Other Decision Criteria

It should be clear from this chapter that the correct decision formula to use in CBA is one based on NPV, with suitable ranking by benefit—cost ratios where necessary. It is possible to modify IRR in such a way that it overcomes most of the generic problems involved in its use, but we have seen that this was somewhat complex. In this final section we look briefly at some of the alternative techniques that have been advocated.

4.7.1   THE PAY-BACK PERIOD

Although not favoured by economists, some industries and even some public agencies continue to think in terms of the period over which they recoup their initial investment. That is, if they can recover the investment in a period of, say, t years, where t is some arbitrarily established 'maximum', they will undertake the project. What this criterion effectively does is to discount returns after the pay-back limit by an infinite amount. If net benefits accrue after the pay-back period they are a fortuitous gain. If net costs occur it is simply hoped that they will not grow to the level where they cancel out the initial recovery of the investment. If, at the end of the pay-back time horizon, it looks as if net costs will occur rather than net benefits, then the agency has the option to close the project down with the comfort of knowing that at least it has not lost its original investment.

Several problems arise. First, a pay-back criterion can easily be quite inconsistent with maximising NPV. Second, the tendency is to opt for very short pay-back periods on the grounds of caution. The paradox here is that projects giving very high returns in the early years will be the only ones that meet this requirement, and yet such projects may be those ones with a high risk of net costs after the pay-back period. This approach has no foundation in any economic rationale for investment. If risk is relevant, then it is best treated in a separate fashion (see Chapter 5).

4.7.2   ANNUAL VALUE

Given a stream of money benefits $B_1, B_2, \ldots, B_n$, these benefits have a present value, $\mathrm{PV}(B)$. Corresponding to the stream of benefits will be an annuity, A_B, which, when discounted, will have the same present value as $B_1 + B_2 + \cdots + B_n$, so that $\mathrm{PV}(A_B) = \mathrm{PV}(B)$. Similarly, there will be an annuity corresponding to the stream of costs, A_K, so that the decision rule is: rank by $A_B - A_K$. Clearly, from the definition of the annuity, the result cannot differ from the present value rule.

4.7.3 TERMINAL VALUE

A terminal value is obtained by *compounding* benefits and costs forward in time to the terminal period (usually the end of the project's economic life), and the resulting rule is to rank by

$$\text{TV}(B) - \text{TV}(K).$$

Formulated in this way, the terminal value approach is formally equivalent to the present value rule. Mishan has, however, suggested added modifications which appear to make the terminal value approach more appealing (Mishan, 1967). His 'normalisation' rules are:

(i) Compound all consumption benefits at the social equivalent of individuals' time preference rates, r (see Chapter 9).

(ii) Compound all reinvestable surpluses and any costs at the opportunity cost rate — i.e. the rate the money could earn if invested again (see Chapter 9). Let this be p.

(iii) Select a common terminal period T for all investments.

(iv) 'Equalise' cost outlays across projects, so that each project has the same present value of costs.

An example shows the results. Table 4.5 shows three hypothetical projects, A, B, C, and their associated benefit streams. Present values are calculated, and ranking by NPV gives B, A, C. Ranking by IRR, however, gives C, A, B, project C having two internal rates, the benefit flow being $-, +, -$.

Now suppose terminal values are calculated and Mishan's rules are adopted. First, expenditures have to be equalised. The cost of A is therefore multiplied by 5, and C is *divided* by 3 since there is a negative benefit flow in period 2 which, when discounted at p and added to the capital cost of C equals 100, the common outlay. Next, reinvestment is allowed for: the 16 in period 2 for

TABLE 4.5

Project	t_0	t_1	t_2	t_3	t_4	*PV(B)*	*PV(K)*	*NPV*	*IRR*
A	-20	15	16	.	.	28.8	20	6.8	0.34
B	-100	.	.	160	.	117.2	100	17.2	0.17
C	-45	351	-402	.	.	319.1	377.3	-58.2	0.46 and 4.56

Source: Mishan (1967, p. 785, with corrections).

project A is reinvestable at p, say 20 per cent, and the 160 in period 3 for project B is reinvestable at some rate higher than p. The 117 in period 1 for project C is reinvested at p. The final table becomes that shown in Table 4.6. The new rankings by NTV are A, B, C. In addition, a 'normalised' IRR, λ, is computed, and this is seen to give an identical ranking. The normalised IRR (IRR*) is defined as the discount rate which makes the *terminal* value of the benefits equal to the *present* value of the expenditure, i.e.

$$ \text{IRR}^* = \sqrt[n]{\frac{TV(B)}{PV(K)}} - 1 $$

where n is the number of years to the selected terminal period, and $PV(K)$ is calculated at the rate p.

The attributes of this approach are claimed to be: :

(i) Identical rankings whatever rule is used: i.e. NTVs, NPVs, IRRs or benefit—cost ratios will all yield the same rankings *provided* they are expressed in normalised form.

(ii) Expressed in normalised form, benefits may be discounted at *any* rate of interest to obtain a normalised present value.

(iii) The normalised internal rate of return 'accords with the popular conception of an internal rate, as an average rate of growth over the relevant period' (Mishan, 1967, p. 788).

(iv) The multiple-roots solution to project C in Table 4.5 disappears in Table 4.6.

The procedure is interesting in so far as it does place the various decision formulae on a comparable basis and in such a way as to ensure equivalent rankings. Without in any way decrying the ingenuity with which the approach has been developed (those with a preference for rates of return approaches, for example, would find the 'normalised' IRR trouble-free), it remains true that net present value approaches, with due allowance being made for reinvestment, will achieve the same results.[3]

TABLE 4.6

Project	t_0	t_1	t_2	t_3	t_4	$TV(B)$	$TV(K)$	NTV	λ
A	−100	75	.	.	115	215	207.4	+7.6	0.207
B	−100	.	.	.	210	210	207.4	+2.6	0.203
C	−15	117	−134	.	.	202	207.4	−5.4	0.192

APPENDIX

Proof that $d_t = e^{-rt}$ implies a constant discount rate

$$d_t = \frac{1}{(1 + r)^t} \qquad \text{or, in continuous form,} \qquad d_t = e^{-rt}$$

Differentiating,

$$\frac{\partial d_t}{\partial t} = -re^{-rt}$$

Expressing the absolute rate of change as a percentage rate of change we have

$$\frac{\dfrac{\partial d_t}{\partial t}}{d_t} = \frac{-re^{-rt}}{e^{-rt}} = -r.$$

Hence the rate of change is a constant r, which is negative.

5 Risk and Uncertainty

5.1 Introduction

Clearly, few, if any, investment decisions take place in a riskless world. Exploration for oil, coal and uranium, for example, involves the risk that nothing will be found, or that what is found will not be in commercial quantities. The decision to opt for one type of nuclear reactor rather than another carries with it the risk that, if the chosen reactor type is 'unproven', it may be subject to many faults which will add significantly to the cost of construction and operation. This was the case in the United Kingdom with the advanced gas-cooled reactor, see for example (Henderson, 1977). Or the reactor choice may be one which involves an unexpected accident which results in a public outcry which in turn increases the demand for better safety standards and thus raises costs. This would be exemplified by the accident to the light water reactor at Harrisburg in the United States in 1979, although views differ as to whether it was an 'expected' or 'unexpected' accident.

Equally, investment in an airport may not see the expected traffic materialising perhaps due to changes of taste on the part of travellers, or to real income changes which reduce the demand for travel. The same could happen with motorways. The examples are endless and tend to concentrate on the risk of *cost* items being higher than planned simply because this tends to be the most familiar type of risk in public investment decisions. Lack of markets — i.e. the failure of benefits to accrue on the scale anticipated — is also a hazard, as in the case of Concorde in the United Kingdom. Constraints of various kinds may also turn net benefit situations into net cost situations as with the building of hospitals for which no trained staff can then be found, and so on.

All this suffices to show that risk and uncertainty are very much the 'order of the day'. The question therefore arises as to how public investment decision rules should be modified to allow for such risks. As we shall see, various adjustments have been proposed, while in the view of some no adjustment is required in many cases because of the alleged special nature of public investment.

5.2 The Meaning of Risk and Uncertainty

It is conceptually useful to distinguish risk and uncertainty. In general, a risky context is one in which the person evaluating the project in question has some idea of the *probabilities* of the various outcomes. For example, the outcome of ultimate interest is the value of the net social benefit (NSB). It may be, therefore, that the decision-maker can attach a probability to the NSBs being, say, £100 m, £50 m, £10 m and £−30 m respectively. If so the *probability distribution* may

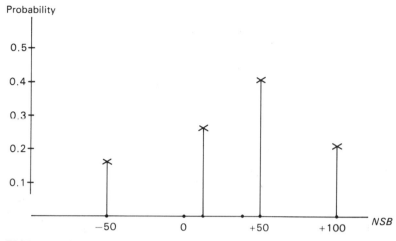

FIGURE 5.1

appear as in Figure 5.1 in which hypothetical probabilities have been assigned to the hypothetical net benefits. Note that these probabilities could be derived from the fact that the investment in question replicates many others of the same kind (motorways, power stations, reservoirs etc.). If so the probabilities in question will be *objective probabilities*. Alternatively, it may be that the decision-maker has no prior experience to go on, or if he has there are reasons for not taking it into account. In this case the probabilities will be *subjective probabilities*, ones placed on the outcomes by the decision-maker himself. For our purposes it matters little which they are.

Uncertainty, on the contrary, relates to a context in which no such probabilities can be assigned. Figure 5.1 cannot be drawn at all, although, of course, it will always be open to a decision-maker to convert an uncertainty context into a risk context by assigning subjective probabilities based on some guesses, intuition etc. The distinction is a useful one however, since, as we shall see, various rules have been designed for dealing with uncertainty contexts and these rules, taken from *decision theory*, are of interest in themselves. It is as well to remember, however, that the literature does not always preserve the conceptual distinction made here.

5.3 Risk-aversion

Confining ourselves to the risk context, some useful definitions can be established straight away. Figure 5.2 shows two probability distributions, this time 'smoothed' on the assumption that the decision-maker has extensive knowledge of the various probabilities attached to the different outcomes. The distributions are purely hypothetical but they have features in common. Both are normal distributions (simply a matter of convenience) and both have the same mean or

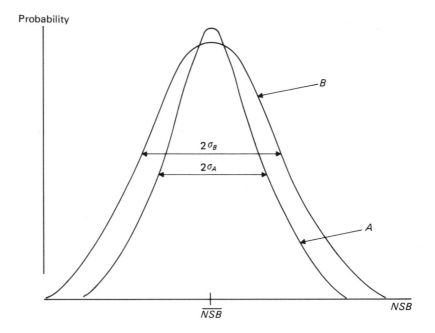

FIGURE 5.2

expected value, $\overline{NSB}$. They differ, however, in that distribution B has a wider dispersion (standard error) than distribution A, that is

$$\sigma_B > \sigma_A .$$

Now, if the decision-maker is faced with A and B as two exclusive projects, which one would he choose? One criterion of choice is to select the project with the highest *expected value* of NSBs. On this criterion the decision-maker would be indifferent between A and B because their expected values are the same at $\overline{NSB}$. Yet we can see that distribution B has a higher range of outcomes and in this sense is more 'risky'. For the decision-maker to be indifferent between A and B he would have to be indifferent to the different levels of risk. If he is, he is described as being *risk-neutral*. Risk-neutrality would seem to be an unreasonable attitude on the part of an individual or a firm. It is largely by extending this view to governments and local governments that the presumption has emerged that governments, too, are not risk-neutral. Later we consider some arguments as to why they might be, in certain circumstances. For the moment we proceed on the assumption that our hypothetical decision-maker is *risk-averse*.

Figure 5.2 is cast in terms of choosing either A or B, with an assumption that $\overline{NSB} > 0$. Risk-neutrality also means that the decision-maker will accept *any* project with a positive expected value of NSB. This means that a project with the probabilities shown in Figure 5.1 would definitely be undertaken. To compute the expected value of that project we simply calculate

$$\overline{\text{NSB}} = 0.2(100) + 0.4(50) + 0.25(10) + 0.15(-50)$$

$$= 20 + 20 + 2.5 - 7.5$$

$$= 35.$$

However, suppose that the decision-maker is very much averse to making any loss. In this case he will tend to 'weight' the probability of losing £50 m somewhat more heavily. We therefore need some objective function other than expected value maximisation to account for this. This is to be found in the idea that what is maximised is not the expected value of money returns, but the expected value of *utility*. Intuitively, we can see that the disutility of the loss of £50 m might well have a much higher 'value' than the utility of a £50 m gain. Of course, we have a problem in defining *whose* utility is in question. Strictly, it should be society's utility function that is used. Chapter 2 discussed the problems of identifying what this would be, or even if it could be defined. In CBA we saw that the social function in use should relate back to some aggregate of individuals' welfare functions. For the sake of this chapter we assume that this aggregation has somehow been completed.

5.4 Expected Utility Maximisation

In the expected value approach we were maximising an expression of the form

$$E = p_1 \cdot Y_1 + p_2 \cdot Y_2 + \cdots + p_n \cdot Y_n$$

where p_1 is the probability of Y_1 occurring, and so on, and Y_1 is one of the outcomes measured in money terms.

In the expected utility maximisation approach what is maximised is an expression of the form

$$E(U) = p_1 \cdot U(Y_1) + p_2 \cdot U(Y_2) + \cdots + p_n \cdot U(Y_n)$$

where U now refers to utility and $U(Y_1)$ reads 'the utility of the money outcome Y_1'. If, for example, Y is income, we are speaking of income utilities.

Now, we need to know something more about the income utility function. The general presumption is that it will slope upwards at a decreasing rate, as in Figure 5.3. This simply reflects the assumption of the *diminishing marginal utility of income*. We can also use Figure 5.3 to illustrate further concepts that will be needed before we can see how the expected utility objective can be translated into a revised CBA decision criterion.

In Figure 5.3 consider the two income levels Y_1 and Y_2 and assume these to be the only two possible outcomes of a given project. The utility levels associated with these income levels are $U(Y_1)$ and $U(Y_2)$ respectively. Suppose now, the probability of Y_1 occurring is unity – i.e. Y_1 is absolutely

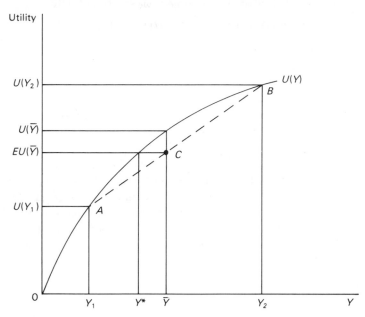

FIGURE 5.3

certain. Then our expected utility formula will be

$$E(U) = 1 \cdot U(Y_1) + 0 \cdot U(Y_2) = U(Y_1).$$

This fixes point A on the diagram. The same exercise with the probability of Y_2 occurring equal to unity will give point B. Now consider point $\bar{Y}$ which is the expected value of Y with possible outcomes Y_1 and Y_2 and given probabilities p_1 and p_2. If $p_1 = p_2 = 0.5$ it is obvious that $\bar{Y}$ will lie exactly midway between Y_1 and Y_2. If the probabilities are 0.4 and 0.6 respectively, $\bar{Y}$ will lie to the right of this midpoint (as shown in Figure 5.3), and so on. The location of $\bar{Y}$ is determined by the respective probabilities, which in turn are given in ratio form by the ratio CB/AC in Figure 5.3. The line AB is in fact the locus of the expected values of the *utility* of the Y_1, Y_2 outcome for various probabilities. That this must be so is seen by inspection of the equation for calculating the expected value of utility.

Thus, to find the *utility* value of the expected value of $\bar{Y}$ we read off the AB segment, as shown in Figure 5.3. If $\bar{Y}$ was a *certain* outcome, however, its utility level would be $U(\bar{Y})$ as shown. What we observe is that the utility value of a certain outcome $\bar{Y}$ is greater than the utility value of a 'gamble' of Y_1 or Y_2 with given probabilities such that the expected value of that gamble is $\bar{Y}$. For any risky context, then, we can always write

$$U(\bar{Y}) > EU(\bar{Y}).$$

This inequality enables us to define the *cost of risk-bearing*. The utility derived from the 'risky' $\bar{Y}$ in Figure 5.3 is $EU(\bar{Y})$. The same utility level could have been obtained from a *certain* income of Y^*. The distance $\bar{Y} - Y^*$ therefore measures what the decision-maker will accept by way of a reduction in income to secure a certain income level rather than the risky income level. Two measures can in fact be observed. These are

(i) $\bar{Y} - Y^* = $ *the cost of risk-bearing*

(ii) Y^* $= $ *the certainty-equivalent income* of $\bar{Y}$.

5.5   Application to Decision Rules: Adjusting Net Present Values

On the face of it, all we have to do is to 'adjust' our decision rule in such a way that the cost of risk-bearing (CRB) is deducted from the expected value of the net social benefit of the project. That is, where before the decision rule for the initial acceptance of a project was

$$\text{NSB} = \sum_{t=0}^{t=T} \frac{B_t - C_t}{(1 + r)^t} \tag{5.1}$$

it now becomes

$$\text{NSB}^* = \sum_{t=0}^{t=T} \frac{B_t - C_t}{(1 + r)^t} - \text{CRB}. \tag{5.2}$$

To put it another way, NSB* is the certainty equivalent NSB.

There are two problems with equation (5.2). The first is that the expression for CRB does not explicitly allow for time: essentially, it has been assumed that the magnitude $\bar{Y} - Y^*$ in Figure 5.3 occurs in an immediate year such that discounting is not relevant, or that the $U(Y)$ function in Figure 5.3 is a utility of *present value* of income function. We therefore need to allow for this fact by writing the CRB as an undiscounted sum occurring each year with a present value of:

$$\text{PV(CRB)} = \sum_{t=0}^{t=T} \frac{k_t}{(1 + r)^t}$$

where k_t is the CRB in year t.

Second, since the context is one of risk, B_t and C_t in equation (5.2) are in fact expected values. To signify this we rewrite them as $\bar{B}_t$ and $\bar{C}_t$ and equation (5.2) now becomes

$$\text{NSB}^* = \sum_{t=0}^{t=T} \frac{\bar{B}_t - \bar{C}_t - k_t}{(1 + r)^t}. \tag{5.3}$$

Equation (5.3) thus provides one way of modifying the basic CBA equation to allow for risk. Note that nothing has been said about how k_t would be estimated *in practice*. Only slight reflection is needed to see that we have a rather serious problem. First, the value of k_t has been obtained in money terms but only by the use of an income-utility function. Unless we can specify that function we cannot estimate k_t. This in turn raises the issues of whether an income utility function can ever be estimated (economists vary in their views on this) and, if it can, whether it exhibits diminishing marginal utility. If it does not, the entire structure so far developed has little value. Second, it will be recalled that in CBA we are dealing with the community as a whole so that the relevant income utility function is that of society. Once again, the issue of the existence of a social welfare function is raised, while, if we argue that it is the decision-maker's utility function that matters, not society's, we will be faced with a possible inconsistency problem discussed in Chapter 2 whereby individual preferences and decision-makers' preferences are added together.

None the less, equation (5.3) indicates the direction in which we need to go *if* risk matters. Before discussing the view that, for social investments, it does not matter, we can see how equation (5.3) might be reformulated so that the CRB is integrated in the discount rate rather than as an absolute reduction in the expected net present value.

5.6   Application to Decision Rules: a 'Risky' Discount Rate

In order to illustrate how the decision rule can be modified by adjusting the discount rate we borrow some concepts from 'state-preference theory' (Hirshleifer and Shapiro, 1963; Hirshleifer, 1965). The essential idea is that it is possible to buy and sell claims to income in future periods where the income in question is contingent upon a particular state of the world taking place. Hence the name 'state-contingent claims'. Thus each claim would command a price in the (hypothetical) market for state-contingent claims. We can write such a price as P_{tx} where P is the price of the claim *now*, t is the period in which the income would accrue, and x is the 'state of the world' necessary for the income to accrue. For example, P_{3x} would be the price now of a claim to £1 in period *3* contingent on state x occurring. We can write

$$\frac{p_{1x} \cdot \text{MU}(C_{1x})}{p_{1y} \cdot \text{MU}(C_{1y})} = \frac{P_{1x}}{P_{1y}} \tag{5.4}$$

and the equilibrium of the consumer (it is convenient to think in terms of the individual for the moment) is as shown in Figure 5.4. Note that C_{1x} is the *claim* to an income in period 1 if the state x occurs.

The diagram is entirely analogous to the standard consumer equilibrium diagram. The choice is between two 'goods': claims to incomes in period 1 where one income is contingent upon state x occurring and the other is contingent upon state y occurring. The budget constraint is given by $P_{1x} \cdot C_{1x} + P_{1y} \cdot C_{1y}$ so its slope is

$$-\frac{P_{1y}}{P_{1x}}.$$

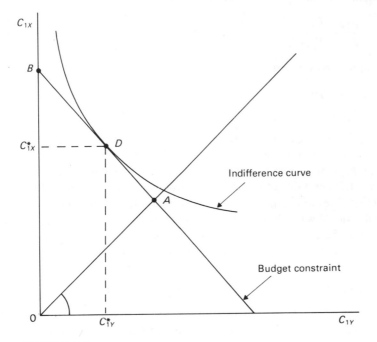

FIGURE 5.4

The individual is assumed to have an indifference map and one indifference curve is shown. At the illustrated equilibrium the ratio of the claims prices is equal to the slope of the indifference curve which is given by

$$\frac{p_{1x} \cdot MU(C_{1x})}{p_{1y} \cdot MU(C_{1y})}.$$

The individual holds C_{1x}^* of claims contingent upon state x occurring and C_{1y}^* claims contingent upon state y occurring.

Note that if the ratio of the prices of claims equals the ratio of probabilities of the states occurring, the equilibrium condition will dictate that $MU(C_{1x}) = MU(C_{1y})$ which means the amount of claims relating to x will equal the amount of claims relating to y. The consumer will be at point A in Figure 5.4 where $C_{1x} = C_{1y}$. His indifference curve will be different to the one shown, i.e. it will be tangential to the budget line at A. At such a tangency, then, the slope of the indifference curve would be

$$-\frac{p_{1y}}{p_{1x}}.$$

The equilibrium in Figure 5.4, however, gives the inequality

$$\frac{p_{1y}}{p_{1x}} < \frac{P_{1y}}{P_{1x}} \tag{5.5}$$

which in turn means that

$$\frac{p_{1x}}{P_{1x}} > \frac{p_{1y}}{P_{1y}} . \tag{5.6}$$

Now P_{1x} is the price of a claim to £1 of income if x occurs. Hence $1/P_{1x}$ is the amount of income, contingent on x occurring, that can be secured for £1, and $p_{1x} \cdot (1/P_{1x})$ must therefore be the expected income secured for £1 if x occurs. Since the left-hand side of the above equation is greater than the right-hand side, the expected returns from type x claims is greater than that from type y claims. If our individual was risk-neutral he would be interested *only* in expected value (see Section 5.3) and hence would buy type x claims only — i.e. he would be at point B in Figure 5.4 and the indifference curve would have to reflect this fact. The equilibrium at D in Figure 5.4 reflects

    (i) the fact that the individual is not risk-neutral but risk-averse;

    (ii) the fact that the expected return on type x claims is higher than on type y claims which puts the consumer on the budget line 'north' of A.

Now, armed with these concepts we can derive a formula for a 'risky' discount rate. Confining ourselves to the two-period case, the formula for the present value of net social benefits is

$$\text{PV(NSB)} = -K_0 + \frac{1}{1+r} \cdot B_1 \tag{5.7}$$

where K_0 is capital expenditure in year 0 and B_1 is the (net) benefit in year 1. The discount factor $1/1 + r$ can be thought of as the price *now* of a claim to £1 in the next period, period 1. This enables us to link the discount factor with the price of a claim on future benefits. We could in fact rewrite equation (5.7) as

$$\text{PV(NSB)} = -P_0 \cdot K_0 + P_1 \cdot B_1 \tag{5.8}$$

where P_0 is the price of a claim on the immediate period, and hence equals unity, and P_1 is the price now of a claim on a *certain* net benefit in period 1. But the context of interest is a risky one so that we need to reformulate the expression for net benefits in period 1 so that equation (5.8) becomes

$$\text{PV(NSB)}^* = -P_0 \cdot K_0 + P_{1x} \cdot B_{1x} + P_{1y} \cdot B_{1y} \tag{5.9}$$

which simply tells us that the claim to the benefit in period 1 if state x comes about has a price of P_1. If he wished to be *certain* of securing £1 in period 1 we would have to hold *both* claims — i.e. the ones relating to contexts x and y.

That is, the price of a *certain* £1 in period 1 is $P_{1x} + P_{1y}$ which we have already seen is equal to the discount factor $1/1 + r$. In equation (5.9), PV(NSB)* is the *certainty-equivalent* present value, a concept already introduced. Quite simply, a 'risky' discount rate — i.e. a discount rate incorporating a risk element to reflect the CRB — is then that rate which, when applied to the stream of the expected value of net benefits, will give the certainty-equivalent value.

The expected value of the net benefit in period 1 will be

$$EV(B_1) = p_{1x} \cdot B_{1x} + p_{1y} \cdot B_{1y}$$

or

$$EV(B_1) = p_{1x} \cdot B_{1x} + (1 - p_{1x}) \cdot B_{1y} \qquad (5.10)$$

because $p_{1y} = (1 - p_{1x})$ since both events cannot occur at the same time. Substituting equation (5.10) in the net present value calculation gives

$$NPV = P_0 \cdot K_0 + [p_{1x} \cdot B_{1x} + (1 - p_{1x})B_{1y}] \frac{1}{1 + r^*} \qquad (5.11)$$

where r^* is the 'risky' discount rate we require. But equation (5.11) must equal equation (5.9) since r^* is defined as the rate of discount which makes the NPV equal to the certainty-equivalent net present value. Hence

$$-P_0 \cdot K_0 + \frac{p_{1x} \cdot B_{1x} + (1 - p_{1x})B_{1y}}{1 + r^*} = -P_0 \cdot K_0 + P_{1x} \cdot B_{1x} + P_{1y} \cdot B_{1y}$$

or

$$1 + r^* = \frac{p_{1x} \cdot B_{1x} + (1 - p_{1x})B_{1y}}{P_{1x} \cdot B_{1x} + P_{1y} \cdot B_{1y}}. \qquad (5.12)$$

Equation (5.12) provides us with an expression for a 'risky' discount rate which is applied to the expected values of benefits. Note that if $B_{1x} = B_{1y}$ — i.e. the benefit flows are *not* contingent upon states of nature: they are certain — equation (5.12) will reduce to

$$1 + r^* = \frac{1}{P_{1x} + P_{1y}}. \qquad (5.13)$$

But $P_{1x} + P_{1y} = 1/1 + r$, as demonstrated earlier. Hence

$$1 + r^* = 1 + r, \qquad \text{and} \qquad r^* = r \qquad (5.14)$$

which is what we would expect. The 'risky' rate reduces to the riskless rate once the risk context is removed.

Once again, while it has been possible to produce a formula (albeit for a limited two-period case) for a risky discount rate it will be evident that the information required is not likely to be any more forthcoming than it was for the absolute measure of the CRB. The problem lies not with the probabilities in equation (5.12) since, *ex hypothesi*, we take these as being known. Rather, it lies with the two 'price' variables. We have no perfectly functioning capital market in which to observe them and hence no obvious way in which we can compute r^*.

5.7   Is the Cost of Risk-bearing Relevant?

Clearly, whatever the theoretical rationale for making some allowance for the CRB in investment appraisal, there are formidable informational difficulties in making one, save in the respect of knowing the likely *direction* of change. In the view of some, however, the empirical difficulty referred to is a non-problem. It arises because a theory largely developed in the context of the theory of the firm has been applied to government decision-making without seeing whether the context alters the applicability of the theory. According to the Arrow–Lind theorem (Arrow and Lind, 1970) allowing for risk is not relevant in such contexts.

5.7.1   THE ARROW–LIND THEOREM

Since governments are largely organisations with massive expenditures on capital projects it can be argued that the risk attached to any *single* project is so small that it is not worth worrying about. This will arise from two aspects of such investments. First, they are but one of many, so that, as with any 'wise' portfolio of investments we can expect those with the risk of losses to be at least balanced by those with a 'risk' of securing higher net benefits than expected. This is known as *risk-pooling*. The requirements for this argument to hold are:

    (i)   that the government's portfolio of capital projects should not be dominated by one or more large projects such that the risk on these projects dominates the general risk structure of the portfolio;

    (ii) that there should be no interdependence among projects or, if there is, it should be such that this interdependence reduces the overall risk attached to the portfolio.

Both requirements are questionable. The governments of advanced countries frequently have major programmes of capital investment which have high risk elements in the sense being considered in this chapter. In the United Kingdom the cases of Concorde and the choice of gas-cooled nuclear reactors have already been cited. In less developed countries large projects such as irrigation, water supply or electrification may also dominate. In these latter cases, however, factors offsetting the risk are, first, that such investments tend not to be high risk investments, the returns being reasonably certain, and, second, that risk is in any event frequently shared by countries offering capital aid. It is also the case that often the returns on a large part of the programme will depend on a few key variables, such as the rate of population increase and of economic growth, since these tend to govern the demand for most products. Unfortunately, forecasts of these variables are notoriously inaccurate, and an overestimate may lead to an excessive expansion of capacity throughout the public sector (or vice versa).

The Arrow—Lind theorem is, however, more concerned with a second kind of risk-reducing phenomenon, the *spreading of risks across people*. The intuitive appeal of the argument is simple — the larger the number of taxpayers in the country, the less is the risk per taxpayer from any given project. The formal proof of the theorem is somewhat complex, however. We may refer to Figure 5.5, which repeats the essentials of Figure 5.4, for an indirect demonstration. The $U(Y)$ function is shown with diminishing marginal returns. Suppose the project in question is being considered by a single person and the outcomes 1 and 2 have probabilities of $p_1 = p_2 = 0.5$ with payoffs of $Y_1 = +50$ and $Y_2 = -20$. Assume the person begins with assets of 100 so that the risky project alone will give an asset outcome of 150 or 80. The expected value of the

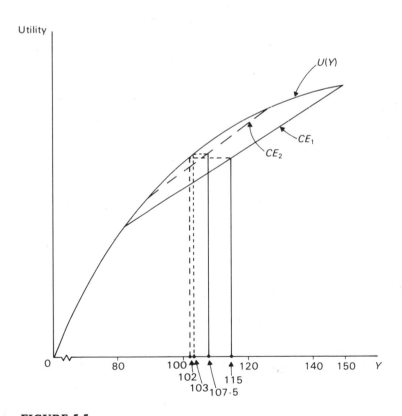

FIGURE 5.5

project is

$$(0.5 \times 50) - (0.5 \times 20) = +15$$

so that the expected value of assets is 115.

However, we need to relate this to a certainty equivalent via the $U(Y)$ function. Reference to Figure 5.5 shows that the certainty-equivalent value of 115 is 102 and this is obtained by reading off the certainty-equivalence line CE_1 (drawn from $Y = 80$ to $Y = 150$). Hence the cost of risk-bearing is

$$CRB_1 = E(Y) - CE(Y)$$

$$= 115 - 102$$

$$= 13.$$

Now suppose a second individual joins in the project and agrees to share the gains or losses equally. We make the heroic assumption that the second individual has the same $U(Y)$ function as the first. Now the pay-offs *to each individual* are +25 and −10 since they share the gains/losses. In asset terms, again assuming individual 2 has initial assets of 100, the pay-offs are $Y_1 = 90$ and $Y_2 = 125$. We therefore draw a new certainty-equivalence line, CE_2, as shown in Figure 5.5. The expected value *to each individual* is

$$(0.5 \times 25) - (0.5 \times 10) = 7.5$$

or, in asset terms, 107.5. To find the certainty-equivalent value we refer to CE_2 and see that it is 103. Hence, the cost of risk-bearing for each individual is

$$CRB_2 = E(Y) - CE(Y)$$

$$= 107.5 - 103$$

$$= 4.5.$$

Now each individual bears this risk so the *project risk* is $2 \times CRB_2 = 9$.

However, this total risk is less than the risk on the project when only one person was involved. By 'spreading' the risk across more individuals the project risk has been reduced. This is the essence of the Arrow–Lind theorem which demonstrates that, in the limit, if the number of individuals tends to infinity the project risk tends to zero.

Now, if the theorem is correct and cannot be challenged in its own context, and if the population in the country undertaking the project is large, we have a rationale for ignoring risk altogether. Given the complexities of empirically estimating the CRB this is rather convenient and we can revert to the use of expected-value procedures. That is, what the Arrow–Lind theorem tells us to do is to treat the government as a risk-neutral investor. Before turning to some theoretical critiques of the theorem, however, we can make a few observations about its empirical usefulness.

First, it matters a great deal what kind of risk we are talking about, since the Arrow—Lind theorem is largely concerned with spreading the *financial cost* of a project across taxpayers. But projects have many types of risk. Consider the reactor accident in Harrisburg in 1979: had that accident been any worse, fairly large numbers of people would have been exposed to excessive radiation. But the numbers would not have begun to approach the number of taxpayers in the United States. That is, as far as the externality aspects of projects are concerned, those risks are very unlikely to be spread across many people. An explosion at a liquid natural gas terminal would be damaging to the local inhabitants, but not to the nation. A blow-out in an oil well could affect hundreds of thousands of tourists, fishermen etc. through its pollution impact, but not an entire nation of taxpayers. A road with a serious accident risk imposes this risk only on those who use it. And so on. If the Arrow—Lind theorem holds for the resource cost of a project, it does not seem to hold for the externality aspects.

Second, we can even question whether it holds for the resource costs. For, as we have seen, governments can only behave as if they are risk-neutral if the population in question is infinite. Obviously, no population is infinite so we must be thinking pragmatically about very large numbers. But would 20 million taxpayers constitute a very large number relative to the size of many public-sector projects? Would 80 million? If not, and these are approximately the taxpayer populations of the United Kingdom and the United States respectively, then the theorem does not permit us to ignore risk.

Third, the Arrow—Lind theorem requires that a mechanism exists for the actual spreading of the risks. What Arrow and Lind postulate is a government that reduces taxes if the net financial flow from their portfolio of projects is positive and raises taxes if the outcome is negative. But while governments are very likely to change taxes in an upwards direction to pay for negative outcomes, they may well do nothing of the sort for positive outcomes. Arguably they would increase government expenditure and thus 'spread' the benefits in this way. Much would depend on the nature of the increased expenditure, however.

5.7.2 THE RELEVANCE TO PUBLIC GOODS

Fisher (1974) has produced an important qualification to the Arrow—Lind theorem in terms of its theoretical validity. For the theorem, if it holds at all, does so only for *private goods* — i.e. those goods which when consumed by any one individual cannot be consumed by some other and where the principle of exclusion applies. In many public investments, however, the goods being provided are not private goods but public goods — those that have at least an element of non-exclusion and non-rivalry. Defence expenditures would be a case in point, as would many environmental improvement expenditures. In such cases, the number of persons does not affect the risk of the project — that risk is invariant with how ever many people there are. If the environmental improvement programme goes wrong, it may well be an entire nation that suffers since, for example, noise is not reduced simply because 100,000 people hear it rather than one.

How relevant Fisher's critique is depends very much on the empirical validity of public good or public bad elements in such projects. Arguably, if they exist they will tend to be localised public bads such as the earlier examples given of radiation risks, gas explosions and so on. None the less, the theoretical point is entirely sound and the Arrow—Lind theorem clearly does not hold if the goods in question are public goods or if the risks in question take on the form of public bads.

5.7.3   OPTION VALUE AND RISK-AVERSION

In order to deal with another line of criticism relevant to the Arrow—Lind theorem we need to make a diversion to explain the concept of 'option value'. For if it can be demonstrated that option value exists then it will be found that it bears a close resemblance to the concept of the cost of risk-bearing and it would have to be deducted from the net present value of the project. An intuitive idea of option value can be obtained by taking the example of whaling. Few of us are ever likely to see a whale, in its natural habitat anyway. The existence of documentary films, television and the general media all serve to inform us that they exist and that many species of whale are subject to the threat of extinction. By and large this threat comes from over-catching despite the existence of a quota system. There exists a substantial body of opinion which believes that these species should be preserved and that if the only way to do this is to reduce the catch rate then that is what must be done. Clearly, these expressions of concern are translatable into losses of utility as the whale populations are reduced, even though the 'good' in question is consumed either indirectly — through TV and so on — or is not consumed at all. That is, all one needs is information about whales to generate the possibility of expressing concern and suffering disutility.

The example illustrates two types of meaning of 'option value'. The first relates to disutility caused through the potential loss of an option to exercise the choice of trying to see a whale in its natural habitat. The second relates to a kind of altruism extended to whales but which we can think of as disutility suffered through the removal of an option to exercise that altruism. Arguably, the second kind of option value is even more important than the first: many people would simply like to think that the whales will continue to exist without any thought that they themselves would wish to see them. In both senses then, we can think of option value as a form of willingness to pay to reduce the risk of options being removed in the future.

To define option value more rigorously we can once again make use of the diagram used to illustrate the measure of CRB. Figure 5.6 therefore repeats the

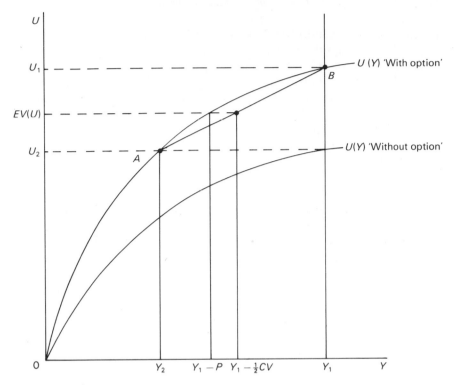

FIGURE 5.6

essentials but this time two $U(Y)$ functions are shown, the upper one relating to a 'with option' alternative and the lower one to the 'without option' alternative. The option in question can be the preservation of whales, the provision of some good, or whatever. Assume that the $U(Y)$ function relates to society as a whole (we have already considered the problems involved in this idea) and that the starting point is an income of Y_1. The corresponding utility levels are U_1 and U_2 for the 'with' and 'without' cases.

Suppose now that society is asked what it is willing to pay to avoid the 'without option' alternative. The answer would be the amount $Y_1 - Y_2$ in Figure 5.6. This is because at income Y_1 the 'without option' alternative yields a utility level of U_2. That same utility level 'with' the option is secured when income falls to Y_2. The sum $Y_1 - Y_2$ therefore corresponds to the income level equivalent to $U_1 - U_2$ with Y_1 as the starting-point. $Y_1 - Y_2$ therefore indicates their maximum willingness to pay to avoid the 'without' alternative. But this is a familiar concept since it is nothing more than the *compensating variation measure of consumers' surplus* (see Chapter 6). We may therefore write

$$CV = Y_1 - Y_2.$$

However, the context we are interested in is one of risk. We therefore introduce the idea that the 'with' and 'without' alternatives themselves have probabilities. Perhaps there is some uncertainty about the size of whale populations, some dispute over the impact of whaling and so on (indeed, this defines the context for the actual example of whaling, although the probability of the 'without' situation occurring would seem rather high). In this case the measure of the surplus, *CV*, has itself to be translated into an *expected value* and this will simply be the probability of the need to take action to secure the 'with option' outcome. If we suppose this to be 0.5 then the expected value of the surplus will simply be

$$E(CV) = 0.5\,CV$$

and the income level corresponding to this is shown as the midpoint between Y_1 and Y_2 – i.e. $Y_1 - 0.5\,CV$. Reference to the certainty-equivalence line between *A* and *B* in Figure 5.6 shows that the utility level corresponding to $Y_1 - 0.5\,CV$ is the expected value of the two utility levels U_1 and U_2.

Now, instead of seeking society's willingness to pay to avoid the 'without option' alternative, we could equally well ask what society is willing to pay for the certain *option* of buying the good in question. This price will be given by $Y_1 - P$ in Figure 5.6 because at this income society will assume it is on the upper $U(Y)$ curve with a utility level corresponding to its expected utility level $E(U)$.

Whereas *CV* was a measure of consumer surplus, *P* is a measure of the maximum *option price* society is willing to pay. Further,

$$P > E(CV)$$

(Since $Y_1 - P$ is greater than $Y_1 - 0.5\,CV$)

which means that society is willing to pay *more* for the assurance that the good will be there (if they want it) than the expected value of their consumers' surplus. Cicchetti and Freeman (1971) term this excess 'true option value'. We can therefore write

Option Value = Option Price – Expected Consumers' Surplus

$$= P - E(CV).$$

What option value is, then, is *the price people are willing to pay for an assurance (an option) that the good in question will be available (at a predetermined price) if they want it.* The assurance is formally equivalent to the removal of the risk of the good not being available. Option value will exist as long as individuals are risk-averse, and Cicchetti and Freeman (1971) provided the first formal proof that this is so. Note in Figure 5.6 that the option price *P* is the certainty equivalent of the expected value of consumers' surplus. Since the price *P* is the sum being paid to remove risk this is exactly as it should be.

If option value exists and if it can be estimated, what is its impact on a CBA decision rule? The answer is that, if the Arrow–Lind theorem does *not* apply, then risk-aversion defines the context of decision-making. If risk-aversion is relevant then so is option value and it should be deducted from the NPV of the net benefits of the project. Note that this is *not in addition* to deducting the cost of risk-bearing since they are really two ways of thinking about the same thing. Note too that all the problems of empirical estimation of the CRB arise in exactly the same way. At best, when we think option value is relevant we should have some idea as to whether the net benefits of a development (e.g. one that reduces whale populations even further) are overstated or not. We shall see that the context of *irreversible costs* provides the most likely one in which option value will exist. We now consider an interesting additional theorem — one that demonstrates that option value exists *even under risk-neutrality*.

5.7.4   OPTION VALUE AND RISK-NEUTRALITY

Arrow and Fisher (1974) have provided a proof that a sort of option value exists even for a risk-neutral investor. This proof requires a level of mathematics well above that used in this text. Accordingly we use an illustrative example adapted from one provided by Krutilla and Fisher (1975). The context is one of a development project which imposes some *irreversible consequences* such as long-run damage to the ecosystem, loss of wilderness, loss of wildlife species etc.

Ignoring the discount rate, we hypothesise a parcel of land for development. Let the proportion of land developed be d and the options are to develop it *all* in period 1 ($d_1 = 1, d_2 = 0$), to develop it all in period 2 ($d_1 = 0, d_2 = 1$), to develop part now and part later ($d_1 > 0, d_2 > 0$ with $d_2 = 1 - d_1$) or not to develop it at all ($d_1 = 0, d_2 = 0$). Let the net benefits of *development* be B_1 and B_2 respectively. Note (i) that development in 1 leaves development benefits occurring in 2, and development in 2 leaves preservation benefits occurring in 1; and (ii) net benefits are defined as the gross benefits of development *minus* the costs of development *minus the benefits of preservation*. That is net benefits are defined as net of costs and net of the benefits of the alternative, in this case preservation.

We now seek two sets of decision rules. The first is produced on the basis of a simple expected value objective assuming B_1 is known and B_2 is subject to a probability distribution such that $B_2 = 1$ with a probability of 0.9 and $B_2 = -8$ with a probability of 0.1. For the moment this is all the information the decision-maker has. The expected value of benefits in year 2 is therefore

$$E(B_2) = 0.9(1) + 0.1(-8) = 0.1$$

which is positive. We can now formulate the first set of decision rules. These are:

(1) *if $B_1 < 0$, $d_1 = 0$.* This is we simply leave development until period 2 when we can 'capture' some expected benefits.

(2) *if $B_1 > 0$, $d_1 = 1$.* This requires a little more explanation: essentially since

no second period losses are *expected* from development in period 1 we proceed to develop now. Note that, had $E(B_2) < 0$ we would have to compare B_1 with $E(B_2)$. For example if B_1 is positive but does not outweigh $E(B_2)$ then $d_1 = 0$.

(3) *if $B_1 = 0$, $0 < d_1 < 1$.* That is the amount of development in period 1 does not matter. If we develop we get the sequence of benefits $(0, 0.1)$ and if we wait to develop to period 2 we get the same sequence $(0, 0.1)$. If we develop some now and some later we get zero benefits in period 1 and the benefits of period 2 of the development in 1 plus the benefits of developing the remainder in period 2 — again the sequence is $(0, 0.1)$.

Now change the context such that by the time period 2 starts we have more information on the benefit. If we know B_2 is going to be negative (it will have a value of -8 in our example) then $d_2 = 0$ — we simply do not develop in period 2. The *sum* of the benefits over the two periods is

$$d_1 B_1 - 8d_1 = d_1(B_1 - 8).$$

Why is $8d_1$ subtracted? Because the negative benefits from development now accrue in period 2 but they relate to the amount of development carried out in period 1 (there being no development in period 2). It is essential to remember this 'carrying over' of benefits if development takes place at all in period 1.

If on the other hand we know B_2 will be positive ($+1$ in our example) then $d_2 > 0$ and the sum of the benefits over the two periods will be

$$d_1 B_1 + (d_1 + d_2)B_2$$

i.e. the benefits accruing from the amount of development in period 1 and the benefits accruing from wholesale development over the two periods. Since $d_1 + d_2 = 1$ and $B_2 = 1$ in our example this can be rewritten as

$$d_1 B_1 + 1.$$

Now reconsider the decision rule as seen at the start of period 1. We seek the expected value of the sum of benefits. We know that if a negative outcome occurs in period 2 it is given by $d_1(B_1 - 8)$ and if a positive outcome occurs it is given by $d_1 B_1 + 1$. It follows that the expected value is

$$E(B_1 + B_2) = 0.1 d_1(B_1 - 8) + 0.9 d_1 B_1 + 1$$
$$= d_1(B_1 - 0.8) + 0.9.$$

Our decision rules can now be reformulated.

(1)' *if $B_1 < 0.8$, $d_1 = 0$.* Quite simply, if $B_1 < 0.8$ then $(B_1 - 0.8) < 0$ and hence development should not occur in the first period.

(2)' *if $B_1 > 0.8$, $d_1 = 1$.* In this case $(B_1 - 0.8) > 0$ and development should occur.

(3)$'$ *if* $B_1 = 0.8$, $(B_1 - 0.8) = 0$ and we have the same situation in rule (3) previously.

Now, how do the decision rules differ? The vital difference is that the value of net benefits of developments in period 1 can on the new formulation be *positive* (but <0.8) but the decision will be to *postpone* development. Second, both sets of rules are based on expected value formulations (risk-neutrality) but *the second gives a different result, one which indicates a loss through the use of the 'simple' expected value formulation*. This loss is a *quasi-option value* and this value (0.8 in our example) needs to be deducted from the NPV of any project. Third, the expected value rules differ in context in that the second incorporates a 'learning' function whereby knowledge of benefits is increased as time goes on.

We have therefore identified an option value cost which is likely to arise in the context of *irreversibilities*. Again, empirical difficulties abound, but we again have some idea that standard-risk-averse and, now, risk-neutral contexts will tend to overstate the net benefits of certain developments.

5.8 Uncertainty

The lengthy discussion of risk contexts has indicated that some form of deduction from the 'orthodox' net present value of a project needs to be made for risk if we are satisfied that the context is properly one of risk-aversion – such a deduction reflecting the option value or cost of risk-bearing in the project – and that such deductions might similarly apply for risk-neutral contexts. The relevance of the second observation, based on the Arrow–Fisher theorem, is that the Arrow–Lind theorem was used to demonstrate that risk *might* not be a legitimate worry of governments engaged in social appraisal because they could act as if they were risk-neutral. The suggestion now is that even risk-neutrality does not obviate the need for some allowance for the risk of loss of options.

Now the risk context has been based on the idea that there is some prior knowledge of probabilities. What happens when these probabilities are not known? This will certainly be the case for many new ventures, new technologies and so on. One hopes that research and development will have indicated some of the probabilities but this will not always be so. In many cases we simply will not know the probabilities and hence we require some rules on how to proceed in such contexts. These rules come from *decision theory* and it is as well to point out at the start that whichever rule is selected is very much dependent upon the outlook of the decision-maker. The argument in this book is that this outlook should take cognisance, as far as possible, of the views of society. If social attitudes appear cautious about new technologies then cautious rules should be adopted. If society appears optimistic, optimistic rules can be adopted. One complicating factor concerns future generations in that the rules to be considered frequently involve the decision being made by one generation with the costs or benefits being borne by the next generation. We shall suggest that this tends to favour the adoption of a particular rule.

5.8.1   THE PAY-OFF MATRIX

The matrix in Table 5.1 shows on the horizontal axis a set of possible states of nature, $N = 1$ to $N = 4$. The probabilities of these states of nature occurring is not known, hence the context of uncertainty. The net social benefits (the 'pay-offs') accruing from each state of nature *are* assumed to be known and these appear in the 'body' of the matrix. They vary according to the strategy chosen and we assume there are four of these, $S = 1$ to $S = 4$. Note that even the amount of information conveyed in this hypothetical matrix is greater than that which may exist in reality. We might for example only have an idea that some states and strategies will give rise to 'better' or 'worse' results than others without being able to quantify the outcomes. There is always the unpredictable and the unknowable. But by definition we cannot modify decision rules to allow for what we cannot know. At worst then we would hope to be able to place some ordinal indicators in the body of the matrix.

We may now consider the main rules that have been suggested for such a context.

5.8.2   THE MAXIMAX CRITERION

On this criterion, the decision-maker simply opts for the highest pay-off which is immediately identified at $S = 3$, $N = 2$ giving NSB = 4. Hence he opts for strategy 3. Clearly this is an optimistic strategy based on looking for the maximum pay-offs of each strategy and then taking the maximum of these. Note how risky this is, since strategy 3 would result in zero pay-off in 3 out of the 4 possible 'states of nature'. None the less we cannot, *ex hypothesi*, say what the probabilities of N_1 etc. are.

5.8.3   THE MAXIMIN CRITERION

On this rule, sometimes called the Wald criterion, we look for the minimum pay-offs in each strategy, and then maximise the minimum pay-off. If we circle

TABLE 5.1

$N =$	1	2	3	4
$S = 1$	2	2	0	1
2	1	1	1	1
3	0	4	0	0
4	1	3	0	0

the minimum pay-offs for each strategy in Table 5.1 we obtain

MINIMUM PAY-OFF

$S = 1$	0
2	1
3	0
4	0

Clearly, strategy 2 is chosen. (If pay-offs are replaced by costs the rule becomes one of looking for the maximum losses and then minimising this loss. In this form it is the *minimax loss* criterion.) The maximin criterion is inherently cautious since the revised matrix shows that it uses only the *minimum* pay-offs over which a decision is to be made. Consistently applied in CBA one could argue that it would lead to under-investment and the inhibition of economic growth.

5.8.4   INDEX OF PESSIMISM CRITERION

This approach, the Hurwicz criterion as it is sometimes known, looks at the best and worst outcomes of each strategy with a prior probability (the 'index of pessimism') being assigned to the worst outcome and, by definition, one minus this probability to the best outcome. Rewriting the matrix in Table 5.1 for the best and worst outcomes gives:

	BEST	WORST
$S = 1$	2	0
2	1	1
3	4	0
4	3	0

Let the index of pessimism be 0.9 so that the index applied to the best outcomes is 0.1, then the matrix becomes:

WEIGHTED INDEX

$S = 1$	$(2 \times 0.1) + (0.9 \times 0) =$	0.2
2	$(1 \times 0.1) + (0.9 \times 1) =$	1.0
3	$(4 \times 0.1) + (0.9 \times 0) =$	0.4
4	$(3 \times 0.1) + (0.9 \times 0) =$	0.3

Strategy 2 would be chosen as having the highest pay-off. Note that if the index had been 0.7, strategy 3 would have yielded a weighted NSB of 1.2 and strategy 2 an NSB of 1.0 so that strategy 3 would have been preferred.

Note that if the index is set equal to unity the Hurwicz rule reduces to the maximin rule. The Hurwicz rule appeals because of its explicit use of the index of pessimism. Equally, one could argue that if states of nature are limited, assignment of such an index is no less difficult than assignment of subjective probabilities. Possibly the index could be inferred from 'implied' values in past decisions — an issue discussed at length in Chapter 2.

5.8.5   THE LAPLACE CRITERION

This criterion takes up the hint made in Section 5.8.3 and simply assigns prior probabilities to the states of nature. However, the probabilities are all equal on the basis that if we know nothing everything is equally probable (the so-called 'principle of insufficient reason'). If we can accept this then the matrix in Table 5.1 becomes:

	$N = 1$	2	3	4	Σ
$S = 1$	0.5	0.5	0	0.25	1.25
2	0.25	0.25	0.25	0.25	1.00
3	0	1	0	0	1.00
4	0.25	0.75	0	0	1.00

Note that these multiplied NSBs are then *summed* to give an expected value. The expected value of strategy 1 is highest and hence 1 is chosen.

One is tempted to favour such a rule for a risk-neutral agency which a government might be if the Arrow—Lind theorem (Section 5.7.1) holds. But this temptation should be resisted, because while the results in the final column of the matrix above are indeed expected values, they are based on probabilities which have no theoretical or empirical justification. This is because the 'principle of insufficient reason' itself has no foundation: simply because we do not know something does not mean that we can behave *as if* we know that events are equiprobable. That is, assigning equal probabilities is making as assertion (or statement) about the world on the basis of no evidence or information of any kind. The Laplace criterion is therefore a dangerous rule to utilise.

5.8.6   THE MINIMAX REGRET CRITERION

On this rule, otherwise known as the Savage criterion, we utilise something akin to the minimax loss principle mentioned in sub-section 5.8.3. The 'losses' are however defined as the difference between the *actual* pay-off and what that pay-off *would* have been had the correct strategy been chosen. We can see this by first constructing the *'regret' matrix* shown in Table 5.2. Thus, if state of

TABLE 5.2

$N =$	1	2	3	4
$S = 1$	0	2	1	0
2	1	3	0	0
3	2	0	1	1
4	1	1	1	1

nature 1 occurs and strategy 1 is chosen, then the *actual* gains are +2. The best that could have been achieved with this state of nature is also +2, so for $N = 1$ and $S = 1$: Potential Gain − Actual Gain = 2 − 2 = 0. Similarly, for $N = 1, S = 2$ we have an actual gain of 1 and a potential gain of 2 (had S_1 been chosen), so the regret is 2 − 1 = 1. And so on.

Now, we aim to minimise the maximum regrets. These are given by:

MAXIMUM REGRETS

$S = 1$	2
2	3
3	2
4	1

So that strategy 4 is chosen.

It can be argued that the minimax regret criterion is again rather cautious, but less so than the maximin. Again, this could be held to be detrimental to long-run growth prospects if applied consistently in CBA programmes. On the other hand it has an equity appeal in that it enables us to avoid the worst disasters. This may be particularly relevant if the investments in question impose costs on future generations. There is uncertainty about what the structure of tastes of future generations will be and we have already seen that where demand is uncertain in a future period there is some loss of option value. There is therefore some reason to err on the side of caution in adopting decision rules.

Others have questioned the internal consistency of the minimax regret criterion in that it appears to be inconsistent with the requirement that such decision rules be independent of irrelevant alternatives. For a formal proof see Dasgupta and Pearce (1972, pp. 191−2).

5.8.7 CONCLUSIONS

With the exception of the Laplace criterion, all the rules presented have approximately equal credentials in that all have some problem associated with them and all rely upon some prior attitude on the part of the decision-maker to determine their choice. However, one could advance the view that the rules need not be used consistently across all public investments, even if total uncertainty characterised such investments. That is, suppose all public projects have uncertainty attached to them. Should all therefore be decided upon by a single criterion? The answer is that it will depend upon the type of negative outcomes we are considering. If, for example, the cost of being wrong in one area — perhaps energy investment — is very large, one is tempted to argue that something like the minimax regret criterion is to be preferred. We could advance the idea of diminishing marginal utility (or in this case, increasing marginal disutility) to defend such an approach. If, on the other hand, the cost of being wrong is quite small we may prefer maximax or more optimistic rules. In other words, it may be desirable to adopt a Hurwicz criterion, with an 'index of pessimism' varying between extreme values of 0 and 1 according to the project under consideration.

6 Valuing Costs and Benefits when Prices Change

6.1 Consumers' Surplus

If all projects were perfectly divisible, one could determine their optimal scale simply by expanding them until the value of their marginal product exactly equalled the value of the inputs required to produce it. There would be no need for a method of valuation for comparing alternative situations in which prices differ. For instance, in Figure 6.1, one would expand output of good X until X_2 is reached. It would be necessary to forecast how prices change when output expands, but no comparison of situations such as $P_1 X_1$ and $P_2 X_2$ is needed.

In practice, CBA has most often been applied to cases where indivisibilities are important — dams, roads, railways, power stations and so on. In many cases, one important question is whether to have the facility at all. If it is decided that some such facility is needed, then there is a choice of scale, but again indivisibilities occur — single or double-track railway, number of electricity-generating sets, number of carriageways and lanes of a road. It is usual in project analysis to examine a number of discrete alternatives, between which prices of the good in question and closely related products may vary significantly. The question then arises, supposing that we have a project which will yield an increment of output $(X_2 - X_1)$, should we value this using the initial price P_1, the final price P_2, or some combination of the two?

The long-standing answer to this question has been to use the concept of consumers' surplus. According to this, we value the increment of output at what consumers actually pay for it, $P_2(X_2 - X_1)$, plus the maximum extra they would have been willing to pay had the seller been able to practise perfect discrimination. This additional amount is represented by the shaded triangle in Figure 6.1. Assuming that the demand curve may be linearly approximated over the range in question, the resulting benefit (B) is:

$$B = (X_2 - X_1)P_2 + \tfrac{1}{2}(X_2 - X_1)(P_1 - P_2) = \tfrac{1}{2}(X_2 - X_1)(P_1 + P_2). \quad (6.1)$$

The increased output is valued at the mean of the initial and final price.

The concept of consumers' surplus was first formulated in terms of cardinal utility, as a money measure of the utility yielded by the change in question. For each level of demand (X_i), the price at which the consumer will purchase that quantity will be given by

$$\left(\frac{\partial U}{\partial X} \right)_{X = X_i} = \lambda P_i.$$

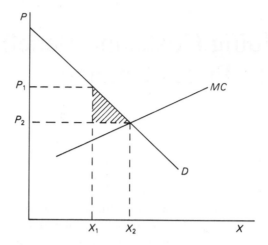

FIGURE 6.1

This may be written

$$P_i = \left(\frac{\partial U}{\partial X}\right)_{X=X_i}\bigg/\lambda. \tag{6.2}$$

(In words, the equation states that the price in question measures the marginal utility of the good relative to the marginal utility of money income.)

Now as we try to aggregate these prices for successive levels of X_i along a normal demand curve (which is plotted assuming that *money* income is held constant), both the purchasing power of money is increasing (as P falls) and the *real* income of the consumer is, as a consequence, rising. These two factors may be expected to change the marginal utility of money in opposite directions but it would be a remarkable accident if, as a result, the marginal utility of money income remained constant. But all our measurements of utility are relative to that of money income. In other words we are measuring utility in terms of a 'measuring rod', the length of which itself changes as we move it along the demand curve! (Pigou, 1920). It may be argued that so long as the price changes are for goods on which only a small part of money income is spent, the change in marginal utility of money income will not be great. However, the change in consumers' surplus may be small too; there is no guarantee that the proportionate error will be small.

In an ordinal framework, such as that implied by the application of the compensation test, the same problem appears in a different guise. Here we need to measure what sum of money will exactly compensate the consumer (that is, return him to his original indifference curve) after a price change. But as he moves along a conventional demand curve, the consumer is able to reach higher or lower-valued indifference curves as a result of the changes in price. Thus the area of the triangle under the conventional demand curve is not an accurate measure of the concept we have in mind. What is needed is the area under a demand curve relating quantity to price, under the assumption that money income is varied in such a way that the consumer remains on the same indifference curve. The name given to this demand curve is the 'compensated demand curve' and the area under it is termed the 'compensating variation' (Hicks, 1943).

The derivation of such a demand curve from an indifference map is illustrated in Figure 6.2. In the top half of the diagram the axes are delineated in terms of

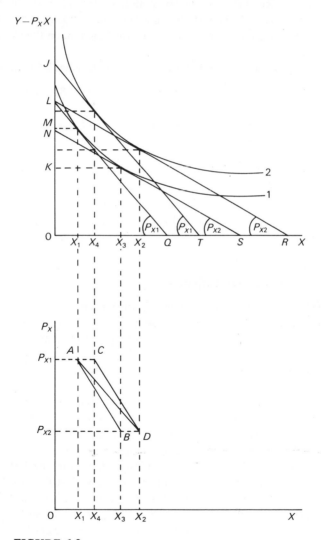

FIGURE 6.2

good X and $(Y - P_X X)$, the amount of money income available for all other purposes after deducting expenditure on good X. The slope of the budget line in this case is equal to $-P_X$. The initial budget line LQ is drawn assuming a money income of $0L$ and a price of P_{X1}. When the price of X falls from P_{X1} to P_{X2}, the budget line pivots to the position LR, and demand (along the conventional demand curve) rises from X_1 to X_2. However, if we reduce money income until the consumer is only able to reach the original indifference curve, the budget line corresponding to P_{X2} will shift to a parallel position tangential to indifference curve 1 (NS) and demand will fall back to X_3. This is the demand resulting from a price of P_{X2} on the compensated demand curve corresponding to indifference curve 1. The conventional (AD) and compensated (AB) demand curves for X are shown in the bottom half of the diagram, on the assumption of linearity.

Relating distances in the top half of the diagram to areas in the bottom half:

LM = expenditure on X at the original levels of price (P_{X1}) and money income ($0L$) = area $0P_{X1}AX_1$;

NK = expenditure on X at the new levels of price (P_{X2}) and money income ($0N$) = area $0P_{X2}BX_3$;

MK = sum of money which is equivalent in terms of utility to an increase in X from X_1 to X_3 on the original indifference curve = area X_1ABX_3;

LN = compensating variation for a fall in price from P_{X1} to P_{X2} when the consumer is held at indifference level 1. Since this equals $LM + NK - MK$, it must correspond to the area $P_{X1}ABP_{X2}$ in the lower half of the diagram.

6.2   The Four Consumers' Surpluses

The compensating variation measure of consumers' surplus measures the maximum sum of money that can be removed from a consumer after a price fall (or the minimum sum of money which must be paid to him after a price rise) in order to leave him on the same indifference curve that he started on. But we may distinguish three other related measures of consumers' surplus (Hicks, 1943).

If we consider a price fall from P_{X1} to P_{X2} in Figure 6.2 which is in practice uncompensated by a change in money income, and then raise price again from P_{X2} to P_{X1}, the compensating variation of this price rise will not equal that of the original price fall. This is because we are now measuring the area under a new compensated demand curve CD corresponding to the higher level of indifference curve 2. To restore the consumer to indifference curve 2 at P_{X1} we should need a parallel shift of the budget line to position JT, corresponding to a rise in money income of LJ. This is equivalent to area $P_{X1}CDP_{X2}$ in the lower half of the diagram. This area could also be treated as a measure of the consumers' surplus accruing from a price fall, and it has been given the name 'equivalent variation'.

In words, it represents the minimum increase in money income that the consumer would be willing to accept to forgo the price fall. Note that the equivalent variation of the corresponding price fall equals the compensating variation of a price rise and vice versa. For a normal good, the demand curve CD corresponding to the higher indifference curve will be to the right of AB; thus the equivalent variation of a price fall will exceed the compensating variation (and vice versa). For an inferior good, point D and demand curve CD will lie to the left of AB, and the equivalent variation of a price fall will be less than the compensating variation. This is because the compensated demand curve shows a pure substitution effect, which is always to increase demand for the good whose price has fallen. The conventional demand curve shows both substitution and income effects. For a normal good, the income effect reinforces the substitution effect and increases demand still further; for an inferior good, however, it works the other way and reduces demand. If the good in question had a zero income effect, then all three demand curves in Figure 6.2 would be identical.

Both the compensating variation and the equivalent variation are computed assuming that the consumer is free to readjust the quantity he consumes of good X when his money income is changed. In other words, they are strictly an evaluation of the price fall from P_{X1} to P_{X2}, not of the quantity rise from X_1 to X_2. If we wished to evaluate the latter, we should have to constrain demand to be equal to X_2 at price P_{X2} and X_1 at price P_{X1}, regardless of which level of money income pertained. The result would be to reduce the compensating variation of a price fall and to raise that of a price rise (since the consumer would no longer be able to adjust optimally to the new situation in which he found himself). The terms given to the quantity-constrained compensating and equivalent variations are those of 'compensating surplus' and 'equivalent surplus' respectively.

We now have four measures of consumers' surplus, each different and none of them exactly equal to the area under a conventional demand curve in the majority of cases. Which should we use? If we are seeking to apply the compensation test, and consumers are free to adjust consumption of the goods in question following price changes, then the compensating variation of a price fall represents the maximum that consumers benefiting from that price fall can afford to pay the losers and still be at least as well off as they were at the original price, whereas the compensating variation of a price rise represents the minimum compensation required for losers from that price rise to be as well off as they were before the change. It appears, then, that if we attach a negative sign to the compensating variation of the losers, the condition $\Sigma CV > 0$ will be equivalent to satisfying the compensation test. Notice that, since ΣEV represents the effect of applying the compensation test to the corresponding reverse move in terms of price changes (only with the signs reversed), and given that for normal goods the equivalent variation of the gainer always exceeds his compensating variation and vice versa for the loser, $\Sigma CV > 0$ implies $\Sigma EV > 0$, and the Scitovsky paradox cannot arise in this case unless inferior goods are present.

However, doubt has been cast on whether $\Sigma CV > 0$ is a sufficient, as well as a necessary, condition for a change to comprise a potential Pareto improvement in welfare (Boadway, 1974). Consider an economy comprising two consumers (A and B) and two goods (X and Y). We wish to evaluate a change in the combination of outputs of the two goods produced. In Figure 6.3, the Edgeworth box corresponding to the first combination of goods is drawn with origins 0_A and 0_B; that corresponding to the second combination has origins 0_A and $0_B'$. Suppose that the actual shift under consideration is from position I on the initial contract curve to position II on the new one. Measured in terms of X, the compensation required by person A to return him to indifference curve a_2 is given by mn. Whether person B can afford to pay this compensation and still remain better off will be determined by the location of his indifference curve b_1 when it is redrawn with origin $0_B'$ instead of 0_B. Suppose that, at the point at which this indifference curve has the same slope as ln, it lies below and to the left of ln, as does b_1'. Then B's compensating variation mp will be less than mn and the project will fail the compensation test. It is also clear that in these circumstances b_1' cannot intersect a_2; thus it is impossible for a position to exist on the new contract curve that is Pareto-superior to point I on the old contract

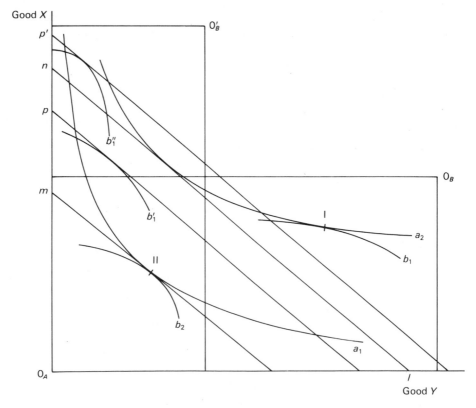

FIGURE 6.3

curve. But suppose that, when drawn with respect to the origin $0_B'$, indifference curve b_1 takes the slope of ln to the right and above the line ln, so that $\Sigma CV > 0$. The new indifference curve b_1 may intersect a_2, giving the possibility of a Pareto-superior distribution of goods. But it need not. It could take a position such as b_1'', in which case mp', the compensating variation of the gainer, would exceed mn, that of the loser, but no distribution of the new bundle of goods in which both consumers are as well off as at position I could be found. Thus the compensation test appears to be a necessary, but not a sufficient, condition for a potential Pareto improvement in welfare.

This proof strictly applies only to the 'batch' compensation test which compares two alternative 'batches' of goods, rather than two alternative sets of prices. It is assumed that after the project to be evaluated is implemented, no further alterations to the batch of goods produced will take place, and compensation is entirely in terms of a redistribution of the existing batch of goods between consumers. If it could be assumed that prices remained constant while production of other goods adjusted to changes in demand resulting from payment of monetary compensation, then the same limitation would not hold when further changes in the batch of goods produced were permitted. But once further price changes are permitted, the compensation test again becomes ambiguous.

If we are not seeking to apply the compensation test, the choice of measure again becomes unclear. Foster and Neuberger (1974) argue that the equivalent variation may be a more reliable welfare indicator since it is at least a monotonic function of the change in utility. As long as the marginal utility of money income is positive, the extra income required to produce the same increase in utility as a price change will be larger, the greater that increase in utility. No such general property holds for the compensating variation as soon as situations where more than one price changes are examined. This is because while the equivalent variation measures the shift in the budget line from a common initial position (in terms of real income and prices), the compensating variation measures the shift from the final position, at which real income and prices differ according to the size of the increase in utility.

Foster and Neuberger also argue that in practice whichever measure is chosen is unlikely to make much difference to the final outcome. Since in most cost–benefit studies, areas under conventional demand curves are used simply because these are easier to measure than any of the Hicksian measures, it is to be hoped that they are correct in this belief. However, the possibility remains that where the income effect for the good in question is large, the choice of measure may take on some significance.

6.3 Aggregation of Surpluses

So far, we have discussed consumers' surplus as though it may simply be measured for each good in isolation and then summed to give an aggregate measure. Where goods are related, so that the price of one good affects the demand for another within the set of goods with which the evaluation is concerned, a difficulty arises. Should we perform the evaluation with respect to the demand curve before the shift or after it?

The problem is illustrated in Figure 6.4, which shows demand and supply curves for two related goods X and Y (in this case substitutes). The project at hand shifts the supply curve of good X from S_{X1} to S_{X2}, causing a reduction in price from P_{X1} to P_{X2}. However, this fall in price will cause a shift in the demand curve for good Y from its initial position D_{Y1}, and by changing the price of Y this will lead to a series of shifts in the demand curve for both goods. The final equilibrium is given by P_{X3} and Q_{X3} on demand curve D_{X3} and by P_{Y2} and Q_{Y2} on demand curve D_{Y2}. Now there are several ways in which we could aggregate surpluses. We could treat the price changes as though they occurred in series, and measure consumers' surplus under D_{X1} for good X and under D_{Y2} for good Y (Hicks, 1956). But it would be just as acceptable to measure the area under D_{Y1} for good Y and under D_{X3} for good X. (To measure both surpluses with respect to the initial demand curve would be overestimating benefits; given that X is available at the lower price P_{X3}, the incremental benefit of a reduction in the price of the substitute Y is less than it would be if the price of X were still at P_{X1}, as implied by demand curve D_{Y1}. A similar argument applies in reverse to the use of both final curves.) Or we could assume that both prices move to their new equilibrium at the same proportionate rate, in which case we could trace out an area of surplus $P_{X1}ABP_{X3}$ and $P_{Y1}CDP_{Y2}$, corresponding to the area under neither set of demand curves. There appears to be nothing to be said in favour of one measure rather than another, yet no reason why they should give the same answer.

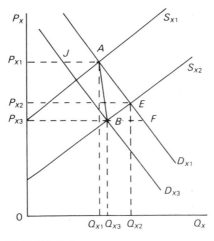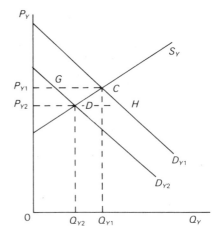

FIGURE 6.4

More generally, what we are seeking to evaluate is the line integral

$$\sum_{i=1}^{n} \int_{P_{i2}}^{P_{i1}} f_i(P_1 \ldots P_n) \, dP_i \tag{6.3}$$

where $f_i(P_1 \ldots P_n)$ is the demand curve for the ith good (Hotelling, 1938). It may be shown that the value of this line integral is independent of the path of integration only if

$$\frac{\partial f_i}{\partial P_j} = \frac{\partial f_j}{\partial P_i} \qquad \text{for all } i, j. \tag{6.4}$$

(This result is demonstrated for the two-good case in the Appendix.) In other words, the cross-price derivatives of the demand curves must be equal for all pairs of goods. This property, known as the symmetry of substitution, holds for demand curves where the income effect is zero, as in the case of a compensated demand curve (Samuelson, 1941). Thus if we are using a measure of consumers' surplus based on a compensated demand curve, it will not matter what path of integration (i.e. which of the methods described above) we use to evaluate it. Otherwise, the measure of consumers' surplus will remain ambiguous, varying according to this arbitrary decision.

The simplest of the above methods of aggregation to handle in most cases is the linear path, in which all prices are assumed to move together. This leads to a total measure of consumers' surplus of $P_{X1}ABP_{X3} + P_{Y1}CDP_{Y2}$ or

$$(P_{X1} - P_{X3})Q_{X1} + \tfrac{1}{2}(P_{X1} - P_{X3})(Q_{X3} - Q_{X1}) + (P_{Y1} - P_{Y2})Q_{Y2}$$
$$+ \tfrac{1}{2}(P_{Y1} - P_{Y2})(Q_{Y1} - Q_{Y2}). \tag{6.5}$$

This result may be generalised to read

$$B = \Sigma Q \cdot dP + \tfrac{1}{2}\Sigma \, dP \cdot dQ \tag{6.6}$$

where the summation is over all goods whose prices change. Thus, as long as we are willing to use a linear approximation to the demand curves, only the initial and final prices and quantities need be known to compute aggregate consumers' surplus.

6.4 Producers' Surplus

Some controversy has arisen over whether there is an analogous area of cost or benefit to be measured with respect to the supply curve. For instance, in Figure 6.5 the demand curve for the product in question has shifted exogenously from D_1 to D_2, raising price from P_1 to P_2. Is the shaded area a benefit,to the producer (producers' surplus) to set against the disbenefit to consumers from the rise in price?

Consider first a pure exchange economy with no production. In this case, the

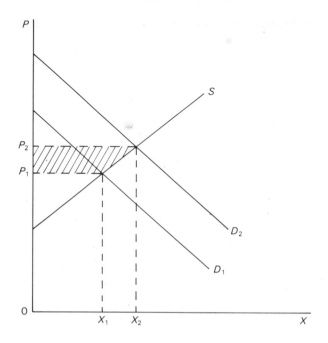

FIGURE 6.5

supply curve represents, for each unit of the good, the minimum price at which the supplier would be willing to part with it. When price rises from P_1 to P_2, the supplier receives an additional payment over and above the minimum necessary for him to be willing to supply the intra-marginal units of the good. One could proceed to partition the increased supply into income and substitution effects, and draw a separate compensated supply curve. For a normal good, this would lie to the right of the conventional supply curve, and the compensating variation for a price rise would exceed the conventional measure of surplus (Mishan, 1959).

Suppose now that the upward sloping supply curve is the long-run supply (equals long-run average cost) curve of a perfectly competitive industry. In this case, is the area in question a surplus accruing to the producers? The short answer is no. This rise in price is associated with an equivalent rise in average cost, leaving the producers with no additional profits. There may, of course, be a benefit to the owners of one of the factors of production, if the rise in average cost was associated with a rise in the price of one of the factors. Indeed, if the sole reason for the rise in average cost was an increase in the rent accruing to the owners of a fixed factor (e.g. land, in the case of agriculture), then the area in question will be a true measure of the extra economic rent. But the rise in average costs could be associated with external diseconomies of scale (in which case, no additional surplus accrues to anyone) or with more general movements in factor prices. In other words, it is necessary to ignore the supposed 'producers' surplus' and trace the effects back to the 'workers' surplus' and 'capitalists' surplus' in the factor markets (Mishan, 1968).

In the presence of monopoly power, it is no longer meaningful to consider producers' surplus in terms of the area above a supply curve, since no supply curve that is independent of the elasticity of demand exists. What is usually meant by producers' surplus when the term is used in these circumstances is quite simply the profit accruing to capitalists or, in the case of a nationalised industry, to government. Strangely, the social surplus is usually defined as the sum of consumers' and producers' surpluses thus measured, workers' surpluses being ignored altogether (Foster, 1960). Presumably, the assumption is that the project in question will always form too small a part of the relevant labour market to affect wages. This is not always the case, however (for instance, the responsiveness of wage rates of bus drivers to the level of service provided, and of coal miners to the level of output planned for, have been contentious issues in recent years). Where wages rates do change, a comprehensive measure of benefit will require the addition of the workers' surplus (the change in area above the appropriate labour supply curve), to the consumers' and producers' surpluses.

In short, then, it is inappropriate to regard the area above the supply curve in a commodity market as a 'surplus' analogous to consumers' surplus. What we should do is trace through comprehensively the surpluses accruing to owners of factors of production — shareholders, workers, landowners, governments. In this process, the term producers' surplus is sometimes used as a euphemism for profit. But in view of the confusion that surrounds it, the term is perhaps best avoided.

6.5 A Comparison between the Consumers' Surplus Measure of Benefits and the Rise in Real National Income

The question may arise as to the extent that a measure of benefits based on the sum of consumers' surplus and rents differs from a simple measure of the change in real national income. It will be seen that as long as factor inputs do not change, the consumers' surplus measure of benefit is equal to the mean of the two alternative ways of measuring the change in real national income.

6.5.1   NATIONAL INCOME MEASURES

The change in the money value of national income is equal to $\Sigma P_2 Q_2 - \Sigma P_1 Q_1$, where subscripts 1 and 2 refer to prices P and quantities Q before and after the change respectively.

To measure the change in real national income, we obviously need to deflate by a price index. We may do this by measuring either:

(*a*) the change in national income at current prices

$$\Delta Y_1 = \Sigma P_2 Q_2 - \Sigma P_1 Q_1 \cdot \frac{\Sigma P_2 Q_1}{\Sigma P_1 Q_1} = \Sigma P_2 Q_2 - \Sigma P_2 Q_1. \qquad (6.6)$$

This is the basis of the 'Paasche Quantity Index'.

(*b*) the change in national income at initial prices

$$\Delta Y_2 = \Sigma P_2 Q_2 \cdot \frac{\Sigma P_1 Q_2}{\Sigma P_2 Q_2} - \Sigma P_1 Q_1 = \Sigma P_1 Q_2 - \Sigma P_1 Q_1. \qquad (6.7)$$

This is the basis of the 'Laspeyres Quantity Index'.

If one were dealing with a single consumer, or a group of identical consumers, then as long as money income remained unchanged, one could assert the following:

(*a*) *If* $\Delta Y_1 > 0$, then consumers have benefited from the move from position 1 to position 2, since they could, at the second set of prices, have bought their original set of goods Q_1 more cheaply than the set they actually chose, Q_2.

(*b*) *If* $\Delta Y_2 < 0$, then consumers are worse off from the move, since at the original prices, they could have bought Q_2 more cheaply than Q_1, yet they chose Q_1.

(*c*) *If both* $\Delta Y_1 > 0$ *and* $\Delta Y_2 < 0$, then consumers are accordingly behaving inconsistently. On the other hand, *if* $\Delta Y_1 < 0$ *and* $\Delta Y_2 > 0$, then we cannot say whether consumers are better or worse off (Samuelson, 1950).

Unfortunately, this approach does not carry over to groups of individuals of differing incomes or tastes, since movements in the aggregate quantities may be associated with shifts in the distribution of goods amongst consumers.

6.5.2   COST–BENEFIT ANALYSIS MEASURES

For simplicity we use a linear aggregation path of the Marshallian measure:

Change in consumers' surplus $\qquad = \frac{1}{2}\Sigma(P_1 - P_2)(Q_1 + Q_2)$

$$= \frac{1}{2}\Sigma(P_1 Q_1 + P_1 Q_2 - P_2 Q_1 - P_2 Q_2). \qquad (6.8)$$

We must distinguish between three cases:

(*a*) *Suppose factor quantities and prices are constant.*
Then $\Sigma P_1 Q_1 = \Sigma P_2 Q_2$. In this case, the change in consumers' surplus

equals the mean of the two national income measures, since

$$\Sigma P_2 Q_2 - \Sigma P_2 Q_1 + \Sigma P_1 Q_2 - \Sigma P_1 Q_1$$
$$= \Sigma P_1 Q_1 + \Sigma P_1 Q_2 - \Sigma P_2 Q_1 - \Sigma P_2 Q_2.$$

There is no change in economic rent to the factors.

(b) *Suppose factor quantities are fixed but prices change.*
If $\Sigma P_2 Q_2 > \Sigma P_1 Q_1$, the change in consumers' surplus is less than the mean of the two national income measures. But the extra factor payments are all in the form of additional economic rent. Thus the full CBA measure requires the addition of this rise in economic rent, i.e. $\Sigma P_2 Q_2 - \Sigma P_1 Q_1$. When this is added in, the measure equals the mean of the two national income measures, since

$$\tfrac{1}{2}\Sigma(P_1 Q_1 + P_1 Q_2 - P_2 Q_1 - P_2 Q_2) + \Sigma P_2 Q_2 - \Sigma P_1 Q_1$$
$$= \tfrac{1}{2}\Sigma(P_2 Q_2 - P_2 Q_1 + P_1 Q_2 - P_1 Q_1).$$

(c) *Suppose factor quantities and prices both change.*
The change in national income equals the change in the value of national output

$$\Sigma W_2 L_2 - \Sigma W_1 L_1 = \Sigma P_2 Q_2 - \Sigma P_1 Q_1$$

where L refers to factor quantities and W to factor prices. Again, if this is positive, the change in consumers' surplus is less than the mean of the two national income measures. The change in economic rent is now

$$\tfrac{1}{2}\Sigma(W_2 - W_1)(L_1 + L_2) = \tfrac{1}{2}\Sigma(W_2 L_1 + W_2 L_2 - W_1 L_1 - W_1 L_2).$$

Now the mean of the two national income measures will exceed the full cost—benefit measure by

$$\tfrac{1}{2}\Sigma(W_2 L_1 - W_1 L_2) - \tfrac{1}{2}\Sigma(W_2 L_2 - W_1 L_1).$$

6.5.3 AN EXAMPLE

Assume an economy produces two goods, X and Y, from two factors, L and K. Prices and quantities in the two situations are:

	P_X	P_Y	Q_X	Q_Y	W_L	W_K	L_L	L_K
1	1	5	4	5	4	2	5	$4\tfrac{1}{2}$
2	2	4	2	8	5	$1\tfrac{1}{2}$	6	4

Thus:

$$P_2 Q_2 = 36 \qquad\qquad P_2 Q_1 = 28$$

$$P_1Q_2 = 42 \qquad\qquad P_1Q_1 = 29$$

$$W_2L_2 = 36 \qquad\qquad W_2L_1 = 31\tfrac{3}{4}$$

$$W_1L_2 = 32 \qquad\qquad W_1L_1 = 29$$

Therefore

the change in national income at current prices = $36 - 28 = 8$
the change in national income at initial prices = $42 - 29 = 13$
the change in consumers' surplus = $\tfrac{1}{2}(29 + 42 - 28 - 36) = 3\tfrac{1}{2}$

If we assume (wrongly in this case) fixed factor inputs,

the change in economic rent would be $36 - 29 = 7$, and
total benefit = $10\tfrac{1}{2}$ = the mean of the two national income measures.

Allowing for changes in factor inputs,

the change in economic rent = $\tfrac{1}{2}(31\tfrac{3}{4} + 36 - 29 - 32) = 3\tfrac{3}{8}$, and
total benefit = $6\tfrac{7}{8}$.

Thus, total benefit is less than both measures of the change in national income and, obviously, less than their mean.

We have shown then that CBA and national income measures differ when changes in factor inputs occur. This is essentially because the national income measure regards the entire value of the increased inputs as a benefit whereas CBA looks only at the change in economic rent. In practice other important reasons for differences between the outcome of a CBA and estimation of the effect of a project on real national income exist in that:

(a) When markets are imperfect, CBA uses shadow prices whereas national income will still be calculated at market prices (Chapter 7).

(b) In the presence of externalities, CBA attempts to value them where national income measures do not. (Chapter 8.)

(c) CBA may embody one of the distributive weighting systems described in Chapter 3.

Thus it is not true to describe the aim of a cost—benefit study as being to measure the effects of a project on national income as conventionally measured. The aim is to achieve a more accurate measure of the effect on social welfare than is reflected in the national income accounts.

6.6   Conclusions

As soon as projects themselves cause prices to change, an element of ambiguity enters with the use of market prices to value costs and benefits. The use of consumers' surplus (and economic rent) is usually put forward as the solution to this problem, but as we have seen in this chapter, these measures involve ambiguities of their own as to exact choice of measure and method of aggregation. Within the framework of the compensation test, the most appropriate choice appears to be the compensating variation, where the aggregation problem then disappears, since all methods give the same result.

In conclusion, it is worth pointing out that there are two broad approaches to the use of surpluses and rents in CBA. The first concentrates solely on quantity changes (outputs and inputs) and values these at market prices plus any surplus or rent on the units concerned. Using the usual linear approximation, the measure would be:

$$\tfrac{1}{2}\Sigma(Q_2 - Q_1)(P_1 + P_2) - \tfrac{1}{2}\Sigma(L_2 - L_1)(W_1 + W_2).$$

With respect to this measure, changes in surplus on the existing volume Q_1 are ignored as representing transfers between consumers and owners of factors of production.

If we are concerned to undertake an analysis of the distribution of costs and benefits in order to apply distributional weights to them, these transfers cannot be ignored. In this case, it is simplest to turn the whole analysis round and concentrate on price changes. Benefits will then be measured as:

$$\tfrac{1}{2}\Sigma(P_1 - P_2)(Q_1 + Q_2) + \tfrac{1}{2}\Sigma(W_2 - W_1)(L_1 + L_2).$$

All consumers' surplus (and economic rent) must now be included whether on marginal units or not.

In aggregate, the two approaches should give the same result, prior to weighting in the latter case. (This may be seen by multiplying out the brackets in the two expressions, and noting that $\Sigma P_1 Q_1 = \Sigma W_1 L_1$ and $P_2 Q_2 = \Sigma W_2 L_2$.) Thus it is only necessary to ensure that one is consistent in one's method of measuring benefits or costs whichever approach is adopted. In practice, most confusion about whether items are being double-counted or not arises from the failure to apply one or other of the approaches consistently across all prices or outputs.

APPENDIX

Equivalence of Alternative Rules of Aggregation, Given Symmetry of Substitution

Suppose we are planning to undertake a project which will affect the prices of two substitute commodities A and B. For instance, one might be improving a road, with the consequences that the flow on an alternative route is reduced, relieving congestion and reducing costs there too (Gwilliam and Nash, 1972). How do we aggregate benefits on the two roads?

Let us call the improved road route X and the alternative route Y in Figure 6.4, and denote their initial and final demand and cost curves by the subscripts 1 and 2 respectively ($S_{Y1} = S_{Y2}$). A seriatim path, beginning with route X, would evaluate the benefits as

$$B_1 = \text{area } (P_{X1}AFP_{X3}) + \text{area } (P_{Y1}GDP_{Y2}).$$

On the other hand, the Hotelling path gives us

$$B_2 = \text{area } (P_{X1}ABP_{X3}) + \text{area } (P_{Y1}CDP_{Y2}).$$

The difference between the two measures is given by

$$B_2 - B_1 = \text{area } (GCD) - \text{area } (ABF)$$

$$= \frac{1}{2} \frac{dQ_Y}{dP_X}(P_{X3} - P_{X1})(P_{Y1} - P_{Y2})$$

$$- \frac{1}{2} \frac{dQ_X}{dP_Y}(P_{Y2} - P_{Y1})(P_{X1} - P_{X3}).$$

Clearly, this will equal zero if

$$\frac{dQ_Y}{dP_X} = \frac{dQ_X}{dP_Y}$$

i.e. if the symmetry of substitution condition holds true.

Similarly, if we took a seriatim path beginning with route B, benefit (B_3) would be:

$$B_3 = \text{area } (P_{X1}CHP_{Y2}) + \text{area } (P_{X1}JBP_{X3}).$$

Now

$$B_3 - B_2 = \text{area } (CDH) - \text{area } (JAB)$$

$$= \frac{1}{2} \frac{dQ_Y}{dP_X}(P_{X3} - P_{X1})(P_{Y1} - P_{Y2})$$

$$- \frac{1}{2} \frac{dQ_X}{dP_Y}(P_{Y2} - P_{Y1})(P_{X1} - P_{X3})$$

$$= 0$$

if

$$\frac{dQ_X}{dP_Y} = \frac{dQ_Y}{dP_X}.$$

Thus if the cross-derivatives are equal, $B_1 = B_2 = B_3$, both seriatim paths are equal to each other and to the Hotelling measure.

7 Shadow Pricing

7.1 The Concept of a Shadow Price

So far, in this book, we have consistently proceeded as though existing market prices (weighted, where necessary, for distributive reasons) were the appropriate valuations to use when performing a social cost−benefit study. In Chapter 3, however, we stressed the restrictive assumptions that are necessary for this to be appropriate. In valuing the outputs of a project, we noted that market prices were appropriate provided that the item in question was one that was to be judged in terms of individual preferences as revealed in the market, and provided that the individual was free to choose how much to consume of the good at a fixed market price. With respect to inputs to the project, the necessary assumptions were stricter: we had to assume that the price of the input in question was equal to the value of its marginal product.

When these assumptions are not fulfilled, market prices will no longer necessarily be appropriate valuations to use in appraisals. In these circumstances, it is necessary to replace market prices by a set of 'shadow prices' (or 'accounting prices') which do reflect the social value of the outputs and inputs concerned.

The term 'shadow price' entered the project appraisal literature via the use of mathematical programming as an optimisation tool. When a resource allocation problem is handled in this way, a shadow price emerges as a marginal valuation imputed to an input or an output at the location of the optimum. The connection with project appraisal is obvious; at the optimum, activities will only be undertaken if the value of their outputs is at least as great as the cost of inputs measured in shadow prices.

Clearly, in this sense, shadow prices exist for all inputs and outputs whether traded or not, and where some combination of market mechanism and government intervention is functioning well, this shadow price will be reflected in the current market price. However, cost−benefit analysts often reserve the term 'shadow price' for a price that is imputed as opposed to being taken directly from market transactions, whether this is because no market price exists, or because the market price is considered to be inappropriate. Nor is the term restricted to valuations in the neighbourhood of the overall optimum; where constraints render optimisation infeasible, it is used of 'second-best' valuations, too. This chapter will consider shadow pricing only in the context of situations where markets exist for the good in question but shadow pricing is deemed necessary as a replacement for existing market prices: the valuation problem posed by externalities and public goods is considered in Chapter 8.

7.2 Market Imperfections

Few observers of the current world can have much confidence in the universality of perfectly competitive markets bringing about an equivalence between shadow prices and market prices. Manufacturing and extractive industry is dominated by an oligopolistic market structure, while the greater number of small firms in the service sector is to a large extent offset by the limited market area each serves. The one sector in which something approaching perfect competition might appear possible, agriculture, is the one in which government intervention to fix prices is most common. Does this mean that market prices are of no relevance in the social appraisal of projects?

This need not be the case. In the first place, unless there is rationing or other interference with consumer choice, prices paid by consumers will still reflect their marginal willingness to pay for the good in question at existing output levels. Of course, these prices will not be the ones that would pertain if resources were allocated optimally throughout the economy, and if one sees project appraisal as part of a programme designed to achieve such an overall optimisation, adjustments to offset the effect of market imperfections will be necessary. But if the aim is the less ambitious one of piecemeal improvements in resource allocation, the existing market prices may be appropriate as a way of valuing additional final output. Unfortunately, this does not apply to intermediate goods and factor inputs.

Second, it may be argued that there are other forces at work which lead to relative prices approximating those of perfect competition. For instance, firms may aim to maximise sales subject to earning a required rate of return determined in the capital market. They may do this because it reflects the aspirations of their non-owner management, because they fear new entry or because of existing or potential government intervention. Whatever the reason, the result may be that relative prices do reflect relative marginal costs at existing factor prices, although if these factor prices are inappropriate, relative prices may still be distorted.

Any comfort produced by such reflections is very limited however. There seems little reason to believe that the outcome of bargaining in the factor markets corresponds to factors receiving the value of their marginal products. Whenever a non-subsidised industry is producing under conditions of economies of scale, price will clearly exceed marginal cost, while other industries may enjoy monopoly profits earned behind barriers to entry. The defence for the use of market prices has often been grounded in the difficulty and expense of doing any better, rather than in a positive belief in the appropriateness of market prices (McKean, 1968). While data on average costs are fairly readily available in company accounts (subject to the usual problems in using accounting data, particularly with respect to the valuation of assets in times of changing price levels), information on marginal cost will require an industry by industry study of production functions and/or cost curves.

A rather different problem arises if market prices are deemed inappropriate in markets related to the project under consideration, not directly by sale or purchase of goods, but indirectly through substitutability or complementarity of demand or supply. If there is distortion in such related markets, then there may be benefits or disbenefits resulting from any changes in price or output in these markets caused by the project in question. For instance, suppose that the additional output of good X produced by a project leads to a rise in demand for, and sales of a complementary product Y. If the price of Y (P_y) is a good measure of its marginal cost, there will be no net benefit resulting from a change in its output; the value of the increased output will be exactly offset by the value of the extra inputs required to produce it (although, if price changes, there may well be a redistribution of income). Now consider the position where the price of Y (P_y) exceeds its marginal social cost (C_y). Even for a marginal change, there will be a net benefit from an expansion of sales of Y, and it may be approximated as:

$$(P_y - C_y) \frac{\partial q_y}{\partial p_x} \cdot \partial p_x. \tag{7.1}$$

Such changes need evaluating and summing for all related goods. As with distributional issues, the acknowledgement of market imperfections and the resulting need for second-best solutions lead to a greater requirement for data and a wider perspective in evaluating the effects of projects.

7.3 The Valuation of Intermediate Goods

The need to look for a second-best solution is particularly acute when one is evaluating projects which buy inputs from, or sell outputs to, firms that are failing to price at marginal cost (Turvey, 1971, ch. 3). Consider first the purchase of inputs from a firm whose price exceeds marginal cost. If the market price of the inputs is used in project appraisal, the opportunity cost of the resources used in the production of the inputs in question will be overstated. The surplus over opportunity cost will accrue to the owners of the firm in question as a transfer payment, and only if (on distributional grounds) benefits to them are to be given zero weighting will it be appropriate to include this surplus as a social cost. The short rule is then that, ignoring distributional considerations, inputs should always be valued at marginal social cost.

The case of outputs of intermediate goods is more complex. If the goods were being sold to perfectly competitive producers, their willingness to pay for such goods would be a reflection of the increased value of final goods produced from them. Where this is not the case, it is strictly necessary to estimate the increased production of final output that will accrue, and to value it at consumers' willingness to pay for it. If price exceeds marginal cost for the final output, consumers' willingness to pay will exceed the market value of inputs; a first approximation of this excess might be derived by multiplying the marginal input—output coefficient for the intermediate good in the use in question by the excess of price over marginal cost for the final output. The problem of valuing intermediate goods is considered in more detail for the case of transport in Chapter 11.

7.4   The Labour Market

The valuation of factor inputs at market prices requires the assumption that these prices represent their opportunity cost in terms of the value of other outputs for whose production they could have been used. The market mechanism will only achieve this result if both the factor markets and the commodity markets are perfectly competitive. If the former hold but the latter do not, then the derived demand curve for the factor will reflect its marginal revenue product; given imperfect competition in the commodity market, this will understate the value of the marginal product of the factor in terms of the willingness to pay of the consumers.

The most obvious divergence between market price and opportunity cost exists in the presence of structural or regional unemployment in the sector of the labour market in question. For then the opportunity cost of labour of the appropriate skills and in the appropriate location is surely zero. Nor is it sufficient to argue that this divergence is only temporary, and that over time the particular workers who would have been employed on this project will retire from the potential labour force or find other jobs. (This has sometimes been argued in the case of the closure of facilities such as coal mines and railways in areas of high unemployment; e.g. National Board for Prices and Incomes, 1970.) As long as there are other potential employees in the categories or areas concerned who remain unemployed, the opportunity cost of that type of labour remains zero; only if some other solution to the problem can be foreseen will the shadow price eventually rise. In fact, if unemployment in the industry in question had downward local multiplier effects (leading to unemployment in the retail trade, for instance), and if the labour thus thrown out of work was also immobile, it would be possible to conceive of labour having a negative shadow price (i.e. employing labour on additional projects might boost production elsewhere, rather than lowering it).

It is sometimes argued that unemployment involves a further additional social cost — the burden of unemployment benefits on the rest of society. This is a misunderstanding however. If there were no taxes or unemployment benefits, then a man on becoming unemployed would suffer a loss of wages (W). In the presence of income tax (T) and unemployment benefit (B), he actually loses ($W - T - B$), while the rest of society loses $T + B$. Unemployment benefit therefore represents a redistribution of part of the cost of unemployment rather than an additional social cost. Of course, unemployment may impose social and psychological costs on the victim over and above the loss of income involved; on the other hand, he may value the extra leisure time.

It may seem perfectly sound to apply the same approach to a situation in which there is national unemployment due to a deficiency in aggregate demand. A problem arises here. If a government fails to use fiscal or monetary policy to prevent such a deficiency in aggregate demand, it is likely to be because, rightly or wrongly, it has chosen to sacrifice full employment to the pursuit of other macro-economic objectives. Should an attempt be made to offset this demand deficiency through project selection, the result may be simply to call forth compensating fiscal or monetary adjustments. Thus if existing macro-economic policy is seen as a constraint whether the policy is sensible or not, the result of shadow pricing labour at zero might be to employ extra workers on one project at the cost of the jobs of those elsewhere. In other words, the extra labour is not at all costless in terms of loss of output elsewhere. The same argument is less likely to hold of regional or structural unemployment however; these are more likely to arise as a result of a lack of instruments to deal with the situation than as a result of deliberate policy decisions on the extent to which relief of unemployment is desirable (Haveman and Krutilla, 1968).

Apart from the extreme case of unemployment, the divergence between shadow and market prices of labour has rarely been allowed for in project appraisal, except in developing countries (see Chapter 10). Presumably, the reason is again the difficulty of doing anything about it. Sometimes, one may be able to estimate the appropriate production function and derive the marginal product of labour directly. Failing that, adjustments may be made for the most obvious divergences; for instance where a particular group of workers appears to be paid substantially more or less than the norm for comparable work elsewhere.

Shadow pricing of capital inputs is usually considered in conjunction with the choice of discount rate, and is therefore postponed until Chapter 8. One particular issue that may be difficult to handle is the shadow pricing of land. Static equilibrium theory would lead us to believe that the market value of the land required reflects the present discounted value of the future stream of benefits that could be obtained from the land in its next best use. A number of difficulties exist however. In the first place, the project will not 'wear out' the land in the same way as it will 'wear out' capital goods (although it may detract from its fertility). Thus it is not the entire value of the land that is to be debited to the project, but the opportunity cost of tying it up for a specified number of years (i.e. interest on the capital value) plus any depreciation in value over the period in question (or less any appreciation). Second, if the market rate of interest is deemed inappropriate (Chapter 8), this will distort the social value of the land, and a correction will need to be applied which raises the value of the land if the market rate of discount is above the social rate and vice versa. Third, the land market is notoriously prone to speculative booms, in which land changes hands at prices based on short-term expectations of what will happen in the property market rather than on the basis of its long-term earning power. Fourth, the social value of alternative uses of the land may differ from its private value in any case, since most uses of land impose externalities (good or bad) on those in neighbouring areas. All in all then, valuation of land is a tricky part of a project appraisal. One thing is certain however: when a public authority already owns the land, the opportunity cost of its use has nothing whatsoever to do with the historic price that was paid for it when it came into public hands, perhaps decades previously (Pearce and Nash, 1973).

7.5 Taxes and Subsidies

The presence of taxes and subsidies raises some interesting questions for the social appraisal of projects. Taxes and subsidies may exist for any of a number of reasons:

(i) *A deliberate attempt by the government to correct for market imperfections.* In this case, provided that the correction is seen as appropriate, market prices including the tax or subsidy may be adopted. If the correction is not seen as appropriate, no doubt the best solution would be to persuade the government to modify it. In the likely circumstance that the project evaluator is in no position to do this, a problem of conflict arises; if he decides to try to offset this effect in his appraisal, he will be forced into the second-best measures discussed below.

(ii) *To raise revenue or redistribute income.* Governments are obliged to take actions which infringe the marginal conditions for Pareto optimality on both of these grounds; in these cases, market prices including the taxes may be inappropriate for social appraisal.

(iii) *As a historical or institutional accident.* Again, if the first-best solution of their removal is not forthcoming, such taxes will require a second-best treatment in project appraisal.

Suppose that a particular final output bears a sales tax for reason (ii) or (iii). If we are considering marginal changes from the existing situation and using consumers' willingness to pay as our numéraire, then it will be appropriate to measure the benefit of an increase in the output in question gross of the tax. Similarly, for intermediate goods, the treatment of taxes will be identical to that of monopoly rents: outputs will be measured gross of taxes and inputs net of them.

The problem of valuation of factor inputs arises again. In an otherwise perfectly competitive industry, the presence of a sales tax would lead to the workers being paid the value of their marginal product less the tax, i.e.

$$W = MP_L(P - t). \tag{7.2}$$

In order to find the true marginal product, we need to add back $MP_L t$. Since

$\text{MP}_L = W/(P - t)$, the shadow wage (W^*) may be computed as:

$$W^* = W + \frac{tW}{P - t} = W\left(1 + \frac{t}{P - t}\right).$$ (7.3)

In other words, the wage is increased by the proportional tax rate. If we could forecast precisely the industries from which labour would be attracted to the project in question, we could measure this exactly. In practice, the best that is likely to be possible is a correction based on the mean tax rate on all goods. The same adjustment will be needed in the valuation of other factor inputs, and thus indirectly in intermediate goods as well. An alternative approach to this problem would be to use factor prices as the numéraire. In this case, instead of scaling factor prices up, we would scale down commodity prices by the amount of the tax. For an example of this approach in the treatment of motor taxes in road investment appraisal, see Chapter 11.

In the view of the producer, income tax does not create a distortion in terms of leading to a divergence between wages and the marginal productivity of labour; thus it is usually ignored in project appraisal, except in considering the distribution of costs and benefits. If the total supply of labour to the economy is elastic, this may be distorted by income tax however, leading to labour being supplied when the value of its marginal product is less than the value of the leisure time forgone or vice versa (Little, 1951). In the absence of evidence of a strong feedback from wage rates to the supply of labour, this effect is usually ignored in practice (Brown and Dawson, 1969).

7.6 International Trade

If all countries were permanently in balance of payments equilibrium, and no country were able to influence the world prices of commodities, the presence of international trade would provide no particular problems for CBA. The current exchange rate would provide an appropriate measure of the marginal rate of transformation of domestically produced goods into goods purchased on world markets. For instance, with an equilibrium exchange rate of $2/£, exports worth £1 in domestic prices (free on board) will earn $2 of foreign exchange; this extra foreign exchange can be used to purchase imported goods worth £1 on the domestic market. Conversely, an extra pound's worth of imports (at domestic prices, cost, insurance and freight) will require extra exports worth one pound to finance it.

Unfortunately, life is seldom that simple, and shadow exchange rates are often required. (For a practical example of the problems of using shadow exchange rates in a policy context, see Posner, 1973, ch. 7.) Consider an economy which is running a balance of payments deficit (analogous arguments could be put forward for the case of a surplus). One is forced to try to predict how the government will react to the situation.

(1) *It may devalue, or permit the exchange rate to fall*

In this case, the analyst's task is to predict the new equilibrium exchange rate for use in evaluations. As a first approximation one may adopt the following procedure. Suppose that the country in question is unable to influence world prices, and has a balance of payments deficit at world prices of $(M - X)$. To eliminate this, an improvement is required such that $\Delta X - \Delta M = M - X$. Let the price elasticity of supply of exports be e_{SX}. The increase in exports brought about by a devaluation will be

$$\Delta X = \left(\frac{r_2 - r_1}{r_1}\right) e_{SX} X \tag{7.4}$$

where r_2 is the new exchange rate, r_1 the original exchange rate and

$$\left(\frac{r_2 - r_1}{r_1}\right)$$

is the percentage change in the domestic price received by suppliers for their exports. Similarly

$$\Delta M = \left(\frac{r_2 - r_1}{r_1}\right) e_{DM} M \tag{7.5}$$

where e_{DM} is the price elasticity of demand for imports. We require

$$\left(\frac{r_2 - r_1}{r_1}\right) e_{SX} X - \left(\frac{r_2 - r_1}{r_1}\right) e_{DM} M = M - X. \tag{7.6}$$

This simplifies to

$$\frac{r_2}{r_1} = \frac{(1 - e_{DM})M + (1 - e_{SX})X}{e_{SX} X - e_{DM} M}. \tag{7.7}$$

If one saw project evaluation as part of an overall optimal economic strategy, and achievement of an equilibrium exchange rate was a necessary part of that strategy, this would always be an appropriate approach. However, given a more piecemeal approach to policy, this cannot be relied on, nor will it always be a sensible policy for the country concerned.

(2) *It may continue to run a deficit*

This may be a very attractive option as long as the deficit can be financed without ill effect! However, not only may the providers of the funds impose conditions on the loans which are damaging to the aims of the government in question, but unless one is able to secure aid in the form of grants, sooner or later the funds will have to be repaid with interest, and it is then that the true costs of the deficit must be borne. Unless one is confident that the economy at that date will be more able to bear the burden of adjustment, so that the current policy is a deliberate and desired redistribution of income from the future to the present, there is clearly a case for adopting a shadow exchange rate to encourage exports and discourage imports. (In other words all flows of foreign exchange to or from the country in question will be converted into domestic currency at a lower exchange rate than that ruling in the market.) The problem is to know how far to go. Adoption of a shadow exchange rate equal to the equilibrium rate would be a minimum step, since this was found to be desirable in situation (1); yet here by contrast with that position, there will be no corresponding contribution made by adjustments in sectors not subjected to social appraisal.

(3) It may impose import duties or quotas, or use export subsidies

Examine Figure 7.1, ignoring initially the lines labelled MR(X) and MC(M). It portrays a situation in which exports (X) would equal imports (M) at an exchange rate of $2/£. However, the government in question is maintaining an exchange rate of $3/£ by suppressing imports to the level M'. The result is that an extra dollar's worth of imports will have a domestic value given not by the existing exchange rate, nor even by the equilibrium exchange rate, but by the exchange rate of $1/£ at which M' would be the equilibrium level of imports.

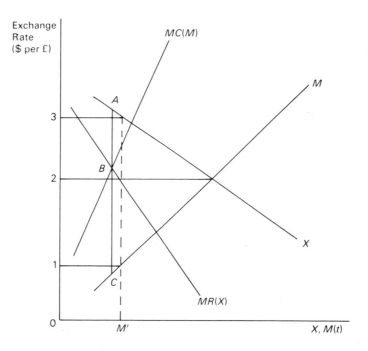

FIGURE 7.1

This surplus will be reaped by the government in the form of duties, or if quotas are used, by the importing companies in the form of economic rent.

The appropriate shadow exchange rate in these circumstances will be that rate which would achieve the same level of imports as that brought about by the existing arrangements, in this case \$1/£. This is the value of the imports which can be financed by an extra dollar's worth of exports, or by saving a dollar's worth of imports elsewhere. In the presence of an absolute constraint on the level of imports, an extra dollar's worth of imports of one commodity requires suppression of another dollar's worth of imports of some other commodity, and these imports forgone are worth £1 on the domestic market. Similarly, an additional dollar's worth of exports will ease the import constraint, permitting the import of goods worth £1 on the home market.

Similar considerations apply to export subsidies. The current exchange rate will understate the value of domestic resources required to earn the foreign exchange necessary to finance a marginal increase in imports. A shadow exchange rate reflecting the degree of this undervaluation will be needed.

Suppose initially that a country is using a combination of tariffs, taxes and subsidies to achieve balance of payments equilibrium in a situation in which it is unable to influence world prices. The equilibrium exchange rate following the removal of those barriers to trade may be estimated as follows (using the above notation):

$$\Delta X = \left(\frac{r_2(1 - t_X) - r_1}{r_1} \right) e_{SX} X \tag{7.8}$$

$$\Delta M = \left(\frac{r_2(1 + t_M) - r_1}{r_1} \right) e_{DM} M \tag{7.9}$$

where t_M is the mean tax/tariff on imports (i.e. the percentage by which the tax raises import prices to the consumer) and t_X is the mean tax/subsidy on exports (i.e. the percentage by which the tax reduces the price received by the supplier of the exports). If $\Delta X = \Delta M$ then

$$\frac{r_2(1 - t_X) - r_1}{r_1} e_{SX} X = \frac{r_2(1 + t_M) - r_1}{r_1} e_{DM} M. \tag{7.10}$$

Or

$$\frac{r_2}{r_1} = \frac{e_{SX} X - e_{DM} M}{(1 - t_X)e_{SX} X - (1 + t_M)e_M M}. \tag{7.11}$$

However, this calculation may be of little relevance if the existing tax/tariff policies are expected to continue.

In this case, it is best to concentrate on estimating at domestic prices the value of the additional imports financed by an extra dollar of foreign exchange.

The result is a price index of the form:

$$\text{Shadow Exchange Rate} = \frac{\sum\limits_{i} P_{Di} Q_i}{\sum\limits_{i} P_{Wi} Q_i} \qquad (7.12)$$

where Q_i is the marginal import of good i, P_{Di} the domestic price of good i (in £) and P_{Wi} the world price of good i (in $).

Such ways of rectifying balance of payments problems as tariffs and quotas may be very much in the interests of countries whose import and export decisions do influence world prices. Subject to the risks of retaliation, they will be able to use tariffs to reflect the difference between price and marginal cost to the country of imports, and taxes to reflect the difference between price and marginal revenue of exports. For instance, if the MC and MR curves are as in Figure 7.1, an import tariff equivalent to a reduction in exchange rate of *BC* and an export tax equivalent to an increase in exchange rate of *AB* will be desirable. The resulting quantity adjustments will turn the terms of trade in their favour. However, the relationship between marginal and average cost and revenue is likely to differ for each commodity. In these circumstances, a different tariff (and consequently a different shadow exchange rate) is likely to be appropriate for each commodity. As long as the existing tariffs, taxes and subsidies are believed to be at the optimal level, it will suffice to use the market prices of the goods in question gross of the tariffs, taxes and subsidies in evaluations, together with the official exchange rate. However, tariffs may exist for quite different reasons including, as with taxes, revenue raising and historical accident. In such cases, it is necessary to take prices net of the tariff, tax or subsidy, and apply a shadow exchange rate reflecting both the divergence between price and marginal cost or marginal revenue for the commodity in question and the overall scarcity value of foreign exchange.

A final comment may be made on the identification of goods to which such a revaluation should be applied. Clearly, it is applicable to goods which are actually imported or exported, but it should also be applied to any commodity where, although the actual units used or produced by the project in question do not enter international trade, other units do. Thus in the absence of the project in question, the inputs could have been used to supplant imported goods elsewhere in the economy or release other units for exports; alternatively, the outputs of this project may have released other sources of supply for export. On this argument, the revaluation would apply to all internationally traded commodities (Little and Mirrlees, 1974, ch. 12). However, if there are institutional barriers to trade, it will be necessary to consider whether such adjustments to trade levels would really have been feasible, and only to treat the goods in question as traded goods if the answer to that is positive.

7.7 Interdependence between Shadow Prices

So far in this chapter we have discussed shadow prices as though individual problems can be considered in isolation and shadow prices calculated one at a time on a piecemeal basis. This is very often done in practice, but it is not really adequate. In particular, when factor inputs or intermediate goods that are used in a wide variety of industries are shadow priced, this will affect the appropriate valuation of the marginal social cost of all their outputs.

For instance, suppose that labour is being shadow priced, and that two goods (e.g. steel and electricity) require, at the margin, inputs of each other and of labour for their production. Their shadow prices (S_1 and S_2) will be:

$$S_1 = a_{12}S_2 + l_1 W^* \tag{7.13}$$

$$S_2 = a_{21}S_1 + l_2 W^* \tag{7.14}$$

where the as are marginal input—output coefficients, the ls are marginal inputs of labour, and W^* is the shadow wage rate. Solving for S_1 and S_2 gives

$$S_1 = \frac{(a_{12}l_2 + l_1)W^*}{1 - a_{12}a_{21}} \tag{7.15}$$

and

$$S_2 = \frac{(a_{21}l_1 + l_2)W^*}{1 - a_{12}a_{21}}. \tag{7.16}$$

Each of these shadow prices can only be calculated given knowledge of the marginal input requirements for *both* commodities. Strictly speaking, a shadow-pricing exercise requires knowledge of marginal input—output coefficients throughout the economy, in order to evaluate a consistent set of shadow prices for all factors and intermediate goods. The latter objective has only really been attempted for developing countries, and will be discussed further in Chapter 10.

7.8 The Problem of Institutional Arrangements

If shadow pricing is to be used in government institutions, at least two institutional difficulties arise:

(i) Determination of shadow prices requires forecasting of and judgement of many other aspects of government decision-taking. In one sense, this should pose no problems. After all, the same government is responsible for determining shadow prices and for other policy decisions. However, these two sets of decisions will normally be taken by completely separate departments within the administration, and there is a very real danger of inconsistent decisions, with one branch of government trying to offset by shadow pricing the results of policies implemented by the other branch. For instance, the department responsible for evaluations will repeatedly have to take a view on the extent to which taxes and tariffs are designed to influence resource allocation, as opposed to these effects being accidental by-products of the pursuit of other objectives.

(ii) Implementation of the decisions requires appropriate financial arrangements. The use of shadow prices in project appraisal will cause governments to systematically choose projects that appear non-optimal in terms of market prices: that is the whole point of the exercise. It is desirable then to ensure that decisions on the use of the asset are taken in the same way. Normal budgetary control (impositions of cash limits for instance) will lead to operating authorities seeking to minimise costs in terms of market prices, and partly offsetting the beneficial effect of shadow pricing in project selection. For instance, a port authority may be instructed to build new labour-intensive cargo handling facilities in view of local unemployment; if given purely financial operating objectives, it may be forced to minimise its use of labour in day-to-day operating decisions. Moreover, if it is required to charge rates which recover total cost, it may lose much of its traffic to competing capital-intensive ports elsewhere (Heggie, 1976). The best solution in this case is likely to be to bring the wages actually paid by the company closer to the shadow wage by means of a government wage subsidy.

Where such subsidies are not expected to be forthcoming, projects can be appraised using shadow prices, but on the assumption that they will be operated on the basis of normal market criteria. This will obviously reduce the benefits from them, however, and offsetting action should be taken if at all possible. All this stresses is that if market prices and shadow prices diverge, the best method of attack on the problem is to seek to bring them closer together; shadow pricing alone in project appraisal is very much a second-best approach.

7.9 Conclusions

We have seen in this chapter that market imperfections and taxes or subsidies may require the replacement of market prices by shadow prices for factor inputs and inputs of intermediate goods. The existence of disequilibrium in international trade may similarly require use of a shadow exchange rate to revalue all inputs and outputs of tradeable goods. The use of shadow prices requires a great deal of extra information, however, particularly since it is unsound to use shadow prices on a piecemeal basis; as soon as some factors or intermediate goods are shadow priced, it is strictly necessary to compute a whole new set of mutually consistent shadow prices. At the same time, shadow pricing poses institutional difficulties, requiring detailed information on other government policies, and for the best results, action to replace market prices with shadow prices in budgeting and operational decision-taking as well. All these difficulties lead to a great temptation to use market prices in the social appraisal of projects even where they are suspected or known to be inappropriate.

8 Externalities and Public Goods

8.1 Introduction

Chapter 7 introduced the concept of a *shadow price*. A shadow price was seen to be the social valuation of an output or input at either the first-best or second-best optimum. In the simplest example of a world where the only costs of production are private costs, the shadow price of an output in the neighbourhood of an optimum will be its *marginal cost*. Various expressions were provided in Chapter 7 for the shadow price of labour and the shadow price of internationally traded goods. The essence of CBA is that all inputs and outputs should, technically, be valued at their shadow prices. Market prices may not therefore be at all relevant if market imperfections, such as monopoly, exist or if market distortions such as output taxes exist.

However, while Chapter 7 discussed shadow prices in the context of *traded* goods and inputs, it hinted that the term is also used for the valuation of goods and inputs which do not have markets, or at least where the market is not an 'overt' one. An example would be peace and quiet — i.e. the absence of noise. We can think of peace and quiet as a 'good' and its obverse, noise, as a 'disgood' or 'bad'. There is no obvious market in peace and quiet — it is not sold in quantities on a readily identifiable market. We could argue that there exists a 'political' market — anti-noise pressure groups exist and while we can hardly describe the civil and military airlines or car and motorbike riders as being 'pro-noise', they are in favour of the products which generate noise and against attempts to raise the cost of their means of transport by noise-abatement measures. (More correctly, their stance is determined by the degree of social responsibility they exhibit, the technical options available, the elasticity of demand for their product, and so on.) But we have already seen (Chapter 2) that the cost—benefit analyst does not like to work with political votes. Are there any other markets for peace and quiet?

We could argue that an effective or 'surrogate' market has emerged. This consists of those who are anti-noise 'voting with their feet' — i.e. simply leaving noisy areas in search of quiet areas. Those less sensitive to noise will then take their place. The market in question effectively becomes the property market, or rather one aspect of it. For we could argue that noise will *partly* determine house prices and hence provide signals to householders in the same way that any other price in a market does. But note that, even if we can sustain this view (and we see later why it poses some formidable problems) the 'price' of peace and quiet is not at all obvious — it will have to be inferred in some fashion from the behaviour of house prices.

If, then, we can identify some such surrogate market for peace and quiet, we may be able to identify its shadow price. Note that a surrogate market may take two forms — an actual market which is not readily apparent, such as the market brought into being by consumers' avertive behaviour if they cannot tolerate noise, or a market that the analyst must invent altogether. An example of the latter might be the valuation of a scenic view interfered with by air pollution which causes a fog or haze to interfere with clear visibility. Possibly we could find a market similar to that for peace and quiet, and in this case people would simply not visit the site so often. Or we might simply have to ask people what they are willing to pay for the preservation of the view. Whatever the case, the essential principle remains that where a good or bad does not have an overt market, what CBA *attempts* to do is to ask either the question 'what price is implicit in consumers' behaviour in respect of this good or bad?' or the question 'what price would rule if a hypothetical market for this good or bad existed?'

Much of the effort in the development of CBA has been in terms of attempts to invent ways of finding these shadow prices. How successful they have been is open to question. Certainly there have been many attempts, and many of these have been 'heroic' in the ingenuity used, but more than occasionally foolhardy in what they have tried to do. The reader is left to decide at the end of the book, and in the light of various case studies, what degree of reliability he or she wish to place on the various estimates obtained.

One final point can be made. The example of peace and quiet and the example of scenic beauty have something in common. Neither will be taken account of if someone is producing a good which has their obverse, noise and destruction of amenity as a by-product. That is, private net benefit maximisation will ignore these bads because they accrue to third parties. We shall see that this is a crucial element in defining an *externality*, for externalities are unpriced goods or bads which accrue to third parties. A second feature is also interesting. If the peace and quiet is shared by, say, two people, the arrival of a third in no way diminishes the amount of peace and quiet enjoyed by each of the first two (assuming the newcomer also likes peace and quiet). We could in fact suggest that hundreds, thousands and perhaps hundreds of thousands of people could all enjoy the same peace and quiet without in any way reducing the amount each individual enjoys. If so, we would have an example of a *public good*, one whose availability to a single consumer is not reduced by having it made available to another consumer. We shall refine these concepts shortly. The amenity example indicates a further possibility. Perhaps a dozen people can enjoy the view and the presence of other people would in no way reduce the pleasure afforded to each individual. But suppose 100,000 people turn up to look at the view? Then what was a public good might easily cease to be a public good. Congestion would occur and the individual utilities would be reduced by the presence of more and more people. The crowded beach or swimming pool might provide other examples, as would the national park, the local forest or whatever. What is required then, is a closer look at the phenomena of *externalities* and *public goods*.

8.2   Externalities and Public Goods: Definitions

We shall say that an *externality* exists when a variable controlled by one economic agent enters the utility function of another economic agent.

Even this simple definition causes some problems, and the reader is warned that different authors define externalities differently. The essence of the condition above is that the interdependence between the two (or more) agents arises from the presence of real variables in the receiving party's utility function. In this way we concentrate on so-called *technological externalities* and avoid *pecuniary externalities* — changes in money variables in the economy which simply have the effect of transferring money sums from one person, firm or sector in the economy to another. Further, by affecting utility we include a firm's utility which, in turn, we take to be dependent on its profits (although it need not be). In this way we recognise as an externality any real variable entering the firm's production function and which variable is chosen by some other firm or consumer. We avoid discussion of whether the interdependence is deliberate or not, since most writers would wish to omit deliberate acts of altruism or malice from the concept of externality. Equally, it is none too clear that the dividing line is easy to draw if, say, a polluter is aware of the effects of his actions on others. Finally, some writers require an additional condition to be present, namely, that the interdependence effect is *unpriced*. This appears to be because if some mechanism is invented for charging the generator of the externality, then we shall in general discover that not all the externality will or should disappear. An 'optimal' amount will remain. Imagine, for example, that what is in question is an *external cost* and that marginal external cost behaves as shown in Figure 8.1. Let the downward sloping curve be a marginal net private benefits curve (in the firm case this will be a marginal profit function if the firm is a profit maximiser). Then, we can demonstrate simply that a Pareto optimum exists where the marginal external cost (MEC) equals the marginal net private benefits (MNPB).

MNPB is defined for the firm as

$$MNPB = P - MC$$

where P is the product price and MC is marginal *private* cost. If then MNPB = MEC, we can write

$$P - MC = MEC \tag{8.1}$$

or

$$P = MC + MEC = MSC \tag{8.2}$$

where MSC is *marginal social cost*. But pricing at marginal social cost is the requirement for optimal 'first-best' shadow pricing. Hence MNPB = MEC is a condition for optimality. In Figure 8.1 we can therefore define:

(1) X_p as the (private) profit maximising output.

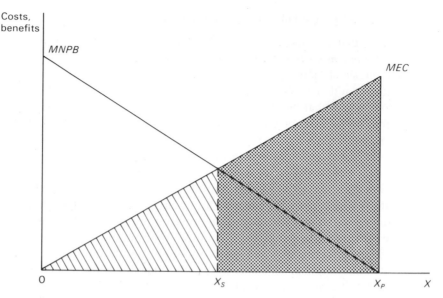

FIGURE 8.1

(2) The area under the MEC curve from 0 to X_p as the level of total externality suffered because output is at X_p.

(3) X_s as the optimal level of output since MNPB = MEC.

(4) The area under MEC between X_s and X_p as the amount of externality that *should* be removed (by a tax, regulation etc.) to ensure optimality. If it *is* removed it is said to be 'internalised' because it becomes a private cost to the externality generator. It is in this sense that this much of the externality no longer exists – it is now 'priced'.

(5) The area under MEC between 0 and X_s as the *optimal level of externality*.[1]

In this book we shall be almost entirely concerned with externalities that result from the activities of the production sector on the consuming sector and, to a lesser extent, on those that result from the actions of the production sector and which impinge on another part of the production sector. This is simply because CBA is largely concerned with investment projects and programmes that postulate some development, although it might well be the creation of a national park, a wilderness area or whatever. To be logically complete, however, we should note that the direction of the interaction could be fourfold:

  (i) producer on producer.
 (ii) producer on consumer.
(iii) consumer on consumer.
(iv) consumer on producer.

Category (i) might include water intake clean-up costs for a downstream producer who is faced with water polluted by an upstream producer. Category (ii) would include noise, loss of amenity through mining, radiation hazards from power stations etc. Category (iii) would include all kinds of activities such as noise from the neighbour's lawnmower, smoke from his bonfire, possibly even dislike of his or her very existence! Examples of category (iv) are not easy to think of, but might include households polluting river water above the supply intake of a firm.

We can link the concept of externality with that of a public good by introducing the terminology due to Baumol and Oates (1975) which distinguishes:

(i) *a depletable externality:* an external effect which takes on the characteristics of a private good or bad such that if consumed or suffered by individual A, it cannot be consumed or suffered by B.

(ii) *an undepletable externality:* an external effect which if experienced by A could also be experienced by B, C etc., since its consumption by A does not reduce its consumption by B etc.

In essence, externalities will tend to take on the characteristics of undepletable externalities (indeed, it is hard to think of depletable externality examples). The 'common consumption' feature is *one* of the two elements typically regarded as characterising public goods. This characteristic is referred to variously as 'common consumption', 'joint supply', and 'non-rivalry in consumption'.

Public goods are usually thought of as having a second feature however. This is *non-exclusion*. What is meant here is that, if in supplying the good to A we end up supplying it to B, we cannot invent a mechanism for excluding B from its consumption. The usual mechanism in mind is the use of prices. But it might equally well be some rationing device such as allowing only some visitors at a time to see the scenic view, and so on. Non-exclusion matters for CBA if it can be shown that it generates a context in which some consumers will not reveal their 'true price' for the good in question. If they do not, we shall be aggregating across a set of true and untrue preferences with little idea of what the real benefit or cost is. For example, if B knows that the good will be provided to A he may well be unwilling to pay for the good in the hope that it will be provided anyway (to A) and thus be provided to him (via common consumption), and that no-one can prevent him from consuming it (by virtue of non-exclusion). He will act as a so-called *free rider*. How serious this problem is we discuss later.

We now have a definition of externality and a definition of a public good. Schematically, they are related as shown in Figure 8.2.

This taxonomy is by no means complete however. Consider a public beach with very few visitors. At first sight it seems like a public good since the addition of an extra visitor does not reduce the enjoyment of the others. If no charging mechanism exists it will also be non-excludable, in fact but not in principle,

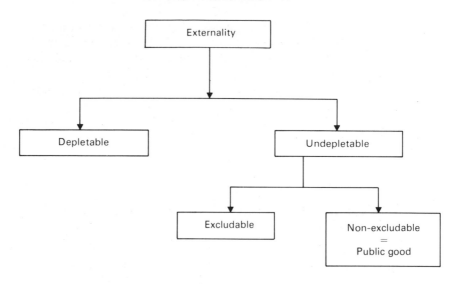

FIGURE 8.2

since we can easily imagine a charging or rationing mechanism to facilitate exclusion. If however the beach becomes crowded, then each new visitor will impose an external cost on the others. Similarly, those already on the beach impose an external cost on the newcomer — a case of *mutual externality*. Our public good is public only up to the point where *congestion* sets in. Such goods are one of a variety known as *impure public goods* and, for the record, we shall see that the *theory of clubs* can be used to identify the optimal number of people using the beach (the optimal size of the 'club').

Second, we have said nothing about the *province* of the public good. The provision of a unit of defence in the North Atlantic could be held to provide the same amount of benefit for someone living in the United Kingdom regardless of where he or she lives. The provision of a public park is less likely to benefit someone living far away from the park than someone living near it. The release of radiation from a nuclear power plant is less likely to harm someone the further they are away from the plant (although there is some randomness in this example since wind speed and direction will be relevant too). In short, we need to define the *locality* or *jurisdiction* of the public good. Few goods are in fact strictly public in the national or international sense. Global pollutants such as atmospheric concentrations of carbon dioxide or fluorocarbons may fit this category. Most public goods and bads, however, are likely to be local in nature. For the purposes of CBA this matters little save to remind us to define carefully how widely we are to cast the net of analysis in 'capturing' costs and benefits.

One other type of public good is also worth mentioning. This is one where there is an element of 'publicness' but where the consumption of the good need in no way be the same for each person. The obvious example is a motorway. For a given time period of say a year, individual A could use it far more than B and both could use it without impairing each other's consumption of it, but of course, the arrival of many other motorists could turn it into a congestion-type public good, although still with variable use being possible.

To try and capture the whole spectrum of goods, from private to public goods via impure public goods consider Figure 8.3.[2] The three areas show:

(a) the degree of rivalry, so that non-rival goods appear on the $0X$ axis *away* from the origin 0;

(b) the size of the group or jurisdiction, so that purely localised goods would appear close to 0 on the axis and global goods at Y_{max} on the Y axis;

(c) the degree of non-excludability on the vertical axis $0Z$, with perfectly excludable goods being close to 0 and totally non-excludable goods at Z_{max}.

Thus, a purely private good has complete excludability and complete rivalry. It is therefore at the origin on the $0X$ and $0Z$ axes. A global public good would have a co-ordinate $(X_{max}, Z_{max}, Y_{max})$ and would therefore appear as a point P. Public goods in general would lie on the axis KP depending on the size of the jurisdiction. An impure public good such as a beach would be fully excludable (in principle) and hence at 0 on $0Z$, partially rival (say at $\bar{X}$ on $0X$) and open to a limited group size (say $\bar{Y}$ on $0Y$). Hence its co-ordinates would be $(\bar{X}, \bar{Y}, 0)$ and it would lie at point B as shown in Figure 8.3.

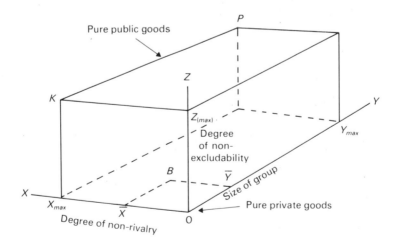

FIGURE 8.3

8.3   Marginal Conditions and Demand Curves

We may now turn to the various marginal conditions and the relevant demand curves for the range of externality—public goods we have identified. The implications for CBA can be spelled out.

8.3.1   PURE PRIVATE GOODS

The Pareto-optimality requirement for an economy with two private goods is

$$\text{MRS}_1 = \text{MRS}_2 = \cdots = \text{MRS}_N = \text{MRT} \tag{8.3}$$

where MRS_1 is the marginal rate of substitution between two goods, say A and B, for individual 1, MRS_2 relates to the same two goods but for individual 2, and so on. MRT is the marginal rate of transformation between the two goods. (No proof is given here — see any basic welfare economics text.)

The demand curves for the two goods in question are shown in Figure 8.4 and to obtain the market demand curve we observe that the curves are added horizontally. Excludability is most simply illustrated by the fact that at price P_1^1 only consumer 2 demands the product, the price being too high for consumer 1. In terms of CBA, the gross consumer surplus from the provision of an amount X^* of good X at zero price would be the area under $D_1 + D_2$ between 0 and X^*. If the supply curve is given by S then the equilibrium price is P^* and net benefits are equal to the area under $D_1 + D_2$ and above S. This will comprise consumers' and producers' surplus, assuming S equals marginal cost.

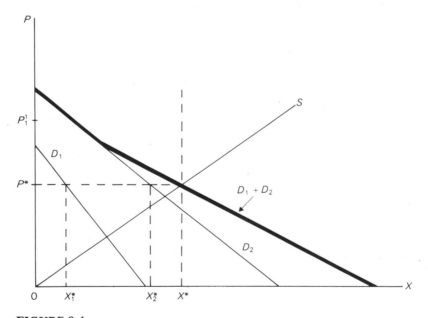

FIGURE 8.4

Note that, at the equilibrium price and quantity, individual 1 consumes $0X_1^*$ and individual 2 $0X_2^*$ and $0X_1^* + 0X_2^* = 0X^*$. We shall see that this contrasts with public goods.

8.3.2 PURE PUBLIC GOODS

The analysis for pure public goods, where non-rivalry and non-excludability are maximised, is slightly more complex. Consider Figure 8.5. The upper half shows a transformation function $T'T'$ between public and private goods (*PUB* and *PRIV*). This function obeys the usual requirement since the presence of public goods in no way affects the technical production relations in the economy. The indifference curve shown is for individual 1. Individual 2's indifference map is shown in the lower half of the diagram.

We select an arbitrary level of utility for individual 1, given by I_1. Take any arbitrary combination of *PRIV* and *PUB*, say A on $T'T'$. Then to keep 1 on I_1, we know that 1 must consume BC of the private good *PRIV*. This leaves AB for individual 2. Note that, hypothetically, 1 is consuming BC of *PRIV* and $0C$ of *PUB*. If he consumes 0_1C of *PUB*, so must 2 since pure public goods imply equal consumption. So, 2's consumption is given by AB of *PRIV*, and 0_2C of *PUB* $(0_1C = 0_2C)$ and this is shown on the lower half of the diagram. If we had begun at D on the top diagram, 2 would have consumed zero *PRIV* and $0E$ of *PUB*. Similarly point F on the upper half would also correspond to 2 having zero *PRIV*, as shown by point G in the lower diagram. In short, we can trace out a locus of a consumption possibility curve for 2 on the assumption that 1's consumption is fixed. This locus is given by the subtraction of I_1 from $T'T'$ in the upper diagram, and is shown as $T_2'T_2'$ in the lower diagram. 2's equilibrium is at H where his indifference curve I_2' is tangential to $T_2'T_2'$. Thus the optimal amount of the public good to 2 is given by the level PUB^* and, of course, this amount is also consumed by 1. To find the distribution of *PRIV* we refer back to $T'T'$ and this tells us that $PRIV_1$ is consumed by 1 (since this amount plus PUB^* keeps him on I_1) and $PRIV_2$ by 2.

Now we are in a position to derive some marginal conditions. Consider the consumption possibility curve $T_2'T_2'$ in the lower part of the diagram. This was obtained by subtracting I_1 from $T'T'$. The slope of I_1 is MRS_1, the marginal rate of substitution for individual 1 between *PUB* and *PRIV*. The slope of $T'T'$ is the marginal rate of transformation between *PUB* and *PRIV*, MRT. Hence we have

$$\text{Slope } T_2'T_2' = MRT - MRS_1.$$

At H, 2's MRS is just equal to the slope of $T_2'T_2'$ so that we also have

$$\text{Slope } T_2'T_2' = MRS_2.$$

Hence,

$$MRT - MRS_1 = MRS_2 \qquad (8.4)$$

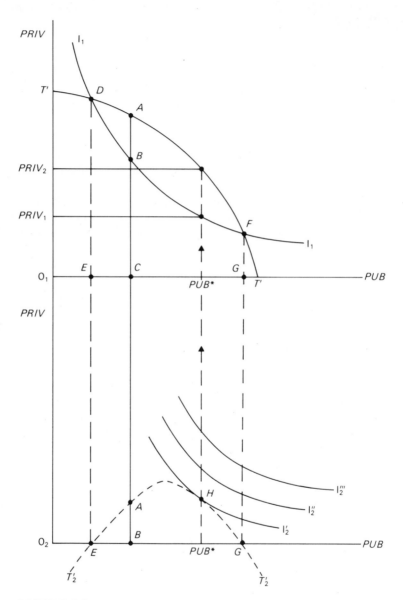

FIGURE 8.5

or

$$MRS_1 + MRS_2 = MRT. \qquad (8.5)$$

We have now derived the marginal conditions for the optimal provision of a public good (first set out in Samuelson, 1954, 1955). They look very similar to the conditions for optimality for a private good. The difference is that the MRSs are *added* whereas they were *equated* in the private goods case.

We know that

$$MRT_{PUB, PRIV} = \frac{MC_{PUB}}{MC_{PRIV}} \qquad (8.6)$$

and, for any individual,

$$MRS_{PUB, PRIV} = \frac{MU_{PUB}}{MU_{PRIV}} = \frac{P_{PUB}}{P_{PRIV}}. \qquad (8.7)$$

We can also write the efficiency condition as

$$\frac{P_{1, PUB}}{P_{1, PRIV}} + \frac{P_{2, PUB}}{P_{2, PRIV}} = \frac{MC_{PUB}}{MC_{PRIV}}. \qquad (8.8)$$

Assuming $P_{PRIV} = MC_{PRIV}$, i.e. marginal-cost pricing is practised in the private sector, we have

$$P_{1, PUB} + P_{2, PUB} = MC_{PUB}. \qquad (8.9)$$

We can now see how this relates to our estimate of net benefits. Figure 8.6 shows the demand curves for the public good by individuals 1 and 2.[3]

Now, if we were to sum D_1 and D_2 in the 'normal' way we would add them horizontally (as was done in Figure 8.4). *But,* any such procedure will violate the condition that *for pure public goods, each individual consumes the same amount.* The procedure is not to add horizontally, but *vertically.* In this way we secure $D_1 + D_2$ in Figure 8.6. Introducing an arbitrary supply curve gives an optimal supply of X_{PUB}^* and a price of P_{PUB}^*. As a check on the validity of the vertical summation procedure, note that P_{PUB}^* is indeed the sum of the two 'individual' prices $P_{1, PUB}$ and $P_{2, PUB}$, just as we require. *These prices are, note, for the same good and in the same quantity but they differ for each individual.* They are sometimes referred to as 'Lindahl prices' after Eric Lindahl (see Lindahl, 1958). While the optimal pricing of public goods is not of major concern to us in this book, we need to note later that a particular problem of measuring net benefits arises precisely because of this important fact about public-good prices.

Putting any such problems aside for the moment we can observe that benefits of the public good to 1 are given by the area under $D_{1, PUB}$ up to $0X_{PUB}^*$ and similarly for 2 the benefits are the area under $D_{2, PUB}$ up to $0X_{PUB}^*$. The sum of

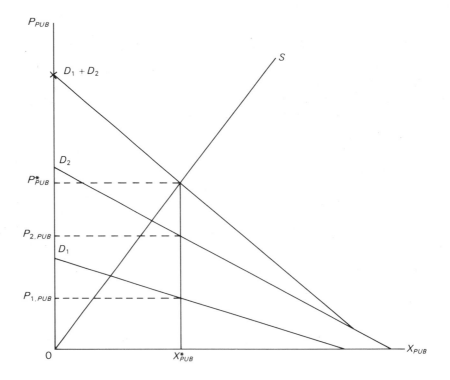

FIGURE 8.6

these two areas corresponds to the area under $D_1 + D_2$ up to X^*_{PUB}. *Net* benefits are of course this same area *minus* the area under the supply curve up to $0X^*_{PUB}$.

8.3.3   IMPURE PUBLIC GOODS

We observed earlier that there exists an entire *range* of goods from private to public, and this was illustrated diagrammatically in Figure 8.3. For current purposes we shall concentrate on just one of these — the case where the good has the *non-rivalry* aspect of a public good up to some limit of the number of persons using it, after which congestion externalities set in. Note however that *excludability* may still be applicable. The use of the term *impure public good* is therefore somewhat unfortunate, but unavoidable given its widespread use in the literature. We ignore the case of the local public good simply because in CBA, its sole importance is to remind us to ensure that we have properly defined the population for whom benefits and costs are being defined. None the less, as we shall see later, the concept of personal mobility has been used to establish the existence of surrogate markets in local public bads — such as noise and air pollution — and we can therefore consider these under the issue of valuation of damage.

The fact that in the impure public good case the net benefits to any one individual will tend to decline as more persons share that good distinguishes it from the pure public goods case. To demonstrate this consider briefly Figure 8.7 which repeats Figure 8.6 but shows a *third* individual 3 being added to the other two. We can summarise the effects of this addition. These are:

(i) With only two consumers the optimal price was P^* and the price to each consumer was P_1 and P_2.

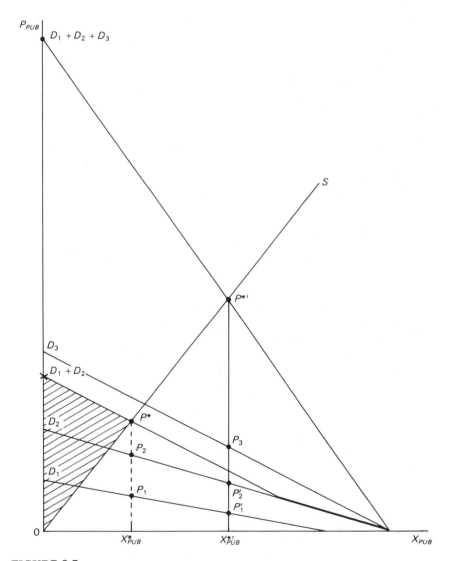

FIGURE 8.7

(ii) The arrival of the third consumer shifts the demand curve to
      $D_1 + D_2 + D_3$. The amount of the public good supplied is increased from
      X_{PUB}^* to $X_{PUB}^{*\prime}$ as shown.

(iii) Everyone gains, as the prices to 1 and 2 are now P_1' and P_2' where
      $P_1' < P_1$ and $P_2' < P_2$. Consumer 3 pays P_3. Net benefits have risen from
      the lower cross-hatched area to the lower area *plus* the upper cross-
      hatched area, the latter being the gain in net benefits.

Fairly simply then, for a pure public good the addition of extra persons not only
causes no problems, but actually secures net gains for the original consumers. If
we think of the consumers as a club, the optimal size of the club is clearly very
large (technically it is infinite).

Now consider what happens in the impure case where the growth in club
membership reduces the benefits to other club members.[4] The marginal
conditions for the pure public good remain valid: no extra amount of the good
should be supplied unless the *sum* of the marginal benefits from the extra
supply equals or more than equals the marginal cost of supplying it. The
optimum exists when $MRS_1 + MRS_2$ etc. = MRT.

Now consider what happens to the demand curve analysis if an extra
consumer is added to the club? We can use the analysis in Figure 8.7 for this
purpose. Figure 8.8 repeats similar features. However, whereas the former
aggregate demand curve was $D_1 + D_2$, the new curve is $\hat{D}_1 + \hat{D}_2 + D_3$ where $\hat{D}_1$
and $\hat{D}_2$ are the *reduced* demand curves of individuals 1 and 2 brought about by
the congestion caused by 3. Now in the case shown, the new aggregate demand
curve $\hat{D}_1 + \hat{D}_2 + D_3$ actually lies below the old aggregate demand curve $D_1 + D_2$.
It will be observed that the new prices for 1 and 2 are lower than they were
before. But 1 and 2 have not gained. To demonstrate this, consider the
consumer's surplus enjoyed by 1 before 3 arrived. This is shown by the light
cross-hatched area. The surplus after 3 arrives is shown by the heavy cross-
hatched area. The latter is clearly less. Had the demand curve for 1 kept its
slope, the surplus would still have been less because the arrival of 3 has actually
decreased the quantity supplied of the public good. Inspection of the surpluses
for individual 2 shows a reduction in surplus there as well. These are not
necessary results, but the diagram illustrates one possible impact of an extra
member. The theory of clubs goes on to define and measure 'optimal
membership'. We omit this theory here, save to remind ourselves that CBA can
and should be concerned with measuring optimal usage. For the theory see
Loehr and Sandler (1979) and for a practical example see Gwilliam and Nash
(1972).

8.3.4 THE 'FREE-RIDER' PROBLEM

The discussion of public goods showed that their optimal provision requires the
charging to *each consumer* of a price equal to the marginal benefit that consumer

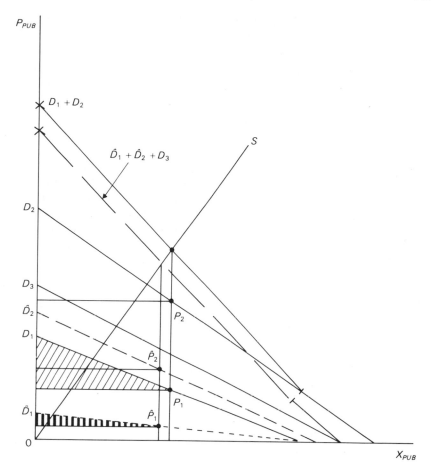

FIGURE 8.8

derives from the consumption of the public good. In terms of Figure 8.6 for example, the price charged to consumer 1 is quite different to that of consumer 2. The only requirement is that the two prices should *sum* to the optimal market price for the public good. Compare this to the private goods context in which the price of the good would be the same for each individual. Why should this requirement of 'differential pricing' be of interest? The first point is that, in practice, no such pricing mechanism where each consumer is charged his own 'personal price' is possible. Everyone pays the same price or because of non-excludability, no price can be levied. Typically, we shall be talking of who bears what tax burden for the provision of the good in the public sector.

Second, for the pure public good there are no additional costs of providing an extra consumer with the good. The marginal cost of adding an extra user is zero.

Note that this is quite different to saying that the marginal cost of expanding the supply of the public good is zero: this is not so.

Third, combining these first two points we can begin to see a problem for CBA. This is that we need to know the marginal benefit (demand) curves for each consumer. Only then can we aggregate them and determine the optimal supply of the public good. But if the good is non-excludable and if it is supplied in some amount X, then an individual can easily express no willingness to pay for the good in the expectation that it will be supplied to others. If supplied to them, it must by definition be supplied to him. He will have got the good, in some quantity anyway, but he will not have paid for it. He is a *free rider*. Figure 8.9 illustrates the problem for the two-consumer case. Two demand curves are shown which are the 'true' demand curves of the consumers for the public good. Hence the intersection of the sum of these two curves $D_1 + D_2$ with the marginal cost of provision MC determines the optimal size of the public good X^* and its optimal price P^*. But suppose individual 1 decides not to reveal his preference in its true form. We can have several situations. Individual 1 could say that he is unprepared to pay anything at all for the public good. In this case the amount supplied will be determined by the 'apparent' aggregate demand curve, which will in fact just consist of D_2. The amount supplied would be X'. Now clearly, individual 1 has lost some benefit

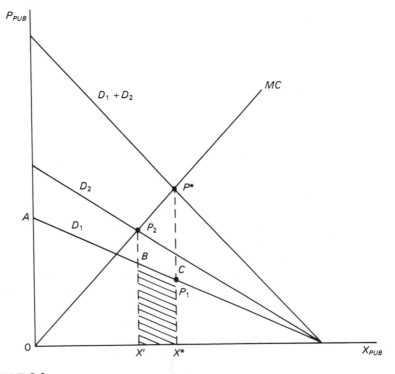

FIGURE 8.9

from the supply of the public good that would have occurred if he had truly revealed his preferences. On the other hand, non-exclusion means that he cannot be prevented from enjoying the amount of the good $0X'$ (indeed, while the term 'free rider' sounds perjorative we should remember that it is not economically rational for him to be excluded, even if it were possible, because the cost of providing the good to individual 1 is zero). Thus, individual 1 forgoes benefits shown by the shaded area in Figure 8.9, but he secures benefits equal to the area under his demand curve up to X' at zero cost to himself. Simple inspection of the diagram shows that by non-revelation of preference he secures a benefit of $0ABX'$ for zero payment, whereas had he 'truly' revealed his preferences and were it possible to invent a pricing (taxing) mechanism that would make each consumer pay according to the benefit received by him, then he would have secured benefits of $0ACX^*$ but would have had to pay out an amount equal to P_1 multiplied by X^*. We can see the rationale of under-revelation of preferences.

Other situations are possible. If the public good is indivisible in the sense that its size cannot be varied (the usual example is a bridge, but note the distinct possibility of exclusion here), then the argument we have just described would hold with even more force because, provided the bridge is built on the basis of other people's revealed preferences, our free rider can enjoy the full benefits of the public good for zero payment. In this case however, the decision-maker does not make a wrong decision because the demands of others are sufficient to indicate that net benefits will accrue from the construction of the bridge. As long as congestion does not occur, it costs nothing to let the free rider use the bridge. In cost—benefit terms we have not affected the decision rule but we have wrongly stated the true aggregate benefits. On the other hand, the investment decision might also be affected. This would occur if under-revelation on the part of the free rider gave an 'apparent' demand curve which indicated net *costs* of providing the public good. Unless some mechanism exists for quickly allowing the free rider to 'vote again', the bridge will not get built and an inefficient decision will have been made.

Finally, the free rider need not reveal a zero preference for the good when his true preference is in favour — he may simply understate the actual level of his demand curve. The result will still be under-provision. Again, net benefits will be wrongly stated and hence our CBA is affected by this phenomenon.

It should also be noted that the converse, overstatement of preferences, can also occur. If people believe that their share of the cost of a public good will be low or zero, they have an incentive to overstate their willingness to pay for it. This problem might also arise if questionnaire techniques are used to assess values.

How serious is the free rider problem? The answer is that we do not really know because no adequate mechanism exists for identifying the 'true' demand curves of individuals. That is, we need to compare what demand actually is with what it would be if only everyone were telling the truth. Some experiments exist to test for the degree of divergences (Bohm, 1971). In so far as they indicate anything, they suggest that under-revelation may not be a serious problem in practice. To be sure however, one would need to implement one of the growing number of 'pricing experiments' suggested in the public-goods literature to see what would happen (Groves and Loeb, 1975; Tideman and Tullock, 1976). Space forbids an examination of these experiments, and, in any event, they lie outside the scope of this text.

8.3.5 THE FORCED-RIDER PROBLEM

We may briefly note that the obverse of the free-rider problem may occur for some public goods. Our presumption throughout has been that what is a good for one individual is a good for the other. But something may be a good for one and a bad for someone else. Loehr and Sandler (1979) point to defence as an example. Thus expanding the defence of a nation amounts to expanding a public good for most people but to those opposed to military activity on, say, moral grounds, the expansion will affect them negatively — they will suffer a welfare loss. If, however, the decision-maker simply assumes that 'votes for' only should be counted, then he will overstate the net benefit for the good — it will be strictly necessary to subtract the net losses of those who would have voted against it had their voice been heard. It may seem odd to hypothesise a situation in which 'votes for' are recorded but not 'votes against'. Our discussion of economic voting mechanisms reminds us, however, that the most someone voting in a market can do is record a zero willingness to pay, since they cannot record a negative willingness to pay. The issue therefore becomes one of ensuring that 'negative votes' can be counted, and this is very much an institutional problem.

8.4 Valuing Externalities: Hedonic Prices

We have now reached the stage of knowing what it is that we wish to measure when valuing externalities and public goods, and of seeing why this may be difficult. The most common approach to the problem is to look for markets in which implicit valuations of such factors may be found. For instance, one widely used technique in seeking monetary estimates of externality relies on the basic idea that any negative externality will affect property prices adversely, and any positive externality will affect them in an upwards direction. The idea is that a house may be thought of as comprising a bundle of 'attributes' — a number of rooms, proximity to city centres, size of garden, central heating, schools etc. The local level of externality is simply one more attribute. The house price is then some combination of the implicit, or *hedonic* prices of the constituent attributes. Thus, pollution is a negative attribute and should therefore have a negative price. Conversely, one can think of the absence of pollution as a positive attribute with a positive price. Effectively, the household is assumed to have a utility function of the form

$$U = U(Y, a_1 \ldots a_n) \tag{8.10}$$

where Y is the bundle of *non-housing* goods consumed, and a_1 is the level of any attribute i. The budget constraint is given as

$$B = P_y \cdot Y + \sum_{i=1}^{n} P_i \cdot a_i \tag{8.11}$$

where P_y is the price of non-housing goods, P_i the implicit price of the ith attribute and B the household budget (income).

Maximising U with respect to the budget constraint yields a function relating the attributes and other commodities to expenditure levels. This function has the form

$$g(a_1 \ldots a_n, Y, B) = 0. \tag{8.12}$$

If the utility function in equation (8.10) is separable between attributes and Y (i.e. the utility derived from the attributes is not dependent on the consumption of other goods), then equation (8.12) can be expressed solely in terms of the attributes $a_1 \ldots a_n$ and housing expenditure H in the form

$$f(a_1 \ldots a_n, H) = 0 \tag{8.13}$$

where $H = B - P_y \cdot Y$. The implicit function (8.13) can be written in explicit form as

$$H = h(a_1 \ldots a_n) \tag{8.14}$$

which tells us that housing expenditure H is a function of the attributes of the house. H is expressed in rental terms. To convert to present value terms we have

$$V = H/r = 1/r \cdot h(a_1 \ldots a_n) \tag{8.15}$$

or

$$V = V(a_1 \ldots a_n). \tag{8.16}$$

Equation (8.16) tells us that the capitalised value of the property (the house price) is dependent upon the levels of the attributes of the house. Since pollution is one such attribute, it follows that the house price is partly determined by the level of noise.

Now, the *marginal valuation* of any attribute i is given by

$$\frac{\partial V}{\partial a_i}.$$

That is, $\partial V/\partial a_i$ measures the marginal willingness to pay for an extra unit of attribute i. It is the *hedonic price*. Hence, to find 'the cost of pollution', equation (8.16) is estimated and the differential with respect to the pollution attribute is taken to obtain the marginal willingness to pay for pollution reduction.

Equation (8.16) is presented in general terms. Its specific form is dependent upon the form of the underlying utility function (8.10). Thus, if the utility function is *linear*, the form of equation (8.16) will be

$$V = b_1 a_1 + b_2 a_2 + \cdots + b_n a_n \tag{8.17}$$

where the bs are constants and, since $\partial V/\partial a_i = b_i$, these constants are themselves the hedonic prices. Effectively then, equation (8.17) can be set up as a regression equation and the coefficients will give the hedonic prices. In this way, we supposedly obtain a 'value' for pollution reduction.[5]

The regression equation (8.17) will look quite different if a different form of utility function is used. For example, a multiplicative utility function yields a log-linear regression equation

$$\log V = b_1 \cdot \log a_1 + b_2 \cdot \log a_2 + \cdots + b_n \cdot \log a_n. \tag{8.18}$$

Note that in this form the coefficients are no longer the hedonic prices. Instead

$$\frac{\partial V}{\partial a_i} = \frac{\partial \log V}{\partial \log a_i} \cdot \frac{V}{a_i} = b_i \cdot \frac{V}{a_i}. \tag{8.19}$$

In this case the hedonic price depends on both the property value V and the level of the attribute a_i.

Note that for the hedonic approach to be tenable on theoretical grounds, consumers must be utility maximisers, and the housing market must contain no imperfections such that individuals are constrained by anything other than their incomes. Of all markets, however, the housing market is the one in which such an assumption is least likely to be met since many factors besides income determine mobility and choice of location.

The actual measurement of hedonic indices can also be troublesome. Not only must all the attributes of the houses in question be identifiable and quantifiable, but we must be able to determine which attributes are important when it comes to housing choice. It is unclear in practice whether every individual has the same set of attributes which he or she considers important.

More seriously, for the hedonic approach to work, restrictions must be placed on the utility functions of individuals before estimating equations of the form of (8.17) or (8.18) can be used. First, *all* individuals must have *identical* utility functions. If this is not so, equations (8.15) and (8.16) will vary from one individual to the next. If the estimated equations are not identical for each individual, the observations used to estimate the equations will in fact be *single observations on many different functions*. Yet what is required is the reverse of this — many observations on a single function. Because of this failing, what the regression equations (8.17) and (8.18) will estimate are coefficients which will in fact be weighted averages of individuals' marginal valuations of noise. This contrasts with what is required, namely single marginal valuations for all levels of the given attribute.

Second, the identical utility functions must also take on a specific form. They must be homogeneous.[6] Non-homogeneity leads to the result that marginal valuations (the hedonic prices) depend on the individual's *level* of utility. Hence, if the sample of households studied contains individuals with different utility levels no unique estimatable price can be obtained.

Third, we need to recall that we obtained the estimating equations for hedonic prices by assuming separable utility functions. That is, the price of Y, the non-housing attributes, was not dependent in any way on the price of housing attributes. However, it is also essential for the separability to apply to the attributes themselves. This means that the price of any one attribute must not be dependent on *any* other factor affecting house price. This seems extremely unlikely: the utility obtained from combinations of attributes (and non-housing commodities) is unlikely to be the same as the sum of utilities from individual attributes.

Fourth, hedonic theory effectively assumes that attributes are exogenously determined on the supply side. Hedonic prices are determined only by demand for the attribute. If endogenous supply of attributes is permitted the estimating procedures will fall prey to the usual problems of econometric identification and simultaneity. Further, all that has been said about utility functions has to be applied to the supply of attributes, with cost being substituted for utility. Only if attributes can be assumed to be completely price-inelastic can we concentrate on a demand-determined hedonic price model. But if attributes are price-elastic, then the supply side must be explicitly considered and the same restrictions that applied to demand must be applied to supply.

Economists differ in their views on the 'meaningfulness' of hedonic prices. For a spirited defence see Freeman (1979) and for a critique see Edwards and Pearce (1979). For a survey of empirical estimates in relation to noise nuisance see Edwards and Pearce (1979).

8.5 A Note on Non-convexity and Optimal Externality

One other issue is worth brief discussion in relation to the optimal externality level. Typically the marginal external cost curve (MEC) is drawn as a rising function of output. This was how it was shown in Figure 8.1 (p. 122). This seems intuitively 'rational' if we think of most externality contexts: the more the nuisance-creating activity occurs, the higher will be the marginal *physical* impact and the more the *value* of extra unit of cost would be as well. The total external cost curve will rise at an increasing rate and hence MEC will appear as shown. There are however arguments to suggest that MEC will behave rather differently.

Figure 8.10 is adapted from Baumol and Bradford (1972). Industry *P* is a

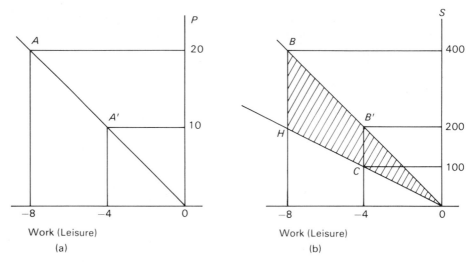

FIGURE 8.10

polluting industry producing some output and pollution as a side effect. This
pollution is suffered by industry S, also producing some output but itself
generating no pollution. $0A$ and $0B$ are the respective production functions.
In industry P, 4 units of labour produce 10 of output, and 8 of labour produce
20 units of output. In industry S, 4 of labour produce 200 of output and 8
produce 400. Both production functions are constant returns functions. But S's
production function changes to $0H$ if P pollutes S — i.e. $0H$ is the production
function *with* the externality and $0B$ is the function *without* the externality. If
we now consider the various combinations of outputs for a limited supply of 8
units of labour we have

   (i)   8 units of labour to P, 0 to S, gives $(20P, 0S)$.

   (ii)   8 units of labour to S, 0 to P, gives $(0P, 400S)$. (S is on $0B$.)

   (iii)   4 units of labour to P, 4 to S gives $(10P, 100S)$. (Because S is now on
        $0H$ and not $0B$.)

If we plot a production possibility curve for these combinations it turns out to be
non-convex — it bends inwards to the origin.

    Figure 8.11(a) shows the production possibility frontiers for the situation
above. Frontier PP_1 relates to a 'no externality' case, and frontier PP_2 shows the
effect for the externality-affected industry S. We can measure the total external
cost (TEC) as S's lost production — i.e. the horizontal distance between PP_1 and
PP_2 as P's output increases. In Figure 8.11(b), if we concentrate on the range of
P output over which TEC increases, we see it does so at a decreasing rate. In
short MEC slopes downwards, as Figure 8.11(c) shows. MEC does in fact
decrease until it becomes negative, a consequence of the TEC curve having the
shape shown in Figure 8.11(b).

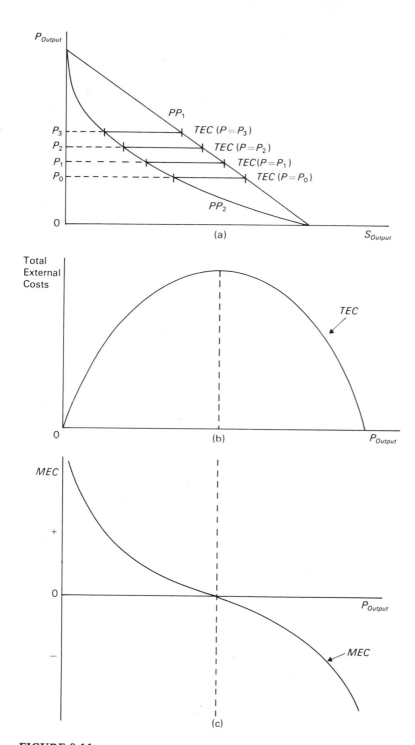

FIGURE 8.11

The possibility of a declining MEC function has more relevance to the mechanisms used for achieving an optimal level of externality than for CBA. In terms of Figure 8.1 for example, the intersection of MNPB and MEC no longer generates the optimal level of externality if MEC cuts MB from above. If MEC cuts MB from below the normal intersection properties remain. As far as the practice of CBA is concerned, the analysis of non-convexity perhaps serves to remind us that we should be sure to calculate externality costs over as wide a range of output as possible: a presumption that those costs will increase with output is not theoretically valid and a presumption that they will increase at an increasing rate is perhaps even less theoretically valid. *Empirically* it is open to question as to whether non-convexity matters much.

8.6   Conclusions

This chapter has done no more than outline the nature of externalities and their close 'relatives', public goods and bads. We observed that externalities tend to have an element of 'publicness' about them and that this in turn can cause problems for the estimation of net social benefits.

There may be no market price, or if one does exist, an element of under-revelation of preferences may be present. Thus, determining the appropriate level of provision may be difficult. Apart from this, most of the problems related to public goods and externality analysis concern the design of optimal mechanisms for controlling their use. Unfortunately, decisions on provision and on the use of public goods are not independent. Failure to optimise the latter results in a reduction in the level of net benefits obtained. In turn, this could affect the investment decision.

9 The Social Discount Rate

9.1 Introduction: Individual and Social Discount Rates

Chapter 4 demonstrated the importance of the discount rate in social investment appraisal. This chapter investigates the various theories that have been put forward to establish how a social discount rate is determined. One immediate problem arises. Chapter 4 proceeded as if the *social* discount rate was some sort of average of individuals' discount rates, and no attention was paid to exactly who the individuals in question should be, nor how the averaging procedure would take place. Implicit throughout, however, was the view that the discount rate must be determined by individual preferences and that the 'social' rate must therefore be linked directly to individual preferences; there can be no question of 'the state' intervening with some discount rate derived from its own preferences, even if speaking of 'the state' as an entity capable of having preferences has much meaning. The social—individual linkage is, of course, entirely in keeping with the underlying Paretian value judgement that individuals' own valuations should count.

Arguably, all individuals' time preference rates will be the same. This would come about because their preference rates will be reflected in their savings behaviour and this in turn will be determined by *the* market rate of interest. Quite simply, all (marginal) time-preference rates would equal the market rate of interest. If they did not, savings behaviour would alter so as to bring the two back into equality.

In practice no single rate of interest exists. There are comparatively 'riskless' rates on government securities, rates which reflect differing levels of uncertainty and so on. Moreover, if individuals are not all *taxed* at equal marginal rates, their time-preference rates will vary. This is because the saver who lends his money gets back the interest on his loan *minus* any tax. If individuals did equate time-preference rates to market rates, then they would be equating them to 'tax adjusted' rates. Again, lenders bear more risk than borrowers, so time-preference rates will differ between the two groups, and so on.

It is more than reasonable then to suppose that no one individual will have the same time preference rate as another. In addition to the factors above, age alone will account for such differences, with older persons tending to discount the future more heavily than younger persons. An averaging process therefore becomes essential. A simple expected value may be calculated, or if it is felt that some individuals are somehow more 'deserving' than others, a weighted average could be obtained. This will be particularly true if, for some reason, the individual's time-preference rate is related positively to his or her income.

However, there are formidable problems in accepting that the resulting average is a social discount rate. First, at any one time we would be averaging rates of time preference (RTPs) for persons who happen to be alive at that point in time. This need not be the same thing at all as securing an average RTP for the persons who will be affected by the project under consideration. People not alive after the project has commenced, for example, will be replaced by new 'voters'. In a simplistic world in which the dead are instantly replaced by the new born, we would be replacing a voter with a high discount rate by someone who has no effective capacity to express a discount rate but which we could reasonably assume would be fairly low! So when we speak of averaging, we must be clear whether we are averaging RTPs at the time of the decision, or over the population alive during the duration of the project. These must be very different.

We could argue that calculating the average at one time-period is sufficient, since at least some of those alive will have *some* concern for those who are 'born into' the new generation. If so, we could argue that the difference in the discount rates between existing and future members of the community is 'internalised' in the existing generation's discount rates. Effectively they will have averaged the RTPs of themselves and the newcomers in the same way that we suggested they should be averaged if only we knew what the newcomers' RTPs would be. This is a satisfying argument but not a very satisfactory one. By and large, we have no real way of telling whether the averaging procedure used by existing voters would amount to the same thing as the averaging procedure suggested whereby we look at the RTPs across all persons affected during the life of the project. We simply do not know what this 'coefficient of concern' is.

One can think of all kinds of complex measures to avoid the problem. Perhaps, for example, the averaging procedure should take place across existing voters at each point of time, with the result that the discount rate obtained might well vary from one year to the next as the age structure of the population changes. Provided this could be done *in advance* of the project, the relevant discount rate could be entered in each relevant year of the project's life. If it cannot be done in advance, and the problems of forecasting population are quite formidable, then the analysts would have to settle for some kind of approximation.

However, even if problems of the kind discussed above could be overcome there is the added problem of what has come to be known as the 'isolation paradox'. In essence the paradox (which in fact is not a paradox at all) is that individuals, taken individually, may well express some set of RTPs. This would reflect their *personal* evaluation of the project, and their own RTP would be used. But if everyone else agrees to invest in the project as well, then the individual in question might well agree to invest in a project which has a negative NPV at his own isolated discount rate, but a positive NPV rate when, because of the agreement of others to invest, he adjusts his RTP downwards. In short, there are *two* RTPs: one when the investor acts 'in isolation', and one when he acts 'socially' with others. The average of the RTPs obtained in one context, where the voter is isolated, may be quite different to the average of the RTPs obtained in a context where the voter behaves as a member of a community. The issue is discussed at length in Sen (1967).

Perhaps the most practical point to make is that while we may have little idea of the extent of 'concern' about newcomers to the community, and hence little idea of the extent to which potential externalities have been internalised, and while we may have even less idea of what a 'collectively' expressed RTP would be compared to one expressed in 'isolation', decisions have necessarily to be made by those with votes at a particular point of time. The context for making that decision will, one hopes, be wide enough to permit the individual to identify as far as possible with the community and with generations to come. If it is not, it seems safe to assume that the social discount rate will in fact be *less* than the one we actually obtain by the averaging process on the grounds that (a) the one observed will not fully account for externalities across generations and (b) no individual will vote 'in isolation' for projects with rates of return lower than the discount rate expressed 'in isolation'. Quite what the magnitude of the adjustment to the observed rate would be is indeterminate, but at least we have good reason to suppose it would be in a downward direction.

Arguably, all the problems noted above favour the view that the choice of discount rate should be left to decision-makers. This would mean that politicians, civil servants, corporate planning divisions of public utilities and so on would choose the rate. Their choice could be argued to be consistent with the fact that, given the complexities of deriving rates of personal expressions of discount rates, these people must choose 'on behalf' of the community. This might be satisfactory if the persons in question were directly accountable for their decisions, but while this may be true of some areas of public choice in for example the United States, it is generally not the case in the United Kingdom. As such, the 'delegated responsibility' approach has some very unattractive features. Unless institutions are devised in such a way that responsibility extends to the community, this delegated approach cannot be held to honour the Paretian requirements for a welfare change.

9.2   A Simple Two-period Model of Discount Rates

Figure 9.1 provides the essential analytical framework for analysing the determination of a social discount rate. The vertical axis shows *consumption* in year $t + 1$ and the horizontal axis *consumption* in year t. Note the emphasis on consumption since, as we shall see, failure to identify exactly what it is that is 'traded off' between periods is held by some writers to have generated a great deal of confusion in the literature on social discount rates. By and large, we select consumption because individuals' welfare is assumed to be determined by their levels of consumption rather than, say, their level of income.

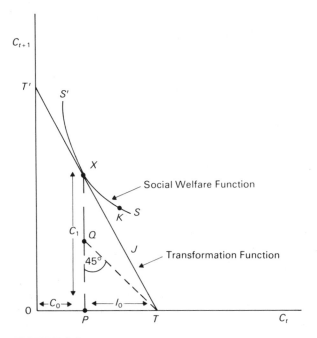

FIGURE 9.1

Our first requirement is for a function which shows us how much consumption can be secured in each period. By definition, if we consume everything in period t, nothing is left for $t + 1$. Point T defines this situation. Equally, point T' defines the situation if everything is consumed in $t + 1$ and none in t. The curve TT' is in fact an *intertemporal production frontier* or transformation function. It could well be a straight line with $0T'$ equal to $0T$. This would simply define a situation in which the sacrifice of one unit of consumption now always enables us to consume that unit in the next period. It is more likely, however, that the sacrifice of one unit now would permit that unit to be used for capital investment which, in turn, would generate that unit again in $t + 1$ *and more*. This is nothing more than the notion of capital productivity. Hence we draw $0T'$ as being greater than $0T$. The linear nature of the frontier is simply there for convenience. The analysis is not altered if we have an 'outward bending' curve such as one would normally expect to find if the frontier obeyed normal assumptions about the diminishing marginal productivity of capital.

Observing the function TT' alone for the moment, the point X would illustrate a point where C_0 is consumed in the first period and C_1 in the second period. What is not consumed in the first period (i.e. $0T - 0P = PT$) must be invested and it is this investment which gives rise to the sacrificed consumption, measured as $PT = PQ$ *plus* the net product of the capital investment, shown as QX. So, we immediately have a measure of the productivity of capital. This is given by

$$\frac{PX}{PT} = \frac{PQ + QX}{PT} = \frac{PQ}{PT} + \frac{QX}{PT} .$$

But since $PQ = PT$ by definition, we have

$$\frac{PX}{PT} = 1 + \frac{QX}{PT} .$$ (9.1)

Moreover, PX/PT is the *slope* of TT', so that

$$\frac{QX}{PT} = \text{Slope of } TT' - 1.$$ (9.2)

What is QX/PT? It is in fact the *net* product of the investment I_0. If we deal with smaller and smaller units of investment, equation (9.2) will still hold. In other words, QX/PT is the *marginal net product of capital* or, to use more familiar language, it is *the internal rate of return* or the *marginal efficiency of capital*. We can write this as r, such that

$$r = \text{Slope of } TT' - 1.$$ (9.3)

Holding equation (9.3) in mind for the moment, let us turn to the issue of what the *optimal* amount of consumption would be in the two periods. To find this we need the concept of an *intertemporal welfare function* and this is shown in the form of a 'social indifference curve' SS' in Figure 9.1. This is shown as exhibiting the orthodox assumption of convexity, but it should be recalled that it is a *social* indifference curve and therefore subject to all the strictures about the construction of such functions (Scitovsky, 1941–2). None the less, the welfare function shown serves a useful didactic function and it will be shown to be a representation of the concept of a social time-preference rate, as discussed in Section 9.1.

The slope of SS' shows the rate at which society is prepared to substitute future for present consumption. By definition, society is assumed to be indifferent (collectively) between a point such as K and another such as X, so long as both are on SS'. Suppose we consider the hypothetical move from K to X. Then we give up an amount of C_t, say ΔC_t, in favour of an amount of C_{t+1}, say ΔC_{t+1}. Let the extra (marginal) utility attached to ΔC_t and ΔC_{t+1} be dU_t and dU_{t+1} respectively. Then, since *levels* of utility at K and X must be the same, we can write

$$\Delta C_t \cdot \left(\frac{dU_t}{dC_t} \right) = \Delta C_{t+1} \cdot \left(\frac{dU_{t+1}}{dC_{t+1}} \right)$$

or

$$\frac{dU_t/dC_t}{dU_{t+1}/dC_{t+1}} = \frac{\Delta C_{t+1}}{\Delta C_t} .$$ (9.4)

Now, $\Delta C_{t+1}/\Delta C_t$ is the slope of SS' so that we can write

$$\text{Slope of } SS' = \left(\frac{dU_t}{dC_t}\right)\bigg/\left(\frac{dU_{t+1}}{dC_{t+1}}\right). \tag{9.5}$$

But SS' is drawn in such a way that as less and less of C_t is consumed, more and more of C_{t+1} is required to compensate for the loss of C_t. We might justify this by arguing that the law of diminishing marginal utility of consumption applies. That is,

$$\frac{d\left(\dfrac{dU_t}{dC_t}\right)}{dC_t} < 0.$$

Letting the excess over unity be given by s we can write

$$\frac{dU_t/dC_t}{dU_{t+1}/dC_{t+1}} = 1 + s \tag{9.6}$$

or

$$\text{Slope of } SS' = 1 + s$$

or

$$s = \text{Slope of } SS' - 1. \tag{9.7}$$

Bringing equations (9.3) and (9.7) together, we have

$$r = \text{Slope of } TT' - 1$$

and

$$s = \text{Slope of } SS' - 1.$$

Observation of Figure 9.1 shows that r, the internal rate of return is, in general, not equal to s, the social rate of time preference. Indeed, they cannot be equal unless the slopes of the two functions TT' and SS' are equal. They are equal at only one point, namely where the level of consumption is optimally allocated between the two periods, or to say the same thing, where the level of investment is optimal. This is at point X in Figure 9.1 and it is easy to see there that s equals r.

What is the significance of this result? Essentially, r measures the opportunity cost of any public investment — it measures the rate of return that could be achieved by sacrificing a unit of consumption now. If that sacrifice is for the purpose of social investment, then we see that the opportunity cost of the investment is measured by r, the forgone rate of return. That rate of return may be forgone in the private sector, or elsewhere in the public sector, an issue we discuss shortly. Assuming for the moment that the forgone investment is evaluated in social terms — i.e. all externalities are allowed for — r is a measure of the *social opportunity cost of capital* (SOC).

What then is s? The answer, as we have already seen, is that s measures the rate at which individuals collectively trade off present and future consumption. It is the *social time-preference rate* (STPR).

The problem is that we now have *two* social discount rates, each with good credentials, as it were. After all, it makes little sense to invest in a project at less than r per cent discount rate since we can always secure r per cent elsewhere in the economy, r per cent being the rate of return on a marginal project somewhere. Equally, if we are to honour the Paretian value judgement that consumers' wants are to dominate, those wants are reflected in the value of s. Of course, we would also expect them to be reflected in r, since the rate of return on the marginal project elsewhere should itself reflect consumer preferences. Quite clearly however, Figure 9.1 demonstrates the possibility that s and r diverge. Only if we can assume optimal investment can we take it that s equals r and 'conflate' our two discount rates to one. But it is precisely because opinion favours the view that economies do *not* operate at the optimal level of investment that two basic schools of thought exist, one favouring the use of r and the other favouring the use of s. As we shall see, since this is a familiar second-best problem — i.e. what rate to use given that the first-best rate (where $s = r$) is not used — the focus of attention has been on devising rules that integrate s and r. What then are the reasons for supposing that the economy operates not at a point like X in Figure 9.1 but rather at a point like J where r is in fact greater than s and the level of investment is sub-optimal?

9.3 The Divergence between STPR and SOC

Baumol (1968) has offered one very straightforward explanation as to why s and r will diverge in practice. Assume the government (responsible for social investment) can borrow at the rate of s, and assume further this government's borrowing rate is equal to the STPR. Let there be a corporation tax equal to t, which is levied on the profits of private industry. From the private company point of view, shareholders will expect at least s per cent, otherwise they will secure better returns by lending to the government. But to provide them with s per cent or more, companies must earn a *gross* rate (r) of $s/1 - t$ since t per cent disappears in corporate tax. Self-evidently,

$$r = \frac{s}{1 - t} > s$$

since t is less than unity. The simple existence of a corporation tax generates a situation where r exceeds s — i.e. at a point like J in Figure 9.1.

This inequality is reinforced if risk is treated differently by investors in respect of the way they view government and private investments. Thus, if they tend to think of government investment as generally 'riskless' the rate s will represent a 'risk free' rate of discount. If they attach higher risk to private investments, then private industry could be thought of as aiming for a rate of return r which is higher still than the rate $s/1 - t$ by some 'risk premium'. The inequality between r and s is widened further.

Next, consider the fact that we have termed r the *social* opportunity cost of capital. For r to be usable however, we must be sure that it is the internal rate of return on the forgone project *assuming all social costs and benefits have been evaluated*. If the forgone project is in private industry there can be no presumption that this is the case. If the balance of these external effects is negative then r will in fact exaggerate the true SOC. If the balance is positive, r will understate the true SOC. Thus, if s is 5 per cent and r is 10 per cent and the balance of external effects is negative, the true value of r would be less than 10 per cent, let us say 8 per cent just as an example.

Finally, note that there is not necessarily a single rate of return on capital. For instance, in comparing public and private investment, comparative rates of return depend on the pricing policy being used in the two relevant sectors. If the private sector is monopolistic in structure while the public sector is required at, say, marginal cost, then profits per £1 invested in the private sector will be higher than in the public sector. On the other hand, if CBA is used in the public sector, this *tends* to give a higher rate of return than that given by purely financial appraisal.

Enough has been said to suggest that, in the real world, we may face a second-best situation with r and s diverging, perhaps markedly, Later on we can see if this is true in practice.

9.4 The Social Opportunity Cost Approach

The SOC school of thought is obviously attractive. No project should be undertaken unless it secures a return at least equal to what could have been achieved if the sacrificed expenditure had gone elsewhere. The problems with the approach are fairly numerous however. A number have been rehearsed already.

What rate of return does one look at to find the SOC? Ideally, one is looking for some rate of return which firms would *wish to achieve* on marginal low-risk investments. The projects must be at the margin since public investment projects can be argued to displace only these projects. They must also be low risk because of arguments to the effect that government investments are low risk due to the 'spreading' of risks across many projects and many people (see Chapter 5, subsection 5.7.1). In fact, some government investments are high risk, reflecting one-off decisions on which there is little or no prior experience (Concorde) or decisions that were simply wrongly made (Advanced Gas-Cooled Nuclear Reactors in the United Kingdom: Henderson, 1977). In the United Kingdom,

TABLE 9.1   Real Cost of Capital in the UK 1960–1975

	Pre-tax cost of capital %	Post-tax cost of capital %
1960	12.5	8.8
1965	9.9	5.4
1970	10.3	3.9
1973	10.2	5.0
1974	14.0	5.3
1975	6.4	5.9

Source: Flemming *et al.* (1976).

such a rate was thought to be in real terms 8 per cent in 1967, 10 per cent in 1969 and 5 per cent in 1978.[1]

Empirical studies of the SOC are many but often difficult to evaluate. A fairly thorough example is provided by Flemming *et al.* (1976) for the United Kingdom. The authors calculate the rate at which future earnings in the private sector are discounted in the capital market. This rate is equal to the ratio of real profits to the market's valuation of the capital stock of industry. Table 9.1 indicates the values obtained. Note in particular that pre-tax rates and post-tax rates are given. The post-tax rates are, according to the authors, easier to calculate because of United Kingdom provisions for deferred tax liability. For our own purposes it is the pre-tax estimates that are relevant however (see the discussion on corporation tax in Section 9.3 above). But Flemming *et al.* caution us that 'It would . . . be unwise to place too much weight on these figures: as markets do, in fact, take tax into account, the pre-tax cost of capital cannot be directly observed' (Flemming *et al.*, op. cit., p. 205).

We may note just two things about the calculations in Table 9.1. First, what is in fact recorded is a set of *average* costs of capital, not the marginal cost which is what we require. The two would be the same only in perfect capital markets. Second, the recorded rates vary significantly from one year to the next after 1973: there is no apparent stability of the rate. These points are raised simply to illustrate the fact that empirically estimating the SOC is in fact not at all easy.

9.5   SOC and Capital Rationing

Chapter 4 demonstrated that, in the presence of a capital constraint, projects cannot be *ranked* by their present net values. Rather, a benefit–cost *ratio* ranking is required (see subsection 4.3.2). We can now look at this same issue of capital constraint in the context of the SOC.

Consider the hypothetical projects shown in Table 9.2. Each has a constant flow of benefits (simply for arithmetic convenience) and the present values are calculated at 10 per cent.[2] The benefit—cost ratios are shown. These favour a ranking of:

A
D
C
B

If we have a capital constraint of, say, £1.6 m, then £1 m should be spent of *A* (NPV = 0.36) and £0.6 m on *D* (NPV = 0.6 x 0.58 = 0.35) to give a total NPV of £0.71 m, the best we can do.[3]

If the capital constraint is relaxed slightly, Table 9.2 indicates that we should invest more in project *D*, yielding an extra £0.23 m over the £1 m extra expenditure. In short, the SOC is £1.23 m. Note, however, that in contrast to the discussion in the previous sections of this chapter, this SOC is *not* expressed as a rate of return, and certainly not as a rate of return on a forgone project in a sector *outside* the one containing projects *A − D*. Two points are therefore worth noting:

> (*a*) the presence of a capital constraint leads us to calculate the *shadow price of capital* ;
>
> (*b*) that shadow price is the price of the last desirable project allowed by the capital constraint and which project is *in the public sector*.

The issue of shadow pricing emerges again later. To see that it gives the 'correct' result, we can present Table 9.2 in a different form, this time with the capital costs expressed in shadow capital cost terms. Essentially, we multiply the capital costs in Table 9.2 by 1.23 and recalculate the NPVs. These are as shown in Table 9.3.

Note that in this revised form the only project to achieve a positive present value is project *A*, the one ranked first by the benefit—cost ratio approach. Project *D* correctly appears as having a zero NPV since what is being said is that *it defines the marginal project in the presence of the capital constraint*. The

TABLE 9.2

Project	Cost £m	Benefits £m p.a.	Life of project (Yrs.)	NPV at 10%	B/C
A	1.0	0.16	20	0.36	0.36
B	1.5	0.12	40	0.17	0.11
C	0.5	0.08	15	0.11	0.22
D	2.0	0.42	10	0.46	0.23

TABLE 9.3

Project	Shadow capital cost (£m)	NPV at 10%
A	1.23	+0.13
B	1.85	−0.68
C	0.62	−0.01
D	2.46	0.00

ranking thus becomes, on NPV terms, A, D, C, B which is exactly what we secured by the benefit−cost ratio approach. The two approaches are entirely consistent.

Lastly, it is worth noting that ranking by the internal rates of return on the projects would have yielded the following (approximate) results: A = 15 per cent, $B = 7\frac{1}{2}$ per cent, $C = 13\frac{1}{2}$ per cent and $D = 18\frac{1}{2}$ per cent, or a ranking of D, A, C and B. These rankings differ from the ones given by the benefit−cost ratios for reasons that differentiate the results obtained from NPV and IRR calculations, and these were given in Chapter 4. In the current case, the IRR is sensitive to the economic life of the projects. Now, much of the project evaluation literature refers to the relevant discount rate in a capital constraint context as the rate of return on the marginal project. But the marginal project cannot be easily defined in terms of a rate of return. If projects are ranked by IRR, D would be the only project undertaken and would therefore also be the marginal project. If projects are ranked by benefit−cost ratios, D would still be the marginal project although A would correctly be undertaken first. Simply pursued, the logic of calling this project the marginal project would mean that the discount rate should be $18\frac{1}{2}$ per cent, and the NPV would in fact be negative. Overall then, it seems more sensible to speak of shadow prices rather than marginal rates of return in such contexts.

9.6 The Social Time-preference Rate

Section 9.1 argued that a social time-preference rate (STPR) must be derived from some average of individuals' rates of time preference, however complex that procedure might be. We can inquire now what the sources of personal time preference are. We can list them as:

(1) *Pure myopia* − people simply prefer the present to the future for reasons which are best judged irrational in the sense that, by adopting such rates, individuals fail to maximise their own welfare over their lifetime.

(2) *Risk of death* − people prefer to have their benefits now rather than later since they cannot be sure that they will be alive later to be in receipt of

them. Indeed, the event in question need not be as serious as death: disease may be age-related and thus prevent the enjoyment of certain benefits later in life. Hence the origin of such exhortations as 'enjoy yourself while you are young'. Note that this form of time preference is entirely rational and reflects risk-averse behaviour in a world of uncertainty.

(3) *Diminishing marginal utility of consumption* — the next generation will be richer than the current one and hence the utility they attach to an extra £1 of consumption will be less than the utility attached to that £1 now. The fact that lower utilities are attached later compared to now is sufficient in itself to discount the future. Note that this argument might well apply to an individual's view of his lifetime earnings — i.e. he may well discount the future on the grounds that he will be richer later on.

We may now look at each of the three rationales in turn.

9.6.1   PURE MYOPIA

If discounting occurs because of irrational judgements by individuals, where irrationality itself requires demonstration (e.g. some deviation from maximum welfare which would have occurred had some other set of decisions been made), then some would argue that it is legitimate to integrate that implied rate of discount into any social discount rate. The legitimacy of doing so arises from the basic Paretian welfare judgement that preferences count since the structure of welfare economics does not 'permit' an assessment of why particular preferences are formed or any judgement as to whether preferences are to be 'allowed' or not.[4] This would be one view. A separate view would argue that the normative paradigms of welfare theory do not in any way preclude us from making 'paternal' judgements about the extent to which irrational preferences shall be allowed to influence a social decision rule (which is essentially what the social discount rate is). Thus, irrationality may dictate very high social discount rates with a corresponding small legacy of capital for future generations. That discount rate may therefore be incompatible with some other value judgement being used. Moreover, the very construction of consumer demand theory is based on assumptions which rule out irrational preferences (e.g. preferences which would permit indifference curves to intersect). Why then suddenly take a moral stance which says that this irrationality will be permitted when calculating a discount rate?

In so far as it matters, the view taken here is the second one, namely that irrational preferences should not dictate the determination of a social discount rate.

9.6.2   RISK OF DEATH

As noted above, this rationale is eminently sensible. Such rates have been calculated for the United States and India by Eckstein (1961), who derived values of 0.4 per cent and 2.15 per cent respectively for the median (40–44) age groups. The rates would seem remarkably low, especially as the rate for the (80–84) age group in the United States was only 7.45 per cent. On the other hand, if this is seen as a *component* of an overall discount rate this may not be so surprising. One immediate problem is that its use could be held to be inconsistent with the idea of a *social* time-preference rate (see Chapter 1).

9.6.3 DIMINISHING MARGINAL UTILITY OF CONSUMPTION

This argument may be either positive or normative. As a positive argument it would proceed as follows:

  (i) future generations will be richer;

 (ii) diminishing marginal utility of consumption exists (both within a generation and across generations);

(iii) individuals are aware of (i) and (ii);

 (iv) hence a positive discount rate is justified if we accept that individual preferences should count.

As a normative argument it would proceed:

  (i) as above;

 (ii) as above;

(iii) individuals are not aware of (i) and (ii);

 (iv) hence it is for social policy to adjust observed discount rates to reflect these phenomena in a normative fashion (Dasgupta and Pearce, 1972, p. 139).

For our purposes it matters little which view we take. We may note immediately, however, that both the positive assumptions (i) and (ii) are questionable. While most people have been raised in the Western world on the expectation of sustained economic growth, that presumption can no longer be so lightly accepted. Large questions exist over whether energy growth can itself be fast enough to sustain economic growth and if not, whether conservation and substitution programmes can do much to affect matters. On the other hand, if such limits to growth exist, it seems reasonable to suppose they will occur in a few decades rather than immediately. None the less, one may want to question just how far the diminishing marginal utility of consumption (DMUC) argument is relevant.

The second problem is that we have unconvincing evidence that DMUC exists (see Chapter 3). Various estimates have been made of the elasticity of an income or consumption utility function and that elasticity is usually given as a negative number, indicating a declining marginal utility. Others have argued that income utilities are simply non-measurable and that casual observation shows various thresholds in which higher and higher incomes generate new wants which need in no way have less marginal utility attached to them. The entire DMUC argument is therefore in question. None the less, historically it has formed the basis for some very elegant 'models' of the discount rate.

9.6.4 A DMUC MODEL OF STPR

Diminishing marginal utility of consumption is illustrated in Figure 9.2. Both total and marginal curves are shown with the lower curve showing marginal utility against marginal consumption changes. Now, Section 9.2 showed that in equation (9.6) we can write:

$$s = \frac{dU_t}{dC_t} \bigg/ \frac{dU_{t+1}}{dC_{t+1}} - 1 \tag{9.8}$$

where s is the STPR and U is utility.

The curve in the lower half of Figure 9.2 is a marginal utility function which we take to have a *constant elasticity* form such that

$$\frac{dU_t}{dC_t} = aC_t^b \tag{9.9}$$

where C is now consumption *per head* and a and b are constants; b is negative and is the *elasticity* of the marginal utility of consumption per head function.[5]

Substituting (9.9) in (9.8) gives

$$1 + s = \frac{aC_t^b}{aC_{t+1}^b} = \left(\frac{C_t}{C_{t+1}} \right)^b = \left(\frac{C_{t+1}}{C_t} \right)^{-b}. \tag{9.10}$$

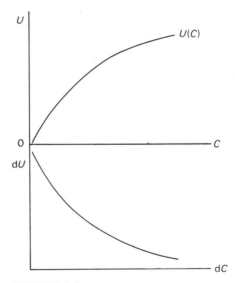

FIGURE 9.2

Now

$$\frac{C_{t+1}}{C_t} > 1$$

so that

$$\frac{C_{t+1}}{C_t} = 1 + c \qquad (9.11)$$

where c is the annual proportional rate of growth of per capita consumption between t and $t + 1$.

Hence, from equations (9.10) and (9.11) we have

$$1 + s = (1 + c)^{-b}$$

or

$$s = (1 + c)^{-b} - 1. \qquad (9.12)$$

The STPR is in fact determined by (i) the rate of growth of consumption per head c, and (ii) the elasticity of the marginal utility function b.

If for example $b = -1$, equation (9.12) would be written

$$s = (1 + c)^{-(-1)} - 1 = (1 + c)^1 - 1 = c.$$

In short, STPR would be equal to the rate of growth of consumption. This special case is sometimes referred to as the *Bernoulli* case. Typically, in so far as anyone regards the value of b as being observable at all, it is thought to lie somewhere between -1 and -2.

There are various ways of 'breaking down' this result to show the separate effects of the rate of growth of *total* consumption and the rate of growth of population. One is to observe that

$$C_t = \frac{K_t}{P_t} \qquad (9.13)$$

where K is total consumption and P is population. Then equation (9.10) reads

$$1 + s = \left(\frac{C_{t+1}}{C_t}\right)^{-b} = \left(\frac{K_{t+1}/P_{t+1}}{K_t/P_t}\right)^{-b} = \left(\frac{K_{t+1} \cdot P_t}{K_t \cdot P_{t+1}}\right)^{-b}$$

$$= \left(\frac{1+k}{1+p}\right)^{-b}$$

or

$$s = \left(\frac{1+k}{1+p}\right)^{-b} - 1 \qquad (9.14)$$

where k and p are the growth rates of total consumption and population respectively.

A brief example may help to illustrate the results obtained by the STPR approach. For the United Kingdom, from 1957–1978 the population grew at $p = 0.39$ per annum on average, and real consumption grew at $k = 2.35$ per cent per annum. Assuming an elasticity of -2 ($b = -2$) we obtain from equation (9.14)

$$s = \left(\frac{1.0235}{1.0039} \right)^2 - 1 = 1.038 - 1 = 0.038.$$

That is, an STPR of 3.8 per cent would be secured in this fashion. Note that, throughout, we have ignored 'pure' (myopic) time preference. Models in which this is included can be found in Feldstein (1965).

9.6.5   AN ALTERNATIVE APPROACH: SCOTT

Scott (1977) has proposed a procedure which, he argues, avoids all the problems raised by the non-equivalence of STPR and SOC in terms of the analysis presented in the earlier part of this chapter. He achieves this by concentrating on *public sector* investment *only* and by looking at the balance between investment and consumption *in that sector*. In essence therefore, he avoids any discussion of the opportunity cost of the investment in terms of spill-overs into the private sector. Scott's 'unit of account' is simply money accruing to the central government. This is not a unit of account which bears much resemblance to those used in SOC and STPR calculations because, as we have seen, these latter values vary across individuals and firms. Instead, we look at how government regards the 'social value' of a unit of account.

To begin with we require the concept of a 'base-level income', and this is defined as an income to an individual such that the government is indifferent to a situation in which an extra pound accrues to the individual or to itself. The 'social value' of £1 is the same regardless of whether the individual or the government receives it. As this base level of income b rises over time the social value of the extra £1 will, from the government's standpoint, decline. The rate at which this weighting declines is the social rate of discount since 'it is also the rate at which the marginal social value of all Government revenue and expenditure is falling' (Scott, 1977, p. 223). This assumes an optimal structure of government expenditure. Now, the faster b the base level of income rises, the faster the rate of fall in the weighting due to diminishing marginal utility of consumption. Thus, if b is the base level of income, its rate of growth is given by

$$\frac{\dot{b}}{b} = \frac{db}{dt} \Big/ b. \tag{9.15}$$

To link this to the rate of fall in the weighting of the extra £s above the value of

b, Scott simply multiplied $\dot{b}/b$ by a factor n, which is the elasticity of the marginal utility of income. Additionally he *adds* pure time preference to this expression so that the aggregate of this declining weighted function and the pure time-preference rate gives the social discount rate: i.e.

$$w = n \cdot \frac{\dot{b}}{b} + d \qquad (9.16)$$

where, w is the social discount rate and d the pure time-preference rate. (Note the similarity between equation (9.16) and equation (9.12).) We have already seen that there are serious arguments for not including d in a formulation of the social discount rate. To estimate $\dot{b}/b$ Scott observes the highest rate of income that past governments have been prepared to subsidise through the system of supplementary benefits (subsidies to individuals based on their income, family dependents etc.). This grew at about 2 per cent per annum until 1939 and 3 per cent per annum in the post-war period. The value of n is something we have already discussed and in our earlier example we used an elasticity of -2. Scott selects -1.5 on the basis of an observation of the literature on the subject, and on an analysis of net-of-tax yields on Consols over a lengthy period. Effectively, the pure time-preference rate is taken to be equal to the net-of-tax yield on Consols divided by the rate of growth of consumption per head. In effect however, n and p are interlinked and the value of one depends on the other.

As a final 'best' guess, however, Scott postulates the following values: $n = 1.5$ (the elasticity of the marginal utility of consumption); $\dot{b}/b = 2-3$; and $p = 1.5$. These values give a range for w, the social discount rate of 4.5–6.0 per cent.

Interestingly, although the three approaches – namely SOC, STPR based on DMUC, and Scott's approach – are quite different, the values obtained for the social discount rate through them yield comparable estimates. Rates between 4 and 6 per cent are given by all the approaches for the time at which the various estimates were made.

9.7 'Synthetic' Discount Rates

So far we have considered approaches based solely on either the SOC or STPR. Considerable attention has however been paid to the devising of second-best discount rates, given that the STPR and SOC are more than likely to diverge for the reasons already stated. These approaches may be dubbed 'synthetic' rates of discount. In effect they prescribe new rules for project evaluation and it is not the case that actual expressions for the social discount rate can be obtained from them. In effect however, the synthetic approaches operate with some average of the SOC and STPR rates, but as will be seen, it is not possible to express the rate as an average in a straightforward manner. We discuss two major approaches, those of Marglin (1967) and Feldstein (1972).

9.7.1   MARGLIN'S APPROACH

The essence of all synthetic approaches is that they differentiate the *sources of finance* for a project. They may also differentiate *types of benefit*. Sources may be broadly split between *taxes* and *borrowing*, while benefits may be differentiated according to whether they generate cash flows which are reinvestable or benefit flows which are not. The approaches also operate with a 'fundamental' discount rate s, which is the STPR (however determined).

Now we can follow Marglin's (1967) derivation. Note that we work with *perpetuities*, since this makes the arithmetic simple. Thus the sum of a flow of benefits $B_1, B_2, B_3 \ldots$ in perpetuity and discounted at s is B/s. Then, the fundamental rule for the *potential* acceptance of a project is, as we know,

$$\text{PV(Benefits)} > \text{PV(Costs)}.$$

Let benefits be constant at B per year, then the left-hand side reads

$$\text{PV(Benefits)} = \frac{B}{s}. \tag{9.17}$$

When looking at *costs* however, we need to consider what proportion of the finance comes from taxes and from government borrowing. The general argument is that *taxes* are at the expense of forgone *consumption* so that the cost is measured in consumption units. *Borrowing* is held to be at the expense of forgone private investment. In reality, there is little to justify this simplistic separation of financial sources — i.e. tax income might well have been invested. Let the total capital cost be K and let it all occur in the very first period, such that

$$K = I + C \tag{9.18}$$

where I is forgone private investment and C is consumption. Then, I can be thought of as earning the SOC r, although we have already seen some of the problems in thinking of SOC as a rate of return. C can be thought of as earning the STPR s. In perpetuity, and discounting at the STPR, we then have

$$K = \frac{I \cdot r}{s} + \frac{C \cdot s}{s} = \frac{I \cdot r}{s} + C. \tag{9.19}$$

The required inequality for potential acceptance of the project is now[5,6]

$$\frac{B}{s} > \left(\frac{I \cdot r}{s} + C \right). \tag{9.20}$$

Note that if $C = 0$, we have

$$\frac{B}{s} > \frac{I \cdot r}{s}$$

or

$$\frac{B}{r} > I \qquad (9.21)$$

which, in the simple case under consideration, is a restatement of the SOC argument.

Now we can consider what happens on the benefit side. For every £1 of benefit flow, assume a fraction b accrues as a reinvestable cash flow and the remainder $(1 - b)$ as a consumption benefit which cannot be reinvested. Then we can write

$$B(\text{£}1) = b \cdot r + (1 - b) \qquad (9.22)$$

where it will be seen that the reinvestable fraction earns a rate of return r when reinvested. Notice again that if all benefits accrue as *non-reinvestable consumption benefits*, b equals 0 and £1 of benefit is simply £1 of benefit. By allowing for reinvestment we have implicitly attached a *shadow price* to £1 of (nominal) benefits. The benefit side of the equation now reads

$$\frac{B}{s} [b \cdot r + (1 - b)]. \qquad (9.23)$$

Substituting equation (9.23) into (9.20) brings both the source of finance and type of benefit issues together. We obtain

$$\frac{B}{s} [b \cdot r + (1 - b)] > \left[\frac{I \cdot r}{s} + C \right]$$

or

$$\frac{B}{s} > \frac{I \cdot r + C \cdot s}{s[b \cdot r + (1 - b)]}. \qquad (9.24)$$

Multiplying both sides by s gives

$$B > \frac{I \cdot r + C \cdot s}{b \cdot r + (1 - b)}. \qquad (9.25)$$

Equation (9.24) describes the essence of the synthetic approach.[7] To check its validity, suppose reinvestment possibilities do not exist. In that case $b = 0$, and equation (9.25) will reduce to

$$B > I \cdot r + C \cdot s$$

or

$$\frac{B}{s} > \frac{I \cdot r}{s} + C \qquad (9.26)$$

which is the same as equation (9.20).

It should be noted that even in this approach, it is assumed that the benefits of the private investment forgone would have been consumed. Similarly, benefits from the public sector project are reinvested once only. Alternative assumptions could be made however. At one extreme it could be assumed that all benefits would be reinvested in perpetuity. Here we hit on a problem however. For as long as benefits are being reinvested they will be growing at rate r. If $r > s$, the present value of these benefits will be growing at rate $(1 + r/1 + s)$. For instance, after n years the present value of B per annum, with all benefits reinvested, will be

$$\sum_{t=1}^{t=n} \frac{B(1 + r)^n}{(1 + s)^t} \, .$$

As long as reinvestment continues, this sum — and hence the present value of the project — grows in perpetuity as n is extended. The present value of the project is infinite. The same could occur on the cost side, if the benefits of the forgone private investment were to be reinvested in perpetuity.

In practice, this problem may be less severe than it appears at first glance. For reinvestment in perpetuity does not make sense of the ultimate aim of the economy, which is consumption — for the consumption is never enjoyed! What it does mean however is that one may have to look far beyond the life of the project itself in order to take account of all reinvestment possibilities. In choosing between projects, one must look at least far enough ahead to ensure that there is no possibility of a rejected project 'overtaking' an accepted one by virtue of unevaluated reinvestment possibilities.

Finally, consider what would happen if *all* costs and benefits were subject to perpetual reinvestment. Our criterion would then become

$$\sum_{t=1}^{t=n} \frac{B(1 + r)^n}{(1 + s)^t} > \frac{K(1 + r)^n}{(1 + s)^t} \, .$$

Or, multiplying both sides by $(1 + s)^t/(1 + r)^t$, we have

$$\sum_{t=1}^{t=n} \frac{B}{(1 + r)^{n-t}} > K.$$

In other words, we have another case in which discounting at r would be appropriate. This is not surprising, given that in these circumstances all costs and benefits up to year n take the form of investment, rather than consumption.

9.7.2   FELDSTEIN'S APPROACH

Feldstein (1972) has proposed an approach in which the *shadow price* of the source of finance is explicitly considered. In exactly the same fashion as Marglin he divides sources of finance into a proportion of forgone investment (*b*) and forgone consumption $(1 - b)$. The forgone investment has a shadow price S which converts it to 'equivalent pounds (£s) of consumption'. Working with the case in which no reinvestment of surpluses occurs, but where there are different sources of finance, the Feldstein rule is then

$$\sum_t \frac{Bt}{(1 + s)^t} > \sum_t \frac{k_t[b \cdot S + (1 - b)]}{(1 + s)^t} \qquad (9.27)$$

where k_t is the cost outlay in period t. Feldstein offers little guidance on the determination of S. However, some light can be shed on the formula by converting equation (9.27) to a perpetuity, rearranging slightly, and setting $S = r/s$ since, as we saw in sub-section 9.7.1, this is the opportunity cost of £1 of forgone investment. Then, since

$$\sum_t k_t/(1 + s)^t = K$$

we can write

$$\frac{B}{s} > K[b \cdot S + (1 - b)]$$

or

$$\frac{B}{s} > K\left[\frac{b \cdot r}{s} + (1 - b)\right]. \qquad (9.28)$$

Now, $I + C = K$, such that

$$I = bK$$

and

$$C = (1 - b)K.$$

and using the equations for I and C, we have

$$\frac{B}{s} > \frac{b \cdot K \cdot r}{s} + (1 - b)K \qquad (9.29)$$

or

$$\frac{B}{s} > \frac{I \cdot r}{s} + C. \qquad (9.30)$$

But equation (9.30) is the same as equation (9.26). Marglin and Feldstein achieve essentially the same result via what appear initially to be slightly different routes.

9.8   Conclusions

It seems fair to say that no single school of thought on discount rates commands consensus among economists. Some still believe in the essential logic of the SOC approach, otherwise resources will be misallocated both within the public sector and between the public and private sectors. Others seek first to honour the basic axiom of 'consumer sovereignty' and adopt the STPR. Still others, as we have seen, seek a modification of the cost—benefit criterion to allow for the shadow price of forgone investment and for the extent to which benefits accrue in reinvestable form. Which view is taken rests very much on the extent to which the respective arguments seem forceful. One thing seems clear however: the issue is one of choosing a discount rate in a second-best world, so that behaving *as if* first-best conditions prevailed (where r equals s) does not seem relevant.

Thus it becomes very much a question of determining what alternatives are forgone and what reinvestment possibilities do exist. To this extent a synthetic approach seems best.

Finally, little has been said about the role of the discount rate when future generations are involved. The interested reader is referred to Page (1977) for an excellent discussion.

10 Social Appraisal of Projects in Developing Countries

10.1 The Special Problems of Developing Countries

There are two good reasons why students of CBA should look at the experience of applying the technique in developing countries, even if they are not specialising in development economics and are never likely to make any practical use of this knowledge. The first is that, by seeing the technique at work in an unfamiliar context, its dependence on the assumptions and value judgements underlying it may be brought out more clearly. The second is that it is in this context that the technique has been developed to the greatest degree of refinement and consistency.

Since the publication of the OECD manual in 1968 (Little and Mirrlees, 1968), the idea has become accepted that substantially different methods should be used for appraising projects in developing countries from those used in developed countries. In particular, shadow pricing — while in practice being limited to exceptional cases in developed countries — has become much more systematically and extensively used in project appraisal in developing countries. One reason for this is that there may be a substantial sector of the economy based on subsistence farming, in which market prices for factors and outputs simply do not exist. Even where they do exist, market prices are often believed to be subject to more distortions in developing than in developed economies. Little and Mirrlees (1974) list the main reasons for this divergence in treatment as being:

(*a*) Rapid inflation, in which time-lags and/or government controls distort relative prices.

(*b*) Currency overvaluation, together with restrictions on imports and the problem of inelastic demand for exports.

(*c*) Imperfect markets in factor inputs, particularly immobility and underemployment of labour.

(*d*) Deficiencies in saving and in government income, brought about by poverty and the difficulties of administering tax systems.

(*e*) Extreme inequality in the distribution of income and wealth, and the problem of business profits belonging to foreign corporations.

Now there is little in these conditions that is entirely unique to developing countries, and a case certainly exists for the wider use of shadow pricing. It is all a matter of degree. Shadow pricing requires a lot of work, and even then the results may not be very accurate. Thus many commentators argue that it is only in the face of the most serious and blatant distortions that it is worth the effort (McKean, 1968).

In this chapter, we first discuss the particular problems of inflation, international trade, the labour market, the savings deficiency and the distribution of income in developing countries. Finally, we bring all these factors together to consider the main alternative approaches in use in shadow pricing in developing countries.

10.2   Inflation

It may reasonably be asked why inflation should be a problem in project appraisal at all. After all, surely all project appraisal should be performed in real prices, so that while forecasting relative price movements is important, general movements in the price level are not.

There are problems caused by a high rate of inflation in terms of the effect on relative prices, however. While in a frictionless model prices may move instantaneously from one general equilibrium position to another, in the real world they do not. Some prices are determined from day-to-day in the market place, others are revised periodically by administrative action. Some prices may be subject to government control, others free to find their own level. In other words, relative prices may fluctuate substantially in a manner totally unrelated to current supply and demand conditions. Even if there are no other causes of distortion, it is difficult to know which set of relative prices to adopt as being appropriate for purposes of evaluation.

In addition, inflation may be a contributory factor in some of the other factors listed above, in particular currency overvaluation.

10.3   Currency Overvaluation

In Chapter 6, it was suggested that the solution to problems of evaluation in the face of an overvalued currency was to use a shadow exchange rate. This may not be a complete answer however. In the first place, many developing countries are heavily dependent for their exports on primary products with inelastic demands, while they import manufactured goods for which they produce no domestic substitutes. In these circumstances only a very large devaluation — implying a substantial reduction in real national income — may be adequate to eliminate a balance of payments deficit. A perfectly appropriate response to this situation may be to seek to manipulate the country's international trade by specific tariffs, controls and subsidies, whose level will vary with the elasticity of demand for the good in question. But given such a system of intervention, it is inevitable that some measures will be ill-judged, and countries may have controls and tariffs which differ from product to product on the basis solely of historical and institutional accident.

The usual approach to this problem would be to estimate the foreign exchange earnings attributable to additional exports or import substitutes, and the foreign exchange costs of any additional imports or goods diverted from export. This would then be converted into domestic currency at the shadow exchange rate (Chapter 6). To it would be added the change in tax revenue resulting from tariffs, taxes or subsidies on the good in question.

The alternative suggested by Little and Mirrlees is to value all commodities that are the subject of international trade at world prices, on the basis that this represents the foreign currency which could be earned by selling them abroad or which could be saved by reducing imports of the good in question. In either case, the figure is an appropriate measure of benefit (or of opportunity cost of domestic consumption). It may be expressed in terms of a foreign currency (e.g. United States dollars) or converted into domestic currency at the official exchange rate, in which case it is given the term border currency (e.g. border rupees).

Clearly, this approach is only appropriate where international trade is a realistic possibility for the good in question, and the separation of 'tradeables' from 'non-tradeables' is a difficult matter of judgement. For instance, India has become a substantial exporter of railway rolling-stock in recent years, but does this mean that her entire output of such equipment could be sold abroad? Probably not, since such equipment is purchased by a process of putting out to tender where price is only one factor that influences the decision. Adjustment is also necessary where the country in question possesses monopoly or monopsony power in international trade in the good in question, so that the volume bought or sold influences its world price. In this case, it is the marginal cost or marginal revenue that is relevant, rather than the price.

Given that a decision to use 'world' or 'border' prices has been taken, the reverse problem to that of shadow wage rates arises when valuing non-tradeables. World prices for these either do not exist or are inappropriate, yet they have to be measured in terms of a common numéraire with tradeables. The solution is to measure their marginal social cost in terms of the opportunity cost of traded goods and factor inputs (the latter being valued at the value of their marginal product in world prices); marginal social benefits of non-traded goods are valued at the maximum consumers would be willing to pay for them in shadow prices. To obtain this from data based on market prices, it is necessary to multiply by a form of price index showing the difference in price level between market and shadow prices, and termed the 'consumption conversion factor'. A similar price index may be used to value inputs where a full evaluation of their opportunity cost is not deemed worthwhile; this index is known as a 'standard conversion factor'.

10.4 The Labour Market

Doubt has often been expressed as to whether the wage rate does (or should) reflect the value of the marginal product of labour in any economy; in the case of developing countries, there is a particular cause for alarm. This is the much discussed phenomenon of a dual economy, the simultaneous existence of traditional and modern sectors. In the traditional sector (mainly agriculture), the family unit works as a team and shares the produce, so that the individual receives the average product of labour. Given the absence of alternative employment, the work is simply shared out among the family and the marginal product of labour may be very low or even zero. In the modern sector, labour immobility, unionisation, state regulation or international pressure may lead to a very much higher wage rate.

Thus when a new project attracts labour from the traditional to the modern sector, the wage rate in the modern sector may be a very poor reflection of the social cost to the economy of the move. Indeed, given diminishing returns in agriculture, the average income in the agricultural sector may itself grossly overstate the lost output. Ideally, the value of the marginal product of the diverted labour would be found directly by the estimation of production functions for agricultural products.

The implication of this approach would be to give strong encouragement to projects which divert labour from the traditional to the modern sector. The supposed procedure is illustrated in Figure 10.1. The size of the box represents the total amount of labour (horizontal axis) and capital (vertical axis) available to the economy. Isoquants for the traditional sector are plotted with respect to

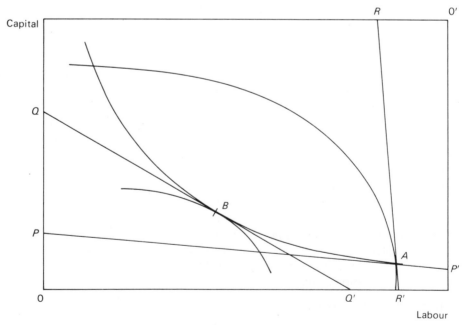

FIGURE 10.1

origin 0 and isoquants for the modern sector with respect to origin $0'$. It is presumed that the economy is at a point such as A, where the slope of the isoquant for the modern sector is far steeper than that for the traditional sector. By transferring labour from the traditional to the modern sector, and capital in the reverse direction, a point such as B may be reached, where agricultural output is unchanged but industrial output is substantially increased.

At position B, the relative shadow prices of labour and capital are given by the slope of the line QQ'. This applies no matter which sector the labour is being transferred from. At position B, the originating sector does matter, however. Factors being transferred from the modern sector have relative shadow prices given by RR'; factors being transferred from the traditional sector have relative shadow prices given by PP'. The justification for a low shadow price for labour is based on the assumption that labour will always be attracted from the traditional sector.

Problems exist however. Labour immobility and lack of appropriate skills may limit the ability of labour to transfer to the project in question. Even if it is possible to overcome these problems with a programme of education and training, doubts have been expressed about the desirability of doing so. In particular, there may be substantial cultural resistance to the change, and even the limited security in the event of sickness and unemployment afforded by the aid of the poor peasant family may have to be given up. Valuation of such factors may again be overstepping the bounds of economic analysis, but it may be worth encouraging other projects to raise labour productivity within the traditional sector rather than by transferring it, even if they do not show the best economic returns.

The approach also ignores the existence of urban unemployment in many developing countries. When this exists, it may be thought that the shadow price of unskilled labour for urban projects ought to be zero. This is only true if the additional projects do not attract additional labour to migrate to urban areas. It has been suggested that on average, creation of one extra urban job attracts more than one rural worker to migrate (Mazumdar, 1974). In this case, extra urban jobs would actually make urban unemployment worse, and the shadow wage would exceed the value of the marginal product of one rural worker.

10.5   The Savings Deficiency

One of the most obvious problems of developing countries is that an improvement in the standard of living is likely to depend, at least to some extent, on an increased rate of investment. Yet in a country where the majority of the population is very poor, voluntary saving will be low. Any attempt at forced saving will be politically unpopular and — if applied to the population at large — cause great hardship. The type of administrative machine necessary for the collection of a progressive income tax is unlikely to exist.

The first implication of this situation is that there may well be a divergence between the opportunity cost of capital and the rate of social time preference; this was discussed in Chapter 9. The best approach there was considered to be to shadow price any costs and benefits which represented investment forgone or reinvestment opportunities. This approach is generally followed in methods of appraisal for developing countries (Marglin, Sen and Dasgupta, 1972), although again Little and Mirrlees reverse the procedure, making investment the numéraire and shadow pricing consumption to express it in common units with investment.

The relevance of this procedure is not confined to the direct effects of the project. Different projects may yield different levels of saving according to the proportion of revenue paid out as profits and as wages to various classes of worker. For instance, consider again the case of a worker diverted from the traditional sector to the modern sector. So far, we have suggested that the shadow price of his labour is the value of his marginal product in the traditional sector (m). It is likely however that this product was committed to consumption, and if the weight attached to consumption relative to investment is $1/s$, this makes the social cost of his diversion (in terms of investment) $(1/s)m$. In the modern sector, he may earn a wage of w. If this is all consumed, there will be a cost of $(1 - 1/s)w$ arising from the commitment of resources involved (i.e. the difference between the social value of w units of investment and w units of consumption). The shadow wage thus becomes

$$w^* = (1/s)m + (1 - 1/s)w = w - (1/s)(w - m). \tag{10.1}$$

More generally, allowing for some saving, the shadow wage will be

$$w^* = (1/s)C_t m + (1 - C_m/s)w = w - (1/s)(C_m w - C_t m) \tag{10.2}$$

where C_m is the average propensity to consume in the modern sector, and C_t the average propensity to consume in the traditional sector. Many alternative expressions for the shadow wage rate are to be found in the literature, depending on the precise assumptions made (Sen, 1972).

Similar considerations apply in the case of profits. These may be reinvested by the company concerned, paid out as dividends part of which is consumed and part saved, or remitted abroad. Tracing through such effects is one of the main difficulties in evaluating the social benefits of private investment.

The presence of a savings constraint may also make it necessary to consider in detail the sources of funds for the projects concerned. It is usual in project appraisal to use a general shadow price representing the opportunity cost of capital for all projects. This will not be appropriate, however, if funds are available from an outside agency (e.g. the World Bank, foreign aid from a specific country, a private firm) and are tied to the project in question. In this case, the opportunity cost of the project may not be in terms of other projects forgone, but simply the future stream of payments of foreign exchange necessary to service and repay the loan. Any constraints introduced by the source of finance (e.g. the need for the project to be commercially viable) must also be borne in mind. It is also usually true that acceptance of one project will have some effect on the ability to borrow abroad to finance other projects, even if there is no clearcut budget constraint.

10.6   The Distribution of Income

We have already commented on the coexistence of mass squalor and extreme affluence in many developing countries. It is likely then that many observers would regard the distribution of income in these countries as being far from optimal. Alternative methods of dealing with the problem of income distribution were discussed in Chapter 3. One possibility which was suggested there was that consumption benefits might be adjusted to represent consumers' willingness to pay for the benefits in question if the distribution of income were optimal. This would be appropriate on the assumption that such an optimal distribution of income would be attained by alternative measures. However, political and institutional barriers make this most unlikely in the case of most developing countries. There appears to be a marked reluctance to tax the richer sectors of the community heavily, and in any event corruption may nullify the effect of attempting to do so.

The best approach to the distributional issue in this context would appear to be some form of equity weighting. Clearly, determining what weights to use for any particular country will be a difficult task. Moreover, this will provide a further reason for requiring the form of analysis discussed in the previous section to trace through the ultimate incidence of costs and benefits. For instance, profits remitted to developed countries may be given a weight of zero, and profits consumed at home a very low weight. (This does not necessarily mean giving profits as a whole a low weight, since a substantial proportion of them may be saved and reinvested.) A higher weight may be attached to extra consumption of workers in the traditional sector than for those in the modern one. Again problems in measuring incidence abound. For instance, a worker moving from the traditional to the modern sector may boost consumption in the traditional sector, both by ceasing to consume more than he adds to production at home and by remitting part of his earnings.

Where the benefits of additional consumption cannot be traced to particular groups, it may be reasonable to assume that the consumption will be spread across all income groups in the same proportion as existing consumption (C). Suppose that the latter follows a Pareto distribution, so that the cumulative distribution of consumption is given by $F(C) = (C_0/C)^\sigma$, (where C_0 is the minimum level of consumption), and that the distributive weights take the form $W(C) = (\bar{C}/C)^\beta$ (Squire and Van der Tak, 1975). The share of consumption going to the group with existing consumption level C' will be

$$\frac{\partial F}{\partial C} \cdot \frac{C'}{\bar{C}} = \frac{\sigma C_0^\sigma \cdot C'^{-\sigma}}{\bar{C}}. \tag{10.3}$$

The social value of the entire increase in consumption will be

$$\int_{C_0}^{\infty} \frac{\sigma C_0^{\sigma} \cdot C^{-\sigma}}{\bar{C}} W(C) \cdot \mathrm{d}C = \int_{C_0}^{\infty} \sigma[C_0^{\sigma} C^{(-\sigma-\beta)} \bar{C}^{(\beta-1)}] \, \mathrm{d}C. \quad (10.4)$$

Since, as long as $\sigma > 1$, $\bar{C} = \sigma C_0/(\sigma - 1)$, this may be written

$$\int_{C_0}^{\infty} \left(\frac{\sigma C_0}{\sigma - 1} \right)^{(\beta-1)} \sigma[C_0^{\sigma} C^{(-\sigma-\beta)}] \, \mathrm{d}C = \frac{\sigma^{\beta}(\sigma - 1)^{(1-\beta)}}{(\beta + \sigma - 1)}. \quad (10.5)$$

The final expression is the weight to be attached to a unit increase in consumption, spread in such a way as not to alter the distribution of consumption.

If the government is allocating its own resources optimally, then any group in receipt of net payments from the government (pensioners, for example) may be considered to take, at the margin, as high a weight in the government's view as does additional investment, which is an alternative use of government resources. Unfortunately, governments do not always behave optimally, and direct estimation of distributive weights is to be preferred to such methods of imputing them.

10.7 Alternative Approaches to the Overall Evaluation

The task of comparing alternative approaches to evaluation in developing countries has been complicated by the fact that different writers have chosen different numéraires; Marglin, Sen and Dasgupta (1972 — referred to in the following as MSD) have chosen aggregate consumption at domestic prices, while Little and Mirrlees (1968 and 1974 — LM) and Squire and Van der Tak (1975) have chosen investment, or more accurately uncommitted resources at the hands of the government, at world or border prices. This masks the strong similarity between all the techniques recommended.

In simple terms, MSD value traded goods at world prices (P_W) multiplied by the shadow exchange rate (SER). Non-traded goods are valued at domestic prices (P_D). Costs and benefits which take the form of investment are multiplied by the shadow price of capital (SPK). Conversely, LM value traded goods at world prices, and non-traded goods at domestic prices multiplied by a consumption conversion factor (CCF). Costs and benefits which take the form of consumption are multiplied by the shadow price of consumption (SPC). In summary, the valuations are

		Marglin, Sen, Dasgupta	Little– Mirrlees
Traded goods	Consumption	$P_W \cdot$ SER	$P_W \cdot$ SPC
	Investment	$P_W \cdot$ SER $\cdot$ SPK	P_W

Non-traded goods	Consumption	P_D	$P_D \cdot$ CCF $\cdot$ SPC
	Investment	$P_D \cdot$ SPK	$P_D \cdot$ CCF

Now if it were true that the shadow exchange rate were the inverse of the consumption conversion factor and the shadow price of capital the inverse of the shadow price of consumption, one could then obtain each item in the LM evaluation by taking the corresponding item from the MSD evaluation and multiplying it by CCF x SPC (or the reciprocal of SER x SPK). If this were the case, both approaches would give identical rankings of projects, and the only difference between them would be in the choice of numéraire. In practice, there are differences in detail on a number of matters, including the methods recommended for the calculation of the shadow exchange rate and the consumption conversion factor. But the methods are sufficiently similar for us not to expect vastly different results, despite the very different appearance of the appraisals.

The main differences of practical importance appear to be in emphasis rather than approach. For instance, LM appear to place considerable emphasis on the importance of traded goods, and the fact that traded goods are so much easier to handle than non-traded goods using their technique suggests that they expect traded goods to dominate. By contrast, it is non-traded goods that are easiest to handle following MSD, and they appear more willing to accept that restrictions on trade such as quotas, imposed perhaps for political rather than economic reasons, may make it appropriate to treat a good as non-traded even when some trade exists. For if imports of a particular good are fixed at a certain level, projects which boost production or consumption of the good in question will simply affect domestic consumption levels rather than foreign exchange earnings. Also, internal transport costs may mean that although some international trade exists, from the point of view of much of the country it is appropriate to treat a good as non-traded.

There is a general tendency in LM towards assuming that optimal policies will be followed with respect to international trade, taxation, and government spending. Thus, for instance, it is recommended that sales taxes should normally be considered as part of the cost of a good (a charge for government services or external effects). Generally, LM are ready to impute shadow prices from past government decisions (Mishan, 1974). MSD are far more inclined to accept political constraints leading to non-optimal policies. The degree to which such constraints should be accepted is always a difficult problem for a project evaluation: ready acceptance of constraints may lead to many desirable actions not even being considered, while on the other hand, projects selected on the assumption that constraints do not exist may be wholly inappropriate to the true situation (Sen, 1972).

Mention of this topic leads on to the question of how those shadow prices known as 'national parameters', which are to be determined via direct value judgement, rather than indirectly on the value judgement that consumer preferences should determine them, are to be obtained. In this category fall items such as the social time-preference rate of discount and distributional weights. Clearly, such items require political judgements at the highest level, and are just as important for national economic planning as for project evaluation. If it could be assumed that a national economic plan existed, and was optimal, these values could be imputed from it. Again, MSD are suspicious of such procedures, regarding the value of the national economic plan as being in the assistance it gives in forecasting, rather than in imputing shadow prices. They are inclined to try to minimise the need to take explicit values of national parameters, by computing instead 'switching values' at which a project switches from being viable to being non-viable, and reporting this to the decision-taker. For instance, suppose a project yields the following stream of net benefits:

$$\text{NPV} = \sum_j \sum_i \frac{W_{ij} B_{ij}}{(1+s)^j} \tag{10.6}$$

where B_{ij} is the net benefit to group i in year j, W_{ij} the weight given to benefit to group i in year j, and s the social time-preference rate of discount. If the set of weights (W_{ij}) were known, the switching value of s would be the value at which the NPV of the project became zero (in other words, it is the internal rate of return). If the weights are not known, however, it is necessary to map out a set of alternative combinations of the set of weights (W_{ij}) and s which represent switching values. Clearly, if many national parameters became involved, the approach would become extremely cumbersome.

By contrast with this 'bottom up' approach, LM see the need for 'top down' decision-making, with national parameters being set up by national planners, and with a central office of project evaluation determining the appropriate set of shadow prices to be used in all project appraisals. MSD would have a similar long-run aim, and their emphasis on 'bottom up' estimation of national parameters with the value emerging from a series of decisions on specific projects appears more as an attempt to deal with the situation in which the decision-taker is unable or unwilling to lay down clear guidance on the values to be adopted.

In short, perhaps the MSD approach has some advantages in terms of practicability, and in the case where it can be explained to politicians and administrators, who may look suspiciously at a technique which appears to judge projects in terms of world prices and the balance of payments rather than domestic consumption benefits. But appropriately applied with regard to the circumstances of the country in question, it should make little or no difference whether the broad approach of LM or MSD is adopted; it is in the precise assumptions made in applying the technique that significant differences could emerge.

10.8   Conclusions

The approach to project appraisal in this chapter, as in the entire book, has concentrated on the economic benefits of projects in terms of additions to consumption. This is so even in the case of the LM approach, despite their choice of resources at the hands of the government as the numéraire. It must be acknowledged that in developing countries as well as elsewhere, political factors may play an important role in project choice. Some of these factors may be quantified in the form of additional national parameters. Unemployment may be seen as a social evil, bringing distress and crime in its wake, over and above the poverty with which it is associated. The shadow price of labour would accordingly be reduced, reflecting a willingness to give up some consumption benefits for a higher level of employment. By contrast, a more conventional economic argument might be that the loss of leisure implied in becoming employed has a value which should be added to the shadow wage. This is less relevant in developing countries where unemployment usually means employment in marginal activities – subsistence agriculture, shoe shining, begging – than in the developed world. The wish for independence from foreign interference may lead to a desire to avoid reliance on international trade, even though that would provide the greatest economic benefit. This would require measures to restrict trade that would be almost certain to convert the appropriate treatment of many goods from being that of traded to non-traded goods.

Such modifications of objectives can be introduced into the general framework we have surveyed. Whatever the objectives of the country in question, it seems clear that these will be better served by evaluating projects using an internally consistent set of shadow prices, than by a mixture of evaluations at market prices and *ad hoc* judgement.

11 Cost–Benefit Analysis in Practice: I. The Social Appraisal of Transport Projects

11.1 Introduction

The first major application of CBA to the appraisal of a public investment project in the United Kingdom was the study of the M1 London–Birmingham motorway (Beesley, Coburn and Reynolds, 1960). (Earlier applications in the United States were mainly to water-resource projects.) The M1 study was in the nature of methodological research, being completed too late to influence the particular decision in question, but since then the economic appraisal of road schemes has become an important part of the decision-taking process, in the United Kingdom and many other countries. CBA has also been applied to many public transport schemes, particularly large indivisible projects and projects in urban areas.

The reason why the application of CBA to the transport sector became accepted so quickly is probably that given the institutional arrangements, it is a clear case where the application of purely financial criteria produces ridiculous results. Except where tolls are charged, revenue is related to the use of roads only through the media of vehicle taxation, licence duty and fuel tax. While road improvements may attract extra revenue by generating additional traffic, to the extent that they reduce costs to existing users by reducing congestion or providing a better quality or more direct route, they will probably reduce fuel consumption and tax revenue. In other words, for existing users the relationship between extra revenue raised and the benefits from a scheme may actually be inverse rather than direct. In the case of public transport projects, there is more scope for recouping user benefits in the form of revenue, but even here it may be neither practicable nor desirable to do so entirely. Moreover, the interdependence between transport modes means that, if price does not equal marginal social cost on one mode, there will be secondary costs or benefits to take into account in evaluating related modes. Finally, transport systems are major creators of external costs in the form of damage to the environment, although the progress made in introducing this factor directly into the appraisal is extremely discouraging.

11.2   Transport as an Intermediate Good

As soon as we try to apply the techniques of the previous chapters to road-investment appraisal, a major problem has to be faced. We have talked largely of measuring consumers' and producers' surpluses in terms of factor and commodity price and quantity changes. Transport, however, is largely an intermediate good. This is obviously the case for freight and business travel, but even private travel is usually undertaken as part of the cost of achieving a desired activity (shopping, visiting etc.) rather than as an end in itself.

In principle, it would be possible to trace through the benefits of a transport investment in terms of its effect on the prices and quantities of all commodities produced in the economy. In practice, this ambitious task has yet to be a attempted. What is usually done is to look solely at the benefits measured in terms of changes in prices and quantities of transport services supplied. The question naturally arises of whether the measurement of benefits in terms of intermediate goods is a valid approach to the social appraisal of projects (Friedlander, 1965). Suppose the economy has constant returns to scale and perfect competition. If one could assume that there would be no change in the volume or composition of final output and in the techniques used in producing it as a result of the transport improvement, the use of transport-cost savings as a measure of benefit would clearly be valid. Suppose, first, that factor prices also remain constant. The effect on the price of the ith commodity of the reduction in the cost of transport will be

$$\Delta P_i = A_{Ti} \Delta P_T \tag{11.1}$$

where P_T is the price of transport services, and A_{Ti} the total direct and indirect input of transport services per unit production i (obtained as the appropriate element of the matrix $(\underline{I} - \underline{a}_{ij})^{-1}$ where $\underline{I}$ is the unit matrix and $\underline{a}_{ij}$ the matrix of the input–output coefficients).

Total benefits will be

$$X_i \Delta P_i = \Delta P_T A_{Ti} X_i \tag{11.2}$$

where X_i is the amount of final commodity i produced. But since $A_{Ti} X_i$ is the total output of transport services, benefit can be measured simply as the reduction in the total cost of transport services, the volume of which will remain fixed.

This approach gives rise to a very simple method of evaluating transport projects. Theoretically, however, it must be incorrect. The measured benefit, in terms of price reductions, is only realised in practice if the resources released are redeployed elsewhere (otherwise, there would be a compensating cut in money incomes). Since virtually all commodities require some transport inputs, there must be an increase in transport demand. Moreover, since the degree of fall in price will be greater the more transport intensive the good in question, the increased output will be more significant for transport-intensive goods than other goods, unless the former have systematically lower price elasticities of demand than the latter. How significant the increased transport demand is, however, is an empirical matter which has not yet been fully resolved.

Suppose we allow for changes in the volume of commodities produced. The extra benefit may be approximated as

$$\sum_i \frac{P_i \Delta X_i}{2}$$

where X_i is the volume of i produced (Chapter 6). Substituting in for P_i, this may be written

$$\frac{\Delta P_T \sum_i A_{Ti} \Delta X_i}{2}.$$

Since $\sum_i A_{Ti} \Delta X_i$ is the change in transport output, this may also be measured simply in terms of changes in prices and outputs of transport services. It is doubtful, however, whether the latter could be predicted very accurately without explicitly solving the entire input–output system.

A further possibility is that the reduction in the price of transport services may lead to the substitution of transport for other inputs. For instance, firms may locate at a greater distance from their market to enjoy lower land or labour prices; they may exploit better quality but more distant sources of natural resources, or they may become more concentrated to enjoy economies of scale in production, at the expense of more extensive distribution networks.

In each case, one would again expect to be able to measure the total benefit simply with reference to the derived demand curve for transport services. The maximum price that firms are willing to pay for incremental transport services will, if they are minimising cost subject to fixed input prices, represent the cost savings in terms of other inputs that this increment permits.

So far we have assumed that factor prices are fixed in money terms. If they alter we shall have to consider the change in economic rent accruing to factors of production. In any case, the rise in real factor prices brought about by the reduction in commodity prices may bring forth an increase in factor supplies. If this happens, a full CBA will need to add in the increase in economic rents to the benefits measured in the transport sector (an evaluation of the effect on real national income would, as shown in Chapter 5, find transport sector benefits alone to be an even greater underestimate).

It will be noticed in the last case that the argument required the assumptions of 'no involuntary unemployment' and 'no power on the part of individual firms to influence input prices'. Clearly then, market imperfections in the labour market as well as elsewhere, could lead to divergences between the benefit as measured in the transport sector and the true benefit. One secondary benefit often claimed for interurban transport projects to or from areas of high unemployment is the reduction of regional unemployment by the attraction of additional firms. However, there is no guarantee that the effect will be in this direction. A reduction in transport cost to a depressed area may make it easier to supply other areas from the area in question, but at the same time it will make it easier to supply that area from elsewhere. It will only be to the extent that the region has other advantages that it is likely to benefit from such a change (Gwilliam, 1970). Since many of the problems of depressed areas can be traced to non-transport factors (e.g. labour productivity, industrial relations) improved communications may do more harm than good. Thus while market imperfections certainly do offer the possibility that transport sector benefits are an inadequate measure of the total benefits of an interurban transport project, the size and direction of the bias both require empirical investigation. Since, in the United Kingdom at least, transport cost is on average a relatively small portion of the total cost (6.5 per cent of value added for the economy as a whole; 9 per cent in manufacturing industry), it would be surprising if the indirect effects of transport cost reductions were great. One study (Dodgson, 1974) has calculated that the greatest reduction in the total cost of manufacturing and distribution in any area brought about by the construction of the M62 motorway would be of the order of 0.33 per cent; for other areas, it was even less. Only very minor effects on local employment levels from improved accessibility could be expected.

The use of benefit measures based on intermediate goods makes it impossible to investigate the incidence of the benefits from interurban transport improvements, however. If this is desired, then it will be essential to trace the effects through to the final commodity market, so that they can be related to the consumption patterns of the different income groups.

11.3   Time Savings in Transport Projects

When one is concerned with passenger journeys undertaken in working hours as part of a person's employment, the man-hours involved appear to be – as with the drivers of freight vehicles – quite simply an input into the production process, to be valued at the value of the marginal product of the labour elsewhere. There are some reservations to be added. Time spent travelling may be usefully employed in reading documents, preparing for meetings and so forth, so that a reduction in travel time may not lead to an equivalent reduction in man-hours required. On the other hand, when fixed hours are not worked (as in many managerial and professional positions), travel time savings may be taken in the form of increased leisure, rather than work. In both cases, there is some reason to suppose that even if labour were paid the value of its marginal product, the hourly wage rate would overstate the value of travel time savings.

The situation regarding non-work travel time is rather more complex however. Time has a scarcity value, inasmuch as it is an essential input into most leisure activities in much the same way as money is. Suppose that utility is a function of time spent in each of n activities (T_i), each of which requires inputs of both time and money (P_i per hour) (de Serpa, 1971). For the nth activity, work, the money input is negative. The consumer will seek to maximise:

$$Z = U(T_1 \ldots T_n) - \lambda \left(\sum_{i=1}^{n} P_i T_i \right) - \mu \left(\sum_{i=1}^{n} T_i - T \right). \qquad (11.3)$$

The two constraints express the fact that the consumer's expenditure $\sum_{i=1}^{n-1} P_i T_i$, is constrained to equal his income $- P_n T_n$, and that the total amount of time available for all activities is limited.

The first-order conditions for a maximum take the form

$$\frac{dZ}{dT_i} = \frac{dU}{dT_i} - \lambda P_i - \mu = 0. \qquad (11.4)$$

Or

$$\frac{dU}{dT_i} = \lambda P_i + \mu. \qquad (11.5)$$

Since λ equals the additional utility that would be obtained by having an extra unit of money to spend, and μ represents that from an extra unit of time, μ/λ may be regarded as the 'pure' value of time in money terms. Equation (11.5) shows that each activity is indulged in up to the point at which its marginal utility equals the opportunity cost of the total inputs of time and money necessary. If we write this equation for activity n (work) and rearrange the terms, we discover that

$$P_n = \frac{\dfrac{dU}{dT_n} - \mu}{\lambda}. \qquad (11.6)$$

Since P_n is the negative of the hourly wage rate, we discover that this equals the pure value of time less the marginal utility of time spent working. Assuming the latter to be negative, the wage rate will exceed the pure value of time. Even the pure value of time is not the appropriate measure of the benefit of travel time savings. A reduction in travel time will not merely yield benefits of μ/λ but also of $-(dU/dT_t)/\lambda$, the marginal utility of time spent travelling (assumed negative) relative to that of money. Thus the net benefit of a unit saving in travel time will be

$$- \frac{dU}{dT_t} \bigg/ \lambda - P_n - \frac{dU}{dT_n} \bigg/ \lambda. \qquad (11.7)$$

Only if $dU/dT_t = dU/dT_n$ (i.e. the marginal utility of time spent travelling equals that of time spent working) would the value of travel-time savings equal the wage rate.

In any case, workers are frequently unable to choose their hours of work. In this case, the above budget constraint is simply replaced by

$$\left(\sum_{i=1}^{n-1} P_i T_i - P_n \bar{T}_n \right) \tag{11.8}$$

where $\bar{T}_n$ is the exogenously fixed value of T_n. The marginal conditions for an optimum are the same for $i = 1$ to $n - 1$, but the relationship between P_n and the value of time no longer holds.

The major conclusion arising from this section, then, is a negative one; it is not appropriate to value non-working time savings at the wage rate. Moreover, the marginal utility of such time savings will vary with factors such as the comfort of the mode in question. In practice, the usual approach is to attempt to impute values to travel time savings from trade-off situations, where the traveller has a choice between a fast expensive mode of travel and a slow cheap one. There is a danger, however, that the resulting value may be distorted by a failure to take into account factors such as the relative comfort of the two modes compared.

11.4 Interurban Road Schemes

The current programme used to evaluate interurban road schemes in the United Kingdom (COBA) concentrates solely on the benefits measured in terms of changes in transport costs and volumes. An estimate of the average breakdown of benefits from interurban road schemes evaluated by COBA is given in Table 11.1. COBA assumes no generated traffic, and it appears that changes in vehicle operating costs are insignificant. Thus the measured benefits are largely confined

TABLE 11.1 Average Benefits from a Road Improvement Scheme

	(% of total)
Accident savings	20
Vehicle operating cost savings	0
Working time savings:	
cars	26
light goods vehicles	11
heavy goods vehicles	11
buses	3
Non-working time savings:	
cars	23
buses	6
	100

Source: *Transport Policy — A Consultation Document* (London: HMSO, 1976) vol. 2, p. 99.

to reductions in journey times and in accidents; these are compared with the
construction cost of the road.

Where journeys are made in working time, whether as part of the person's
occupation (driver or conductor) or as business travel to or from a meeting (but
not commuting journeys outside working hours), the time savings are costed at
the wage rate (plus overheads such as insurance payments that are directly related
to the size of the labour force). The two assumptions involved here are that any
time savings are utilised to perform more work, and that the gross wage rate
measures the value of the marginal product of labour. Thus the higher a person's
earned income, the more valuable his working time is deemed to be.
Imperfections in the labour market would provide a good case for shadow
pricing.

Non-working time savings are valued on the basis of the results of behavioural
studies, as mentioned above. While the relevant value must be expected to vary
with trip purpose, time of day, length of trip and comfort of mode used, a
number of empirical studies (mainly confined to commuting trips) have thrown
up a value of around 25 per cent of the wage rate, and this is the figure used
(Harrison and Quarmby, 1969). The implication that the value of travel time
savings will rise at the same rate as real wages has not been adequately tested,
however.

Use of such a formula without weighting would attach a higher weight to
time savings the higher the income of the traveller, and hence favour car users
over bus passengers, and affluent regions over less affluent ones. In practice this
is not done; evaluations adopt the same value of leisure time savings, based on
mean income of the community as a whole, no matter who experiences them.
This is equivalent to either carrying out evaluations as though the distribution of
income were optimal (on the value judgement that an egalitarian distribution of
income is optimal) or adopting a set of 'equity' weights of the form $W_i = (\bar{Y}/Y_i)$.
(See Chapter 3.) Unfortunately, a weighting system is only adopted for this one
item; money cost savings to low income groups, for instance, are not given
increased weight. On the assumption that an egalitarian distribution of income is
not about to be achieved, this inconsistency could lead to misallocation of
resources; for instance a scheme which gives the poor time savings at an
increased money cost of travel could be selected in circumstances in which they
would rather forgo the time savings for the sake of cheaper travel.

With respect to accidents, a major problem arises. Certain of the costs of
accidents (damage to property, medical expenses) simply represent resource
costs to be valued at market or shadow prices as appropriate. When persons are
injured, their labour inputs are lost for a certain period of time and should be
valued at the marginal value product of labour. This is usually assumed to be
represented by the wage rate (although this poses difficulties where, for instance,
housewives are involved!). The same argument is used for the loss of output
when people are killed, although for the surviving population as a whole, this
lost output is partly compensated for by the smaller population to be supported.

Implicitly then, the loss of consumption benefits is treated as part of the cost to an individual of being killed!

What this approach leaves out, clearly, is any assessment of the pain, grief and suffering occasioned upon those involved in road accidents and their relatives and friends, plus any intrinsic value society attaches to human life. Whether there is any way of assessing the monetary compensation such persons would require to restore them to their former level of welfare and whether indeed such a statement has any meaning (particularly for those killed!) seems highly doubtful. An approach which has been suggested is to examine situations in which the traveller can trade off different degrees of risk against other benefits (e.g. driving speed on motorways) but the accuracy of the results depends on the traveller having the knowledge and ability to weigh up the probabilities involved (Mishan, 1971; Ghosh, Lees and Seal, 1975). At present, United Kingdom practice is to allow for these factors by the addition of a politically-determined lump sum to the costs. Thus the valuation of accident cost savings is qualitatively different from the other items in an interurban road investment appraisal, in that it represents, in part, a straight political valuation.

There has been much criticism of this evaluation procedure in recent years (Leitch, 1978). This in part surrounds the accuracy of the traffic forecasts and the assumption of no generation of traffic, but it has also concentrated on the limited scope of the appraisal: for instance, the effect on other modes of transport is ignored. This can only be justified if cross-elasticities of demand are virtually zero, or if other modes are subject to constant returns to scale and marginal cost pricing. Otherwise, there will be losses of consumers' and/or producers' surpluses on other modes of transport. Moreover, improvements to other modes of transport are usually assessed on purely commercial criteria.

COBA also excludes from economic evaluation the environmental effects of interurban road schemes. Such schemes may have both beneficial and harmful effects on the environment. For instance, a new road may take traffic away from shopping or residential areas, relieving them of noise, fumes, vibration, visual intrusion and disruption of pedestrian movement. At the same time, they may inflict all of these costs on persons previously unaffected, and in addition their construction may destroy buildings and recreational facilities and disrupt agriculture. A great deal of effort has been put into trying to find suitable trade-off situations in which consumers may reveal their preferences with respect to such items — for instance purchase of double glazing to ameliorate noise nuisance (Starkie and Johnson, 1975), and comparison of house prices in areas with different environmental qualities (Edwards, Pearce and Harris, 1979). The results have always been so specialised and subject to so many possible distorting influences (for instance, double glazing also affords a degree of heat insulation, but it fails to improve the noise environment outside the house), that while many of these factors may be quantitatively assessed and the results pre-sented to the decision-taker, finding appropriate ways of assessing shadow prices to enable them to be introduced into the formal CBA has not proved possible.

Thus the economic appraisal of interurban road schemes offers only a partial measure of the costs and benefits of alternative schemes, in which many important factors are left out. Any tendency to place more weight on valued than on unvalued items would lead to systematic biases (for instance, too many resources being devoted to the rural sections of interurban routes and too few to by-passes for urban areas).

11.5   Urban Transport Evaluation

The application of CBA to urban transport investments in the United Kingdom was pioneered in the study of the Victoria Line Underground Railway in London (Foster and Beesley, 1963). Since then it has become the normal method of appraisal of alternative urban transport plans (involving both road and public transport proposals) as well as being applied to certain types of individual public transport projects (e.g. urban railway upgradings, railway-closure decisions, new bus stations and interchanges). Clearly, in this sector CBA is being applied to public transport decisions where the traditional method of appraisal has been a simple financial analysis.

A purely financial appraisal of urban public transport projects would lead to an expansion of capacity and quality of public transport on each link as long as the extra revenue generated (by some combination of increased traffic and the ability to charge a higher fare) exceeds the extra costs. In CBA, additional items will be included. Many public transport projects (for instance, the introduction of a new rail service) consist of large, indivisible blocks of output (either because of technological indivisibilities, or because economies of scale mean that if it is sensible to introduce the service at all, then it is sensible to introduce it on a large scale). Therefore their introduction may yield substantial amounts of consumers' surplus to travellers on the route. Where the quality of an existing service is improved, unless price is simultaneously raised to the level which completely offsets the quality improvement (and there is no reason to expect this to be a desirable pricing policy even on grounds of profitability) consumer benefits will result. Indeed, the increased frequency and density of services resulting from an expansion in output almost inevitably improves quality at the same time.

A further factor is that prices rarely equal marginal costs in urban public transport, because of the complexities that would arise from having varying tariffs by time and route. Thus if traffic is diverted from substitute public transport routes, or attracted to complementary public transport routes (feeder services, or city-centre distributors) there is likely to be a change in consumers' surplus and/or profits on these routes.

All this applies to interurban as well as urban public transport (although perhaps it is in practice less significant in the former). Yet CBA has not normally been applied to interurban public transport projects. Why does this difference in treatment exist?

The answer appears to lie in the greater degree of traffic congestion in urban areas, and also in the belief that there exists a greater degree of substitutability of public transport for the private car in such cases. In situations of congestion, the marginal social cost of private transport exceeds the marginal private cost, since an additional user imposes increased costs, in the form of delays, on all other users of the route (Walters, 1961). Thus a change in public transport services or fares, which affects volumes of road traffic, will yield external costs or benefits to other road users. This can be of considerable importance, particularly in the case of high-quality services which are able to attract considerable numbers of commuters who have the option of using a car. For instance, Foster found that two services in the Manchester area which between them showed a financial deficit of some £3/4 m were worth retention and indeed improvement, when social appraisal techniques were employed (Table 11.2).

The divergence between price and marginal cost on roads will also mean that urban road improvements yield costs and benefits on other roads to which they attract additional traffic or from which they divert traffic. These changes in traffic flows will alter the speed of traffic and hence the generalised cost (i.e. time plus money costs) on each route. As a result, a system of appraisal which aggregates benefits on all routes simultaneously is needed, and since its introduction in the London Transportation Study (LTS) the formula based on a linear path of integration (Chapter 5) has been used (Gwilliam and Nash, 1972):

$$\text{Benefit} = \tfrac{1}{2}\sum_j \sum_i (T'_{ij} + T_{ij})(C'_{ij} - C_{ij}) \qquad (11.9)$$

TABLE 11.2   Net Benefits of Two Railway Services

	£ million	
	Retained and improved	*Retained*
Road congestion cost	12.4	5.9
Additional journey time	0.7	−0.4
Additional vehicle operating costs	2.4	1.2
Operating costs of extra buses	0.9	1.1
Bus capital cost	0.4	0.5
Cost of substitute car journeys	1.9	0.9
Accident cost	0.3	0.2
Total	19.0	9.4
Less avoidable costs of rail service	6.0	4.9
Net benefit	13.0	4.5

Source: *Social Cost/Benefit Study of Two Suburban Surface Rail Passenger Services* (London: British Rail 1974) Part 1, pp. 35–6.

where T_{ij}, T'_{ij} is the volume of traffic from i to j before and after the change respectively, and C_{ij}, C'_{ij} the generalised cost of travelling from i to j before and after the change respectively.

A number of other issues concerning urban transport appraisal came to the forefront during the debate on the LTS. An unusually large proportion of the benefits (78 per cent) from the proposed Inner London motorway system comprised of benefits resulting from generated traffic (this is no doubt due to the heavy constraint placed on existing traffic volumes by the high level of congestion in the area at present); 13 per cent of the benefits comprised of additional tax revenue, resulting from diversion of expenditure from low-taxed products to highly-taxed petrol (Table 11.3).

Whether the latter is to be considered a benefit at all depends on whether tax is regarded as a pure revenue-raising measure, or as an attempt to adjust the market price of fuel to reflect externalities imposed by its use (excluding that of congestion, which one hopes is measured directly elsewhere). Doubt has also been cast on whether users benefit from generated trips. In the first place, there is a widespread view that motorists in general under-perceive the financial costs of additional journeys. Second, one way in which major transport improvements generate additional traffic is by the relocation of land use (growth of low-density suburban housing estates, hypermarkets, and peripheral industrial estates). Yet the benefit formula given above assumes users to be choosing freely between alternative destinations whose characteristics (other than travel cost) remain constant. Some additional or longer motorised trip may be forced on users simply by the decline in local facilities for work, shopping and leisure activities.

Two further important general problems with urban transport appraisal may be raised. First, if one simply compares a single plan or small group of plans with a 'do-nothing' option in the face of rising traffic congestion and declining public transport, these plans are almost certain to show some benefit. But the 'do-nothing' option is so far from optimal that a wide range of measures − road construction, public transport improvements, traffic restraint, changes in relative prices − is likely to show benefit. The difficulty is to evaluate a sufficient range of options to find the best 'mix' of measures. The prices assumed to pertain in future years are particularly significant, since many of the external costs and benefits of transport projects discussed above would be largely eliminated if price could be set equal to marginal social cost throughout the transport sector. Even on an individual congested transport link under consideration, part of the benefit of an increase in capacity may be alternatively obtained by raising price to curtail demand (Gwilliam and Nash, 1972). The difficulty again arises in administering systems to do this; a comprehensive system of road pricing by time and location would require substantial metering costs, and one is almost always thrown back on parking charges, special licenses and non-price methods of traffic restraint (Thomson, 1967). But the point that the outcome of an urban investment appraisal depends critically on the prices and traffic volumes

TABLE 11.3   First-Year Costs and Benefits from Inner London Motorways*

	£ million
Capital costs:	
construction of motorways	1330
construction of secondary roads	50
parking	100
blight	9
disruption	8
traffic delays during construction	12
uncompensated housing loss	26
infrastructural costs in resettlement of displaced residents	54
investment in public transport	—
total	1589
annual capital cost, i.e. capital cost expressed on a perpetual annual basis	170
Current costs:	
accidents	5
house waiting costs	4
public transport losses	40
road maintenance and lighting	4
police	4
unperceived costs of generated traffic	73
total	130
Benefits:	
net savings to common and diverted traffic	20
benefits to generated traffic	58
tax benefit	12
total	90
Annual net loss on current account	− 40
Annual net loss overall	−210
Annual rate of return (%)	− 2½

*estimates for 1991 of differences between official transport plan and alternative without inner motorways.

Source: London Amenity and Transport Association (1970, ch. 6) reprinted in J. M. Thomson, *Modern Transport Economics* (Harmondsworth: Penguin Books 1974) p. 217.

assumed should not be disregarded; there may be very much cheaper ways of achieving the end in view than by large-scale new construction.

Finally, but of great importance, are the environmental effects of alternative urban transport plans. The reduction of traffic on existing roads will reduce the noise, air and visual pollution, social disruption and danger inflicted on residents, workers and visitors to the area concerned. On the other hand, construction of new transport infrastructure will itself bring such disamenities to locations previously unaffected as well as involving destruction of property and amenities. Moreover, it may attract additional traffic on existing roads which are used as feeders to the new facility. All these effects will vary from project to project, probably being least harmful for a new rail scheme which uses existing rights of way or is placed underground, and most harmful for an urban motorway. Thus they should affect choice of project, but little progress has been made in introducing them into a conventional economic appraisal (Stanley and Nash, 1977).

The main quantified effect of transport projects in urban areas is usually to give small time savings to large numbers of commuters on a daily basis. Whether this is a factor of great significance in comparison with the environmental effects is a matter of judgement, but it seems that — even more than in the case of interurban schemes — the quantified costs and benefits of transport projects are only one aspect of the evaluation process, and as such only a partial guide to decision-taking in this field.

11.6   Transport Projects in Developing Countries

When one turns from developed to developing countries, one expects the importance of the social appraisal of projects to become much greater, since it is generally argued that the need for shadow pricing is stronger. There is some dispute as to how significant the divergence between market prices and shadow prices is, however. For instance, Sudhir Anand (1976) applied the Little–Mirrlees approach to the valuation of a highway project in West Malaysia. A standard conversion factor of 0.9 was estimated for converting domestic prices into world prices. A more detailed analysis of major items of construction cost and vehicle operating cost, which broke these down into their component inputs of tradeables and factors of production, yielded similar figures. The shadow price of labour was estimated as being the marginal product of labour in agriculture plus certain extra food and transport costs; at domestic prices, this gave a figure of $70 m, equal to 50 per cent of the amount actually paid. This was then multiplied by 0.9 to convert it to world prices. Since it was asserted that there was no problem of under-investment, and the distributional issue was ignored, no weights were applied to this figure. The resulting shadow wage was applied both to the labour used in construction, and to working time savings resulting from the use of the road. For skilled workers, the market wage was assumed to equal opportunity cost. Leisure time savings were assumed to have no social value in a poor country.

The result of shadow pricing in this particular case was to multiply both costs and benefits by a similar factor, having virtually no effect on the social returns from the project. However, this evaluation both assumed away many of the usual justifications for shadow pricing, and was based on the use of a single technology. Had alternative techniques which exploited more unskilled labour relative to other inputs been available, the low shadow price imputed to this form of labour might have raised the social returns on the project, particularly if one placed a weight of more than unity on additional income for such workers.

The possibility that alternative labour-intensive techniques of road building might be desirable in the case of Iran was explored by Irvin (1975). He found that the maximum degree of labour intensity possible would add approximately 22 per cent to the financial costs of the planned highway programme, or RLs (rials) 40,000 per man-year of employment created. This compared favourably with the costs of job creation in the modern industrial sector and, on the assumption that in computing the shadow price of labour a relatively high weight is to be given to the benefits of additional consumption by unskilled workers, appeared to satisfy the social appraisal criterion.

Distributive weighting systems may have a substantial impact on project selection too. In both developed (Dalvi and Nash, 1977) and developing (Thomas, 1977) countries the user benefits from new road schemes are heavily concentrated among high income groups. If such benefits are given low weight, the schemes in question will appear much less attractive, unless they are regarded primarily as a source of government revenue. The case for tolls on new roads, which is usually weak on pure efficiency grounds, may become much stronger when distributive factors are taken into account (Thomas, 1977).

Similarly, use of shadow prices may lead to different decisions on choice of mode (a study of the Ghana timber industry reported in Little and Scott (1976) found a shadow price of 0.767 for road transport but 0.258 for rail) and choice of traction; while electric traction is more capital intensive than diesel, it economises on the use of skilled labour for maintenance work, as well as in many cases permitting the use of a socially cheaper fuel (Majumdar, 1973).

Thus it is important when using shadow prices not simply to re-evaluate a given set of projects which have been prepared in accordance with normal financial cost-minimising criteria. Many of the benefits from the use of social appraisal techniques in developing countries may come from the adoption of technologies more appropriate to their circumstances, and this will only be found if shadow prices are used not just in project selection, but also in the design stage of project preparation.

11.7   Conclusions

Although appraisal of transport projects is one of the most long-standing and well-used applications of CBA, there are still many problems to be overcome. Even the evaluation of direct transport benefits is still subject to uncertainties, particularly with respect to the valuation of time savings. The wider aspects of land use and the environment are not usually incorporated into the formal analysis. Thus while economic evaluation has established itself as a useful tool in this area, its limitations must be recognised, and its results weighed with other evidence before project selection can take place.

12 Cost–Benefit Analysis in Practice: II. The Social Appraisal of Materials Recycling[1]

12.1 The Desirability of Recycling

In a world of impending materials shortages, various measures have been proposed, or are under active pursuance, to reduce the use of primary materials and energy. Such measures include plain 'good housekeeping' whereby the same economic output is achieved with less input of energy simply by limiting energy use to the minimum level necessary to achieve a given output. They include the redesign of products to make them last longer and so reducing the throughput of materials and energy over long time-periods, and the redesign for recyclability — the construction and manufacture of products in such a way that their reuse commands less of an input to separate components than would otherwise be the case (single-metal cans, for example). Finally, and given a fairly distinct but not inevitable link between GNP and materials usage, one might seek to reduce economic growth for the deliberate purpose of 'stretching the lives' of materials.

All these alternatives have numerous obstacles. Extending product life could have employment implications, although these would be fairly trivial in comparison with the economic growth reduction option. Less obviously, extending product life may merely swap one problem for another: if anti-corrosives such as zinc, lead or cadmium are used to make products last longer, there may be associated pollution problems. Direct conservation measures seem to work only on a 'once-off' basis — an initial bout of enthusiasm being followed by a return to 'normal' patterns of behaviour — and, in any event, reach a 'natural' limit when the maximum conservation consistent with social objectives is reached.

One of the most countenanced 'solutions' to resource scarcity is recycling — the reuse of a material that would otherwise be thrown away. This reuse may be in the original form — lead from car batteries being used to make further car batteries, for example — or it may involve a change of use such as the use of waste lubrication oil as a fuel ('one-off' recycling since, once burnt it cannot be recycled again). Note too that recycling also tends to aid the pollution problem, for by preventing wastes from reaching the environment and returning them to the production process, it thus prevents pollution. How far this generalisation holds in practice depends on the nature of the recycling process itself.

TABLE 12.1   Recycling Rates 1974—5 (% of total material used)

	Aluminium		Copper		Lead		Paper	
	1974	1975	1974	1975	1974	1975	1974	1975
Germany F.R.	28.2	28.8	32.4	30.5	23.8	25.6	31.9	33.1
France	20.3	20.6	41.4	39.5	17.9	20.7	30.6	32.7
U.K.	30.3	37.2	40.5	38.8	60.2	60.6	27.6	28.8
Italy	24.9	22.1	29.3	25.2	23.3	20.3	27.8	32.1
Japan	29.9	25.6	10.5	4.7	21.7	23.7	39.2	—
U.S.A.	18.2	23.5	49.4	53.5	47.4	57.4	22.3	18.8

Source: Adapted from R. Grace (1978).

One immediate problem is that recycling already takes place on a fairly significant scale, as Table 12.1 indicates. The table shows the ratio of recovered material used to the total of that material used in selected years and for six different countries. Note, for example, the very high proportion of lead demand that was met from recycled lead in the United Kingdom in the selected years, over 60 per cent. This is explained by the comparative high density of population in the United Kingdom, the well developed market for secondary (scrap) lead and the fact that secondary and primary lead are direct substitutes. By contrast, aluminium cannot be so readily recycled. This is because in its secondary form it is more brittle and cannot be a direct substitute for everything that primary aluminium is. Indeed, secondary aluminium is largely confined to the 'forgings' market and for this reason alone its recycling potential is limited.

However, Table 12.1 illustrates one other issue. Since recycling already takes place, and since, by and large, there are no subsidies for recycling (indeed, in a number of countries, tax laws discriminate against recycling), it seems reasonable to assume that what does take place is profitable. While we cannot assert that what is not recycled is *not* profitable, we are reasonably safe in concluding that it will be more expensive.

What we illustrate in this chapter, then, is the kind of study a cost—benefit analyst would mount to try to see if extra recycling, in addition to that already taking place, is worthwhile. To do this we concentrate on one product, waste paper. The example illustrates once more the problems of intangibles, but also serves to show what problems can arise when data limitations apply.

12.2   The Cost—Benefit Model

The objective is to secure a given amount of paper product, say newsprint, at least at social cost. The technologies available are assumed to be two only: 100 per cent use of virgin wood pulp and 100 per cent use of secondary fibre (waste paper). Consider each technology in turn. The virgin fibre technology (VFT) has the following costs:

(a) V_c, the cost of a unit (tonne) of virgin fibre;

(b) V_p, the pollution impact of processing one tonne of virgin fibre;

(c) V_f, the loss of amenity by having to fell the requisite amount of timber to supply one tonne of virgin fibre.

The secondary-fibre technology option (SFT) has the following costs:

(a) S_c, the cost of a unit (tonne) of secondary fibre delivered to the paper mills, where $S_c = S_k + S_s + S_t \cdot S_k$ is the cost of collection, S_s the cost of separation and baling and S_t the cost of transport to the mill.

(b) S_p, the pollution from the use of 1 tonne of secondary fibre.

Now, a simple comparison between VFT and SFT is not yet possible because we have another cost function for waste disposal *without* recycling. We can write this as

$$D_c = S_k + S_d$$

where D_c is the disposal cost, and comprises S_k the cost of collection, and S_d the cost of disposal (to the land, incinerators or whatever).

Hence we have three social cost functions:

$$SCV = V_c + V_p + V_f \tag{12.1}$$

$$SCS = S_c + S_p \tag{12.2}$$

$$SCD = S_k + S_d. \tag{12.3}$$

By assumption, S_k is the same for disposal as it is for recycling (we relax this assumption later) and it will be recalled we also have

$$S_c = S_k + S_s + S_t. \tag{12.4}$$

We can now establish the objective of minimising the net social cost (and hence maximising the net benefits) of recycling one extra tonne of paper. This can be stated as

$$NBER = SCV + SCD - SCS$$

where NBER is the 'net benefit of extra recycling'. This expands to

$$NBER = V_c + V_p + V_f + S_k - S_c - S_p + S_d. \tag{12.5}$$

Substituting equation (12.4) in (12.5) gives

$$NBER = V_c + V_p + V_f + S_k - S_k - S_s - S_t - S_p + S_d. \tag{12.6}$$

This can be simplified and rearranged to give

$$NBER = (V_c - S_s - S_t) + (V_p + V_f - S_p) + S_d. \tag{12.7}$$

Equation (12.7) is now the relevant estimator for the net benefits of extra recycling. We can investigate each item in turn.

The expression $V_c - S_s - S_t$ is a private cost component reflecting the difference between the cost of virgin fibre and the cost of delivered waste paper *net of collection costs*. This expression can be estimated by comparing the price of one tonne of mechanical pulp (the form of pulp used to make newsprint) and the baling, processing and transport costs per tonne of waste paper.

The expression $V_p + V_f - S_p$ represents the net pollution and amenity benefit of recycling, but is not easily estimatable in monetary terms. The use of recycled fibre reduces most pollutants but *may* increase waterborne pollutants, depending on the technology used. Effluent control in modern de-inking plants (where the ink is removed from old newsprint so as to ensure the recycled product is reasonably 'bright') is now advanced and complete water recycling is possible. But, we have as yet no reliable way of attaching a price to waterborne-pollution reduction and the only possibility lies in the use of the pollution-control cost estimate as a proxy variable, on the assumption that control is socially desirable.

Item V_f in the above expression is controversial. Timber is grown for use as wood and the debarked sidecuts are used for pulp. Sometimes the whole tree, suitably debarked, will be used for pulp. The argument that recycling 'saves trees' is not straightforward. If paper recycling takes place to any significant extent, planting programmes will be reduced and the trees will simply not exist. That is, it is arguable that the use of virgin pulp *rather* that recycled paper encourages afforestation and not the other way round. Thus there could be an amenity loss in terms of fewer trees which could be a cost of any recycling programme. On the other hand, if there is excess demand for pulp, increased recycling will not result in fewer trees, and hence we have a benefit, particularly if the excess demand spills over into the cutting of 'natural' forests. Additionally, afforestation of moorland areas is widely regarded as a disamenity. Current economic evaluation techniques do not permit us to say what V_f would be 'per tree'.

This leaves us with the final item S_d. This refers to the savings in waste *disposal* costs due to the recycling of paper. That is, since the paper does not enter the flow of waste to the environment it saves the cost of disposal. Disposal costs vary widely according to location and method of disposal. However, the use of average figures for the United Kingdom is legitimate since we have not posited any specific location for the hypothesised extra recycling to take place. The Society of County Treasurers' survey of local authorities suggests the costings in Table 12.2.

For our purposes we shall consider only landfill, shredding plus landfill, and incineration. The reason for this is the vast proportion of waste is landfilled in the United Kingdom and composting and separation plus incineration are comparatively rare.

Note one final point before looking at the actual magnitudes involved:

TABLE 12.2   Average Waste Disposal Costs in the U.K.
1976—7

	£ *(1977 prices)*
Landfill	1.54
Shredding plus landfill	4.92
Separation and incineration	12.27
Direct incineration	9.95
Composting and other	10.09

Source: Society of County Treasurers and the County
Surveyors' Society, *Waste Disposal Statistics* 1976—7.

equation (12.7) explicitly sets the costs of collecting waste paper at the same
level as those of collecting domestic refuse. This is unrealistic and we must now
relax this assumption. The unreality arises because there are three methods of
collecting waste paper. The first would be via mechanical separation at the point
of disposal, or at some intermediate point. In general, however, mechanical
separators have not yet demonstrated that the paper fraction is reusable for the
manufacture of paper products.

This leaves two alternatives. First the paper can be collected at the same time
as domestic refuse, but this implies prior separation on the part of the waste
generator (e.g. the householder). Many such schemes have been tried and are
still in existence, the collectors placing the paper in trailers or 'racks' on the
collecting vans. This adds to collection time and hence to costs, as well as adding
to capital and operating times. Second, a separate collection may be undertaken.
What these costs are appears not to be known with certainty since experience
varies widely. Certainly, a number of studies suggest that many local authorities
engaged in waste paper collection appear to lose money, even in major boom
years (Pearce, 1979). Whatever the situation, recycling must generally be
expected to *add* to collection costs. This additional cost (C^*) should therefore
be debited. Separate waste paper collection schemes are likely to have higher
costs than paper collection schemes which are integrated with general refuse
collection operations.

12.3   The Cost—Benefit Study

We may now summarise the relevant magnitudes of the CBA in Table 12.3.

Table 12.3 suggests that there are net benefits associated with all of the
generalised recycling options presented. Given the quality of the data available,
however, more importance should be placed on the ranking orders of the
options rather than on the actual magnitude of the net benefits. It seems fairly
clear that voluntary agencies working with merchant middlemen can perform a
useful collecting role. The local authority case is less clearcut especially given the
diversity of collection costs. Nevertheless, many authorities have in the past and

will continue in the future to generate substantial net benefits through their paper collection schemes. The results for the Oxfam 'Wastesaver' operation are disappointingly low. In fact the collection system in operation when the data was collected has since been substantially modified.

The pollution aspects are recorded in Table 12.3 as 'not known'. However, it is possible to say something qualitative. Midwest Research Institute (1972) concluded that overall, pollution is reduced if repulped waste paper is substituted for virgin pulp in the manufacture of low-grade paper products. Further, most pollution impacts are also reduced if higher-grade paper is manufactured, but the de-inking process in the latter case gives rise to significant increases in process solid wastes and in waterborne suspended solids. In both cases energy 'costs' are reduced. Other work by Bower *et al.* (1971 and 1973), and Bower (1975) suggests that very detailed studies are required before any generalisation is reached. Much depends on 'consumer acceptance' of product specifications. Thus, if paper brightness is reduced, a less 'aesthetic' product is obtained but it would be one that permits an increased use of secondary fibre. As far as newsprint is concerned the brightness specification has to be reduced considerably for residuals generation to change. In tissue manufacture a reduced brightness will lead to reductions in sulphur dioxide, dissolved solids and biochemical oxygen demand but an increase in suspended inorganic solids. The exact magnitudes of these changes in the residuals are however not known with any great certainty.

Table 12.3 shows the results for *one tonne* of paper. To secure an absolute order of magnitude we need to ask what a feasible recycling programme would be in the United Kingdom. We can take two approaches. The first rests on the idea of setting a feasible target for what is recoverable from municipal waste without asking whether the amount recovered would in fact find a use. The second approach looks at likely demand and any shortfall in supply and then asks what the costs and benefits would be of meeting the shortfall by an extra recycling programme.

In respect of the first approach, there is a fairly wide consensus that something like 25 per cent of paper in the municipal waste stream not currently recovered could be recovered. Pearce (1979) estimated that in 1975 some 3.6 million tonnes of paper waste were discarded to the general waste stream, and forecast that the figure would be 4.2 million tonnes in 1980. The equivalent figures for the municipal waste stream are approximately 3 million tonnes and 3.5 million tonnes. On the basis of a hypothetical 25 per cent recovery drive Table 12.4 shows the potential tonnages of paper available and the net monetary benefits.

The second approach is perhaps more realistic. Forecasts vary but previous work suggests a demand in 1980 of 2.4 million tonnes. Much depends on technological progress and, in particular, the rate at which a de-inking plant is commissioned. Pearce (1979) has shown how technological progress will affect demand. His work suggests a shortfall of 0.3 million tonnes by 1980 with limited technical change and up to 1 million tonnes with very rapid technical

TABLE 12.3 Net Social Benefit of Recycling One Extra Tonne of Waste Paper *(1977 prices)*

OPTION	$V_c{}^a - S_s{}^b - S_T{}^c$	$+B_p{}^d$	$\pm V_F{}^e$	$+S_D$ *estimated costs (1977 prices)*	$-C^{*f}$	NBER
(1) Prior-separation and separate collection (Local authority)						
Landfill disposal	85.8 − 15 − 5	N.A.	N.A.	+1.54	−35	32.3 (21.5)g
Shredding + landfill	85.5 − 15 − 5	N.A.	N.A.	+4.92	−35	35.7 (24.9)
Direct incineration	85.8 − 15 − 5	N.A.	N.A.	+9.95	−35	40.7 (30.0)
(2) Prior-separation and integrated collection						
Landfill disposal	85.8 − 15 − 5	N.A.	N.A.	+1.54	−29h	38.3 (27.5)
Shredding + landfill	85.8 − 15 − 5	N.A.	N.A.	+4.92	−29	41.7 (30.9)
Direct incineration	92.6 − 15 − 5	N.A.	N.A.	+9.95	−29	46.7 (35.9)
(3) Prior-separation and separate collection (Oxfam)						
Landfill disposal	85.8 − 30i − 5	N.A.	N.A.	+0.25j	−35i	16.0
(4) Prior-separation and separate collection (Boy Scouts etc.)						
Landfill disposal	85.8 − 6k − 5	N.A.	N.A.	+1.54	−4l	72.3
Shredding + landfill	85.8 − 6k − 5	N.A.	N.A.	+4.92	−4	75.7
Direct incineration	85.8 − 6k − 5	N.A.	N.A.	+9.95	−4	80.75

Notes to Table 12.3

(a) V_c the average price of mechanical pulp was £117.62 in 1977. (See *Overseas Trade Statistics*, HMSO, 1977.) However, it takes more than 1 tonne of de-inked paper waste to produce 1 tonne of pulp. We assume an average loss of 27%. Thus if we recycle one tonne extra of waste paper we save £85.8.

(b) S_s (£15)   processing and baling costs in 1977. This is an average intra-regional figure for local authorities collecting waste paper in the Yorkshire and Humberside region of England. (Source: Yorkshire and Humberside Waste Advisory Council, *Waste Paper Salvage Report*, Feb. 1977, see table 5.)

(c) $S_t = £5$ transport costs of baled waste paper from the collector (charity or local authority) to the mill.

(d) V_p the pollution damage costs associated with the use of virgin pulp.
$\quad S_p$ the pollution damage costs associated with the use of repulped waste paper. In general, $V_p > S_p$ (Turner, Pearce and Grace, 1977).

(e) V_f amenity cost ($-$) or benefit ($+$) of a recycling programme in terms of forestry resources.

(f) C_f^* collection costs for separate waste paper collection systems = £35 per tonne – average intra-regional figure for local authorities collecting waste paper in the Yorkshire and Humberside region. (Source: Yorkshire and Humberside Waste Advisory Council, *Waste Paper Salvage Report*, Feb. 1977, see table 5.) There is in fact a wide variation in the individual authority costing returns.

(g)   the NBER figures in brackets are net of administration costs for the collection and processing operations.

(h) C^* in option (2) refers to the waste paper collection cost element of an integrated refuse and waste paper collection system. £29 per tonne is an intra regional average figure for local authorities in the Yorkshire and Humberside region. (Source: Yorkshire and Humberside Waste Advisory Council, op. cit.)

(i)   both the processing and collection cost figures in this option have an administrative cost element already included. All other collection and processing cost figures without brackets in Table 12.6 do *not* include an estimate for administration costs. The different treatment arises because of the varying data sources.

(j)   the West Yorkshire Metropolitan Council estimate that Oxfam's waste paper recycling drive in their area saved them £0.25 per tonne in landfill disposal costs.

(k)   voluntary agencies collect and sell *un*baled waste paper to the waste paper merchants. £6 per tonne represents the average baling and processing costs being borne by merchants.

(l)   the time spent by, say, boy scouts in collecting waste paper is assumed to have a zero opportunity cost. Transportation to some central collection point may involve parents' vehicles and thus some resource cost. The trip may well be for a combination of purposes, however, i.e. shopping and thus the cost element credited to paper collection is often negligible. £4 per tonne is an average collection-cost figure for voluntary agencies in general which is quoted in paper industry sources.

TABLE 12.4

	1975	1980
	m. tonnes	
Paper in waste stream	3.0	3.5
Extra recovered	0.75	0.9
	£ million	
All options assumed associated with landfill disposal		
NBER, option (1)	24.2 (16.1)	29.1 (19.3)
option (2)	28.7 (20.6)	34.5 (24.8)
option (3)	12.0	14.4
option (4)	54.2	65.1
All options associated with landfill disposal		
NBER assuming 0.5 m.t. shortfall		
option (1)	16.2 (10.8)	
option (2)	19.2 (13.8)	
option (3)	8.0	
option (4)	36.3	

Note: bracketed figures are net of administration costs. For nature of options see Table 12.3.

change. Clearly, the very rapid change scenario is not the correct one for 1980. Hence the shortfall is unlikely to exceed, say, 0.5 million tonnes and could be zero. In Table 12.4 we show the results of assuming the shortfall to be 0.5 million tonnes.

12.4   Conclusions

Numerous caveats must apply to the cost—benefit results secured here. In the first place both prices and costs change over time. Pulp prices can change and, indeed, are expected to run slightly ahead of the rate of inflation in the United States (Little, 1975). Equally, collection costs can change as fuel and operating costs rise. The use of voluntary labour is obviously one mechanism for keeping this cost down. If we expect *relative* prices to change, then this must be allowed for in the cost—benefit outcome.

The use of *averages* in both the price and cost data included in the tables above means that the results should be treated only as broad indicators. There is a distinct lack of waste-paper collection and processing-cost data. The figures used in the table are reasonably reliable although they tend to be based on returns from local authorities confined to one particular region. Wray and Nation (1976) have examined statistical information on collection costs for eight United Kingdom local authorities operating separate waste-paper collection schemes in 1974. Total collection costs then ranged from £10.68 to £16.61 per tonne.

The technological assumptions in the analysis are also not entirely realistic. Very few if any products can be manufactured from 100 per cent low-grade waste paper due to various technical constraints, risk considerations (due to possible contaminants in the waste-paper furnish) and final product consumer acceptance standards. A 'furnish' made from 100 per cent mechanical pulp would be very costly.

Overall, however, it would appear that there are clear benefits to be gained by encouraging charity organisations like the Boy Scouts to collect waste paper. A combined recycling drive by charities and some local authorities would probably be more than sufficient to meet forecast increases in the United Kingdom demand for waste paper. The government, however, would have to be much more selective in its encouragement of local authority waste-paper collection schemes. There are wide intra-regional and probably inter-regional variations in costs and operating conditions for such schemes (Turner, 1978). The average figures in Table 12.3 will mask much of these real world variations.

13 Cost–Benefit Analysis in Practice: III. The Social Appraisal of Nuclear Power

13.1 Introduction

It was argued at the outset of this book that, if nothing else, CBA helped to 'order' the issues relevant to any social evaluation of a project. This attribute can be well illustrated by considering how a cost–benefit analyst might go about the assessment of a nuclear power programme. In doing so the procedure also highlights the problems that arise when the 'intangibles' extend to such issues as personal freedom, and the creation of facilities that could increase the risk of war or successful terrorism. Perhaps above all, the expansion of nuclear power illustrates the ethical complexities that are generated by the adoption of positive discount rates.

13.2 The Nuclear Fuel Cycle

To provide a background to the CBA approach to the appraisal of a nuclear power programme we first need a brief overview of the 'nuclear fuel cycle'. Precisely what this cycle looks like depends upon the nature of the nuclear reactors installed and planned and upon particular policy decisions. Thus, virtually all nuclear reactors in operation are thermal reactors and use uranium as their fuel. The main stages in processing uranium ore up to the stage where it is suitable as a fuel are shown in Figure 13.1. The fuel is enclosed in 'fuel rods' and, depending on the type of reactor (basically classified according to their use of different coolants: water or gas), will become 'spent' after 2 or 3 years inside the reactor. They are then removed. It is here that the major policy decision comes in. The spent rods can either be disposed of or they can be 'reprocessed'. In the latter case the spent fuels inside the rods are removed. The end product of this 'recycling' process is recovery of uranium which can be refabricated into new fuel, a relatively small amount of plutonium (relative to the uranium recovered, that is) and some waste products which have no use. In short, one route − the so-called 'throwaway' cycle − produces waste fuel which has to be disposed of, while the other produces reusable fuels and waste. The relative volumes of waste are actually disputed since reprocessing requires additional inputs which themselves become wastes. The problem with these wastes is that they are radioactive, and in varying degrees. Some will decay rapidly within days or months, while others like Plutonium 239 have a half-life of 24,400

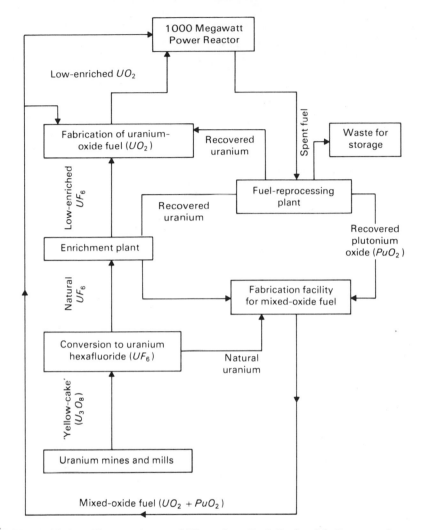

FIGURE 13.1   The Uranium and Plutonium Fuel Cycle with Reprocessing

years. Clearly, long-lived wastes present a waste management problem. Since
radiation is a known cause of cancers, the health risks of not managing the
wastes properly are obvious. Under the reprocessing route there is what some
would regard as an additional problem. The plutonium recovered can, if suitably
treated, be used to manufacture an atomic weapon. If released in such a way
that it is inhaled, it will also cause cancers. It therefore has to be handled and
transported with care and it must be monitored to ensure that significant
quantities, and these may be quite small for bomb-making to be possible, do
not go 'unaccounted for'.

Equally, plutonium is a highly efficient fuel. At least, it is if it is used in another kind of reactor, the 'fast reactor'. This reactor is specially designed to use plutonium and its efficiency in generating energy is perhaps 40 or 50 times greater than that of a thermal reactor. Note too that its fuel comes from other reactors so there is no need to buy new uranium supplies to feed it. Indeed, the 'ideal' state as far as advocates of nuclear power are concerned is one in which the 'balance' of thermal and fast reactors is such as to minimise the use of 'fresh' uranium.

What happens to the highly radioactive waste under either cycle? It must be stored. At the moment it is stored in nuclear power stations under water on reactor sites or at special sites specialising in storage. This cannot, however, be a permanent solution; the containers will eventually corrode and the waste must be transported to new ones, and so on. Although storage of this kind for very long periods is not impossible, the industry prefers to consider processes whereby the waste is solidified and embodied in artificial blocks which are melted, mixed with the waste, and reformed as solid blocks on cooling. The actual processes are complex, but this is the essential idea. They are then stored in this solidified form. The storage options under investigation are deep-clay deposits, granite formations, the sub-seabed, salt mines and salt formations. Once stored in this way, they will not, it is argued, be retrievable and thus cause no problem.

This is the briefest of outlines of nuclear fuel cycles but it will suffice for our purpose.

13.3   The Application of CBA

CBA attempts a comprehensive assessment of costs and benefits. By this we mean that we try to capture all the preferences for and against the option both *spatially* and *in time*. The spatial dimension of nuclear power is not particularly problematic, save that in many cases the 'nation' ceases to be the proper province of concern. As we shall see, this is the case with nuclear power if specific fuel cycles are chosen. The temporal dimension is far more complex. If we recall that costs and benefits are defined with respect to preferences, we have an immediate problem in deciding *whose* preferences are to count. The practical problem is that only the existing generation (and then only part of it) has the capacity to express a view. Yet, with many technologies, including nuclear power, future generations are affected in that they inherit the expanded energy and capital base brought about by the development of nuclear power, and the costs of managing, and possibly suffering the effects of, the inherited wastes. Somehow, then, the value axiom of CBA to the effect that individuals' preferences should count, must take account of what future generations may want. Since they are not here to vote, there is an immediate problem of discovering what their wants will be. This point is developed later.

As conventionally practised, however, CBA can effectively 'dispose' of the intergenerational problem. The incorporation of a positive discount rate in CBA can quickly make a problem disappear. By way of example, consider a case in which a nuclear power programme generates wastes which have to be managed only 50 years from now. Bearing in mind that I-129 has a half-life of 16 million years, neptunium-237 of just over 2 million years and plutonium-235 of over 24,000 years, our example is being fairly generous to those who feel that the nuclear waste management problem is none too serious. Now the cost to the generation in existence 50 years from now is, let us say, £100 m per annum. This is highly conservative as an estimate of managing even existing wastes let alone those of an expanded nuclear programme. But, through discounting, this cost can be made insignificant. At a 10 per cent discount rate the cost that enters the CBA balance sheet is not £100 m but £100 m divided by a discount factor of 1.1 to the power of 50. This is equivalent to multiplying the £100 m by 0.009 to give us a cost of £900,000. Obviously, for years beyond year 50 the cost becomes insignificant.

The problem is that the alternatives to discounting present us with equally perplexing difficulties. If the discount rate is zero, we are obliged to enter every cost that can be debited to the expanded nuclear programme regardless of when it occurs in time and we must then aggregate those costs through time at their absolute magnitudes as perceived by the generation at the time. In our simple example, the £100 m in year 50 would appear as £100 m; a further cost would be entered for year 51, and so on, to some year thousands of years hence, depending on how tractable we think the waste management problem becomes in that time scale. Clearly, then, if we take a discrete 'lump' of nuclear power, say a programme of reactors from 1980 to 2000, CBA may well dictate a clear 'no' to that programme.

The suggestion, made by Freeman (1977), is that we should not forget that discounting is simply the inverse of compound interest. By setting aside £900,000 now at 10 per cent, this will cumulate to £100 m in year 50. We can therefore make due provision for future costs by debiting the nuclear programme not with a whole stream of waste management costs but with £0.9 m in year 1. The theoretical attraction of this is that it invokes the Kaldor—Hicks compensation principle and is therefore in keeping with the conceptual foundations of CBA. Of course, just as no *actual* improvement takes place unless actual compensation is paid, so no actual compensation will occur unless funds are deliberately set aside for such purposes.

Where the 'intergenerational compensation' fund becomes difficult to envisage is when it relates to risks of damage to future generations. We might make reasonably good guesses at waste-management costs. We are on less sure ground if there is any reason to think that radiation levels will create genetic damage, or any reason to think that waste stores will themselves have associated risks. Arguably, the issue is more complex still for stored plutonium if a plutonium recycling fuel cycle is opted for. It is not clear what the cost to future generations would be, nor, even if they were known, what their probabilities of occurrence would be. Even then, if both the scale of hazard is known and the probability distribution of its occurrence is known, do we set aside a compensation fund that cumulates to the expected value of the damage, or some weighted mean that reflects the higher damage costs even if they have low probabilities attached to them? Almost certainly, views on what should happen will be dictated by views on what these risks and hazards are.

Do these problems render the CBA framework invalid even before we go on to consider the nature of costs and benefits in nuclear futures? The suggestion here is that there are certain virtues in the approach which should lead us to retain at least the *format* of CBA. These virtues are (a) that the technique forces us to list the advantages and disadvantages; (b) that CBA teaches us to embrace all affected parties including those across national boundaries and (c) that it impels us to face up to the 'generational' problem.

13.4   The Costs and Benefits of Nuclear Futures

We now turn to the actual costs and benefits of nuclear futures. We consider each item in turn.

13.4.1   THE DEMAND FOR NUCLEAR POWER

The dominant benefit from nuclear power is electricity, and we proceed on the assumption that more, not less, electricity is demanded by the individuals who comprise society. Some will see this as a naïve assumption. They will point to the potential for overestimating demand in official forecasts. They might also argue that people do not 'demand' electricity; it is foisted upon them in order to maintain given industries, and in unnecessary quantities given that electricity is often used for purposes that could have as their energy source some non-electrical base. This is a problem in assessing how wants and preferences are formed, something that was discussed in Chapter 2. Note that already we have a problem of deciding whether a benefit really is a benefit.

We can now proceed on two assumptions. First, let us assume that there is some alternative way of generating the electricity thought to be required by, say, the year 2000. This may be coal-fired plant, wave energy or whatever. In the United Kingdom context, the demand projections by the Department of Energy include the continued use of coal-fired power stations, but the proportion of electricity so generated by the year 2000 actually falls as nuclear power is assumed to grow very rapidly. In turn, this implies that electricity demand cannot all be met from non-nuclear sources and this 'justifies' the nuclear programme of some 41 Gigawatts (GW) of nuclear capacity by the year 2000 (Department of Energy, 1978). We now have another problem. Essentially, the Department of Energy is saying that there is no alternative way of meeting electricity demand without nuclear power. If there were, the CBA would proceed by looking at the difference in the costs of meeting that demand by using various sources and this cost differential would appear as a 'disbenefit' to the higher-cost source. Again, critics will say that the forecasts of electricity demand are exaggerated. They will point to the repeated downward revision of energy forecasts over the past few years and to the possible underestimation of 'saturation' effects. There is certainly some reason to expect that the underlying economic growth forecasts (they are policy objectives rather than forecasts) will not materialise. However, let us again assume the Department of Energy is correct. Moreover, let us fill the so-called 'policy gap' of some 15 GW in year 2000 with nuclear power since, if it occurs, it is not readily apparent how else it will be filled. Note that if it does not occur, the economic growth objectives will not be met unless, that is, we have found some way to drastically reduce the energy/output ratio. So we now have a new programme of some 56 GW as implied in the official policy.

If that official policy is correct, we cannot proceed on the assumption that the demand will be met from some other source. Many alternative technologists will dispute this, even if they were to accept the demand figures which they generally do not anyway. Now, recall that CBA asks the question 'what is the cost of not adopting the programme?'. If there are no alternative sources, the cost will be forgone electricity. Now the energy sector is of special interest because it not only supplies final demands like domestic heat, it also 'supports' other industrial sectors in so far as energy is an output which is combined with capital and labour to produce goods which individuals demand. The cost of not having a nuclear programme is therefore likely to be the gross domestic product we go without. We can make what are literally 'back of the envelope' calculations in order to get some idea of the magnitudes we are talking about.

In 1975 the United Kingdom consumed something like 340 million tonnes coal equivalent (m.t.c.e.) of primary energy. For the year 2000 the forecasts suggest a consumption level of 560 m.t.c.e., an increase of some 64 per cent. The underlying economic growth assumption is that GDP will rise by 3 per cent per annum to 1990 and 2.4 per cent between 1990–2000, which is equivalent to nearly doubling the absolute level of GDP in 25 years, a 97.5 per cent increase to be exact. If we relate these two percentage increases, we get a kind of average energy coefficient of 0.66 (i.e. percentage growth in energy divided by percentage growth in GDP). Now, of the 220 m.t.c.e. *increase* in energy consumption by the year 2000, no less than 120 m.t.c.e. would come from nuclear power if the policy objectives are fulfilled and the 'policy gap' is met from nuclear sources. If the 'policy gap' is met in some other way, then nuclear's contribution is reduced to some 80 m.t.c.e. Supposing now that we abandon the nuclear programme immediately, then, making a few adjustments for existing ordered capacity, we see that the increase in energy consumption could only be some 100 m.t.c.e. to the year 2000, or about a 30 per cent increase. Relating this to GDP via our average energy coefficient means that GDP could rise by only 45 per cent compared to the 97.5 per cent in the official scenario.

In approximate terms, therefore, the 'cost' of going without our nuclear future could, on this basis, be expressed as a halving of the United Kingdom overall economic growth rate between 1975—2000. In annual terms an average annual growth rate for the period 1975—2000 of 2.75 per cent is reduced to 1.50 per cent, a loss of 1.25 per cent per annum.

The caveats to our GDP calculations are important. We do no more than list them here. We have assumed that GDP approximates in some way some gain in national welfare, that the official energy forecasts are correct, that the demand for electricity cannot be constrained by diverting some of its current uses to other sources, and that all non-nuclear energy sources combined cannot take up *any* of the demand assumed to be met by nuclear power; we have also assumed an immutable energy coefficient. To illustrate just one problem noted when we discussed the nature of cost—benefit, consider whether or not the 'lost' GDP is actually a cost or not. For we are all aware of a school of thought that declares economic growth to be *undesirable*. There can be no question that growth brings problems in the shape of depleted resources, pollution, congestion, social stress and so on. It may also bring added benefits in permitting us to remove or reduce inadequacies, improve health standards, and so on. This is no place to enter into this extensive and complex debate. It does serve to show, however, that what we have called a benefit from nuclear power will not be seen by some as a benefit at all. At the very least they would want to argue that we should subtract the costs of growth from the benefits. That is surely correct. Unfortunately, despite some heroic efforts (Nordhaus and Tobin, 1972) we have no real idea of what these costs are. We simply enter them in our balance sheet as a cost.

13.4.2   ROUTINE RADIATION

The expanded nuclear power programme will add to the routine release of radiation, the amount permitted by whatever safety standards are applied. There are any number of problems in handling this cost in a CBA study. The first is that we do not have scientific agreement of what the dose relationship is for low levels of radiation. The problem of course is that to find the scale of the incidence of morbidity and mortality, it is necessary to extrapolate backwards from high-dose experiences and to use the very limited evidence available on low-dose situations. On one analysis, that relationship is linear and goes through the origin, On another, there is a non-linearity which raises the incidence levels at low doses. Now, since our decisions about nuclear programmes may not wait for the 20 or even 50 years it will take to resolve this problem by monitoring the incidence of cancers in general and workforce populations, the best bet is to take a range of incidence as given by an optimist's and pessimist's view of the evidence.

The second problem is what to do about the money value of human life. But what the finite value of a life is remains problematic. The United Kingdom Department of Transport values a human life at about £40,000 when it evaluates road programmes. Court awards reveal an enormous disparity, while studies of 'implied' values — values obtained by looking at a life-saving or expending decision and seeing what that decision cost — reveal figures ranging from £50 for a child's life in the United Kingdom (implied by the decision *not* to enforce the use of childproof drug containers) to about £7 million in the United States (implied by the use of successional tests for colonic cancer). For discussion of implied values see Mooney (1977).

The third problem is that our extended nuclear programme will incur these mortality costs during and after the actual expansion phase. The power station built in the year 2000 will probably still be producing electricity and routine radiation releases in 2025. If we recall our earlier problem with the discount rate, we again see that the costs can be made to 'go away' if we use a positive discount rate.

Conceptually then the fabric of CBA is preserved. We take a range of mortality and morbidity probabilities as dictated by the scientific evidence, multiply this through to secure the total number of persons likely to suffer and multiply again by either a single valued estimate or a range of values for human life. In practice, it is questionable in the extreme if the 'monetisation' part of this exercise makes much sense, even if we accept, as we must, that life is not of infinite value.

13.4.3 NON-ROUTINE RADIATION

Along with routine radiation releases, we also have radiation arising from non-observance of safety levels. These may be accidents in the genuine sense, or culpable events that arise from a failure to observe safety regulations, or from a failure to ensure safety of design before construction, and so on. In most respects the problem for CBA is much the same as that for routine discharges.

13.4.4 WASTE MANAGEMENT

In discussing CBA in general terms we observed that the costs of waste management might be known with far more certainty than the probabilistic costs of radiation releases. The problems lie mainly with medium-active and high-active wastes. Much discussion has taken place on the disposal of high-active wastes in vitrified form to land-based or under seabed repositories. Less seems to be written about medium-active wastes (such as fuel element cladding) and which constitute about three times the volume of high-active waste for a given GW(e) of energy generation (Roberts, 1979). At the moment both types of waste are held in containers at various sites. The current objective in the United Kingdom is to dispose of high-active waste in vitrified form and for this purpose a vitrification plant is being built at Windscale, in Cumbria. The Marcoule site in France is apparently already experimenting with commercial-scale vitrified waste storage. It is unclear, at least to the outsider, what the 'final solution' is intended to be for medium-active waste. Sub-seabed disposal raises as many issues of concern as does land-based disposal, if not more so given the common property nature of the seas (Deese, 1978). Once again, this technological uncertainty makes the cost of waste management difficult to estimate.

13.4.5 PROLIFERATION

The risk of the diversion of plutonium (or for that matter, uranium) for military or terrorist use has attracted extensive attention. The reasons for the concern are readily found in the important papers by Nye (1978) and Gilinsky (1977). To put the matter in perspective, plutonium diversion is not the *only* way of increasing the risk of nuclear weapons proliferation. Indeed, Marshall (1978) may well be right in saying that it is not the most important. None the less, it has been seen as sufficiently significant for the United States actually to declare a policy of caution on the reprocessing fuel cycle. The significance of that decision can be measured by further considering that it implies possibly extensive delay in a fast-reactor programme (the delay depends on existing stocks of plutonium and the demands for military use).

As far as CBA is concerned all that matters is that there is a *positive* risk associated with the reprocessing option. To say that other risks are more important, or that the additional risk is small, does not obviate the fact that it exists as a cost to be debited to nuclear power programmes. Proposals have been made for making fuels in store or under transport 'too dangerous' to handle, but there again appears to be extensive dispute about 'spiking' proposals and certainly no indication of their cost which could be enormous if special fabrication plant is required.

So, if the risk is positive we need to consider the hazard — i.e. the actual cost of damage if the risk materialises. Here the process of monetisation stops. The risk might after all be one of a war between any two nations. The risk of world war would seem remote if only because plutonium diversion would be required on a vast scale to establish an armoury of nuclear weapons of any significance. Again, human life does not have infinite value so that even a national war, or terrorist threats that cause loss of life on whatever scale, have finite cost. But it would be fanciful to suggest that that cost is quantifiable.

13.4.6 CIVIL LIBERTIES

An expanded nuclear-power programme necessarily involves an increase in the infringement of civil liberties. This much has been accepted by the United Kingdom Royal Commission on Environmental Pollution (1976), and by Mr Justice Parker in his report on the Windscale Inquiry (Parker, 1978).

Widdicombe (1978) has pointed to the need for such surveillance given the small quantities of plutonium needed to demolish a city block with a homemade bomb, the capability for which unquestionably exists. If no threats against governments have been made in the United Kingdom, they have in the United States where more than forty 'nuclear' threats have been made against industrial plants or cities since 1970 (Widdicombe, 1978). Moreover, the threat is sufficient, since without an accounting convention that locates and identifies the amount of plutonium in store or transit down to the last kilogramme, threats made without possession of plutonium are at the very least credible.

13.5   The Cost—Benefit Balance-sheet

We can now draw up an outline CBA balance-sheet. As soon as it is drawn up it will be easy to see just how intractable the issue of evaluating nuclear futures in economic terms is. We then consider a somewhat different framework that bears on the intergenerational problem and finally look at what it all might mean for decision-making procedures.

Benefits	*Costs*
(1) Gain in GDP	(2) The social costs of the extra GDP (not known)
	(3) Routine radiation (equal to a range of probabilities of death for an individual multiplied by individuals at risk multiplied by the value of human life — quantifiable in principle)
	(4) Accidents and human failure (probabilities themselves uncertain)
	(5) Waste management (quantifiable, but note relevance of discount rate)
	(6) Proliferation (neither risk nor cost quantifiable)
	(7) Civil liberties (neither risk nor cost quantifiable)

Note all the caveats that have been made with respect to the various items, especially the GDP calculation. With these in mind, we can at least ask the question — are items (2) to (7) worth the gain in GDP? Having asked it, we can see that even this piece of contingency analysis hardly helps. What it does do is 'order' the issues and remind us that there is a cost of going without nuclear power, assuming of course that economic growth is a 'good thing'. Note too that the answer to the question would almost certainly be easier to give if we accepted the use of positive discount rates. For then many of the costs simply vanish because they are borne decades hence and not now.

13.6   A Regret Matrix Approach

Throughout, we have noted the relevance of discounting to the decision in question. The use of a positive rate is obviously unsatisfactory if we have any concern for future generations. Is there any way of considering how they might be integrated? Page (1977) has proposed that we adopt the approach suggested by Rawls (1972) in which we imagine ourselves in some kind of intergenerational assembly, but in such a way that each representative cannot be sure to which generation he will be allocated when 'returned' to society. In this way each one is forced to consider the interests of each generation since he will end up being a member of any one of them. In these circumstances it is argued that he will opt for a choice which minimises the cost across generations. They may well involve sacrificing the forgone GDP for present and immediate generations in favour of 'benign' (i.e. renewable) technologies in later generations.

Another way of presenting the picture is in the form of a 'regret' matrix. This shows us the cost to any future generation if we make a decision now which they disagree with or agree with. Such a picture is outlined below.

EXISTING DECISION ON NPP[1]	FUTURE GENERATION DECISION ON NP[2]	IS THERE FUTURE GENERATION REGRET?	OPTION AND NET COST TO FUTURE GENERATIONS
Yes	Yes	No	Proceed. Net cost = 0
Yes	No	Yes	Halt NP. Net cost = inherited waste and damage, plus decommissioning
No	Yes	Yes	Begin NPP. Net cost = forgone economic benefits before NPP 'on stream'
No	No	No	Proceed. Net cost = 0

Notes

(1) NPP — expanded nuclear-power programme. All answers assume *net* benefits have been evaluated with respect to the voting population.

(2) NP — inherited nuclear-power programme.

Again, the matrix does not solve any problems. But what it does do is spell out the exclusive options and costs of having generations disagreeing with each other on a nuclear-power programme. Note that in the two 'regret' contexts, the trade-off can be presented in terms of forgone GDP and the cost of inherited waste and decommissioning: that is, a 'no' decision now is assumed here to be based on an assessment of the *net* costs to the current generation, so that the cost of this decision *to the future generation* is the forgone GDP *to them* if they vote for nuclear power and have to wait for a programme to be implemented. A 'yes' vote now can be reversed by a future generation but they cannot reverse the problem of managing and perhaps suffering from inherited waste. If this inherited waste problem is judged more important than forgone GDP to future generations, then a heavier weight would be attached to the regret in the yes/no sequence than in no/yes sequence. The highest net cost then occurs if the current generation votes for a nuclear programme that the next generation does not want. If forgone GDP is judged more important, then the highest cost will occur in the no/yes sequence.

Quite what future generations will want is of course an unknown. We do not dwell on the issue here save to make two points. First, what they want could well be decided by what want-information procedure we adopt now. In this respect, the future generation is 'educated' to accept the decisions of their predecessors. Second, generations overlap so that we cannot avoid judging *for* future generations. Decisions made now are decisions for our children and grandchildren: if we care about them at all we should at least ask the questions implicit in the regret matrix approach.

Notes

Chapter 1

1. Anyone doubting the significance of this remark should read the excellent analyses of the U.K. decisions to build Concorde and to adopt the Advanced Gas-Cooled Reactor nuclear programme. See P. D. Henderson, 'Two British Errors: their Probable Size and Possible Lessons', *Oxford Economic Papers*, **29**, 2, July 1977.

Chapter 4

1. The sections of this chapter on the internal rate of return closely follow the discussion in Hawkins and Pearce (1971) and Dasgupta and Pearce (1972). Mishan's terminal value approach is discussed in his article, Mishan (1967), and a more extended discussion can be found in Mishan (1975). For programming treatments of the more complex problems that arise with such problems as multi-period rationing see Weingartner (1963). On optimal time-phasing see Marglin (1963). Numerous books exist on project evaluation criteria for private investment – see Merrett and Sykes (1963); Bierman and Smidt (1975).

2. Real numbers consist of any integers (1, 2, 3, . . .), any ratios of integers (fractions) and any 'irrational' numbers – i.e. numbers in the integer continuum but which cannot be expressed as integer ratios.

Chapter 8

1. Because of the confusing terminology that has arisen, one may find the whole externality up to X_p in Figure 8.1 being defined as 'Pareto-relevant' since it is clearly relevant to determining the optimum, or just that part between X_s and X_p, since the optimal level of externality is 'Pareto-irrelevant' in that it does not affect the Paretian conditions for optimality overall. Again, readers are warned of the differences in terminology in the literature.

2. Slightly modified from figure 2 in Loehr and Sandler (1979).

3. We do not specify here the *nature* of these demand curves. The measure of net benefits secured will depend on whether they are income-compensated curves, Marshallian demand curves, etc.

4. The use of the word 'club' is more than illustrative since what is being discussed are the elements of the *theory of clubs*. For the seminal article see Buchanan (1965).

5. For more detail and a critique of hedonic theory in respect of noise nuisance see Edwards and Pearce (1979).

6. Taking a utility function of the form $U = U(a_1 \ldots a_n)$, then the function is homogeneous if multiplying the independent variables $a_1 \ldots a_n$, by some factor d enables us to alter the value of the function itself by d^k. That is, $U(dc_1 \ldots dc_n) = d^k \cdot U(c_1 \ldots c_n)$. The power k is the degree of the function – i.e. in this case the utility function is homogeneous of degree k.

Chapter 9

1. U.K. Treasury (1978), *The Nationalised Industries*, Cmnd 7131 (London: HMSO).

2. A worked example may help. For project A we have a benefit flow of:

$$-1.0 + 0.16 + 0.16 + \cdots + 0.16 \text{ to year 20.}$$

Discounted at 10% this flow becomes:

$$-1.0 + 0.16 \sum_{t=1}^{t=20} \frac{1}{(1+0.1)^t}.$$

To find the value of the last expression (a geometric progression) we may calculate it directly or refer to discount tables most of which give values for the sum of discount *factors* where the sum in any year, n, is given by

$$S = \frac{1 - (1+r)^{-n}}{r}.$$

Thus, the above cash flow reduces to

$$-1.0 + 0.16 (8.51) = -1 + 1.36 = 0.36$$

which is the NPV shown in Table 9.2.

3. Note that we have assumed D is *divisible* and, in addition, that returns per unit of expenditure on D are invariant with the size of that expenditure. In practice, *both* assumptions are likely not to be realised.

4. The literature is somewhat confused on the nature of value judgements in Paretian theory. The essential value judgement is that individuals' preferences shall count. This need not be at all the same thing as saying 'consumers are the best judges of their own welfare'. The two are frequently treated as if they are the same statement and both are referred to as 'consumer sovereignty'. In fact only the former is relevant to consumer sovereignty since the latter is not, strictly, a value judgement at all. It is a descriptive statement which reduces to 'the individual knows what he wants' or, even more simply, to 'I know what I like'. These statements are positive statements.

5. Elasticity is given by

$$e = \frac{d^2U \cdot dC}{dU \cdot dC^2} \cdot C$$

and we have

$$\frac{d^2U}{dC^2} = b \cdot a \cdot C^{b-1}$$

and

$$\frac{dC}{dU} = \frac{1}{a \cdot C^b}$$

so that

$$e = \frac{b \cdot a \cdot C^{b-1}}{a \cdot C^b} \cdot C = \frac{b}{C} \cdot C = b.$$

6. Alternatively, we can think of $\lambda = I/K$ as a shadow price of capital such that the right hand expression in equation (9.20) would be

$$\left[\lambda \cdot \frac{r}{s} + (1 - \lambda) \right]$$

7. In some printings of Pearce (1971) and Dasgupta and Pearce (1972), some of the equations relating to this derivation are misprinted so that the left-hand side includes the discount rate *s* twice. This is incorrect and the correct formulation is given here.

Chapter 12

1. This chapter is based on earlier work by D. W. Pearce and R. Kerry Turner of the School of Environmental Sciences at the University of East Anglia. Special thanks are owed to Kerry Turner for permitting the material to be adapted for this use, not least since a major part of the contribution is his.

References

Chapter 1

Graaff, J. de V. (1957), *Theoretical Welfare Economics* (Cambridge: Cambridge U.P.).

Hicks, J. R. (1939), 'The Foundations of Welfare Economics', *Economic Journal*, **49**, June.

Kaldor, N. (1939), 'Welfare Comparisons of Economics and Interpersonal Comparisons of Utility', *Economic Journal*, **49**, Sep.

Little, I. M. D. (1957), *A Critique of Welfare Economics*, 2nd ed. (Oxford: Oxford U.P.) (1st ed. 1951).

Chapter 2

Arrow, K. J. (1963), *Social Choice and Individual Values*, 2nd ed. (New York: Wiley).

Dasgupta, A. K., and Pearce, D. W. (1972), *Cost–Benefit Analysis: Theory and Practice* (London: Macmillan).

Harberger, A. C. (1971), 'Three Basic Postulates for Applied Welfare Economics: An Interpretative Essay', *Journal of Economic Literature*, **9**, Sep.

Hunt, E. K. (1968), 'Orthodox Economic Theory and Capitalist Ideology', *Monthly Review*, reprinted in Hunt and Schwartz, op. cit.

Hunt, E. K., and Schwartz, J. (1972), *A Critique of Economic Theory* (Harmondsworth: Penguin Books).

Peacock, A., and Rowley, C. (1972), 'Pareto Optimality and the Political Economy of Liberalism', *Journal of Political Economy*, May/June.

Peacock, A., and Rowley, C. (1975), *Welfare Economics: A Liberal Restatement* (London: Martin Robertson).

Self, P. (1972), *Econocrats and the Policy Process* (London: Macmillan).

Sen, A. (1970), 'The Impossibility of a Paretian Liberal', *Journal of Political Economy*, Jan.

Wildavsky, A. (1966), 'The Political Economy of Efficiency', *Public Administration Review*, XXVI, **4**, Dec.

Williams, A. (1971), 'Cost Benefit Analysis: Bastard Science or Insidious Poison in the Body Politick?', in *Cost Benefit and Cost Effectiveness*, ed. J. N. Wolfe (London: Allen & Unwin).

Chapter 3

Atkinson, A. B. (1973), 'How Progressive Should Income Tax Be?', in *Essays in Modern Economics*, ed. M. Parkin (London: Macmillan).

Boadway, R. (1976), 'Integrating Equity and Efficiency in Applied Welfare Economics', *Quarterly Journal of Economics*, **90**, Nov.

Brown, C. V., and Dawson, D. A. (1969), *Personal Taxation, Incentives and Tax Reform* (London: Political and Economic Planning).

Dalvi, M. Q., and Nash, C. A. (1977), 'The Redistributive Impact of Road Investment', in *Urban Transportation Planning*, eds. P. Bonsall, M. Q. Dalvi and P. J. Hills (London: Abacus Press).

Feldstein, M. S. (1972), 'Distributional Equity and Optimal Structure of Public Prices', *American Economic Review*, **62**, Mar.

Foster, C. D. (1966), 'Social Welfare Functions in Cost–Benefit Analysis', in *Operational Research and the Social Sciences*, ed. J. Lawrence (London: Tavistock Publications).

Harberger, A. C. (1971), 'Three Basic Postulates for Applied Welfare Economics', *Journal of Economic Literature*, **9**, Sep.

Hicks, J. R. (1939), 'The Foundations of Welfare Economics', *Economic Journal*, **49**, June.

Kaldor, N. (1939), 'Welfare Comparisons of Economics and Interpersonal Comparisons of Utility', *Economic Journal*, **49**, Sep.

Krutilla, J. V. and Eckstein, O. (1958), *Multiple Purpose River Development* (Baltimore: Resources for the Future Inc.).

Lichfield, N. (1968), 'Economics in Town Planning', *Town Planning Review*, **39**, Apr.

Little, I. M. D. (1957), *A Critique of Welfare Economics*, 2nd ed. (Oxford: Oxford U.P.).

Mishan, E. J. (1974), 'Flexibility and Consistency in Project Evaluation', *Economica*, **41**, June.

Musgrave, R. A. (1969), 'Cost–Benefit Analysis and the Theory of Public Finance', *Journal of Economic Literature*, vol. 7, no. 3.

Nash, C. A., Pearce, D. W. and Stanley, J. K. (1975), 'An Evaluation of Cost–Benefit Analysis Criteria', *Scottish Journal of Political Economy*, June.

Samuelson, P. A. (1950), 'The Evaluation of Real National Income', *Oxford Economic Papers*, N.S., **2**, Jan.

Scitovsky, T. (1941), 'A Note on Welfare Propositions in Economics', *Review of Economic Studies*, **9**.

Theil, H. and Brooks, R. B. (1970), 'How Does the Marginal Utility of Income Change When Real Income Changes?', *European Economic Review*, **2**, Winter.

Weisbrod, B. (1968), 'Income Redistribution Effects and Benefit–Cost Analysis', in *Problems in Public Expenditure Analysis*, ed. S. B. Chase (Washington: Brookings Institution).

Chapter 4
Bierman, H. and Smidt, S. (1975), *The Capital Budgeting Decision*, 4th ed. (London: Macmillan).

Dasgupta, A. J. and Pearce, D. W. (1972), *Cost–Benefit Analysis: Theory and Practice* (London: Macmillan).

Hawkins, C. J. and Pearce, D. W. (1971), *Capital Investment Appraisal* (London: Macmillan).

Marglin, S. (1963), *Approaches to Dynamic Investment Planning* (Amsterdam: North-Holland Publishing Co.).

Merrett, A. J. and Sykes, A. (1963), *The Finance and Analysis of Capital Projects* (London: Longman).

Mishan, E. J. (1967), 'A Proposal Normalisation Procedure for Public Investment Criteria', *Economic Journal*, Dec.

Mishan, E. J. (1975), *Cost–Benefit Analysis*, 2nd ed. (London: Allen & Unwin).

Weingartner, H. M. (1963), *Mathematical Programming and the Analysis of Capital Budgeting Problems* (New Jersey: Prentice-Hall).

Chapter 5
Arrow, K. and Fisher, A. C. (1974), 'Environmental Preservation, Uncertainty and Irreversibility', *Quarterly Journal of Economics*, May.

Arrow, K. and Lind, R. C. (1970), 'Uncertainty and the Evaluation of Public Investment Decisions', *American Economic Review*, **60**, June.

Cicchetti, C. J. and Freeman, A. (1971), 'Option Demand and Consumer Surplus: Further Comment', *Quarterly Journal of Economics*, Aug.

Dasgupta, A. and Pearce, D. W. (1972), *Cost–Benefit Analysis: Theory and Practice* (London: Macmillan).

Fisher, A. C. (1974), 'Environmental Externalities and the Arrow–Lind Theorem', *American Economic Review*.

Henderson, P. D. (1977), 'Two British Errors: Their Probable Size and Possible Consequences', *Oxford Economic Papers*, **29**, 2, July.

Hirshleifer, J. and Shapiro, D. (1963), 'The Treatment of Risk and Uncertainty', *Quarterly Journal of Economics*, **77**, 4.

Hirshleifer, J. (1965), 'Investment Decisions Under Uncertainty: A Choice–Theoretic Approach', *Quarterly Journal of Economics*, **79**, 4.

Krutilla, J. and Fisher, A. C. (1975), *The Economics of Natural Environments* (Baltimore: Johns Hopkins Press).

Chapter 6

Boadway, R. (1974), 'A Note on the Welfare Foundations of Cost–Benefit Analysis', *Economic Journal*, **84**, Dec.

Foster, C. D. (1960), 'Surplus Criteria for Investment', *Bulletin of Oxford University Institute of Economics and Statistics*, **22**, Nov.

Foster, C. D. and Neuberger, H. (1974), 'The Ambiguity of the Consumers' Surplus Measure of Welfare Change', *Oxford Economic Papers*, N.S., **26**, Mar.

Gwilliam, K. M. and Nash, C. A. (1972), 'The Evaluation of Urban Road Schemes – A Comment', *Applied Economics*, **4**, Dec.

Hicks, J. R. (1940), 'The Rehabilitation of Consumers' Surplus', *Review of Economic Studies*, **8**, Feb.

Hicks, J. R. (1943), 'The Four Consumers' Surpluses', *Review of Economic Studies*, **11**, Feb.

Hicks, J. R. (1956), *A Revision of Demand Theory* (Oxford: Oxford U.P.).

Hotelling, H. (1938), 'The General Welfare in Relation to Problems of Taxation and of Railway and Utility Rates', *Econometrica*, **6**, Apr.

Mishan, E. J. (1959), 'Rent as a Measure of Welfare Change', *American Economic Review*, **49**, June.

Mishan, E. J. (1968), 'What is Producers' Surplus?', *American Economic Review*, **58**, Dec.

Pigou, A. C. (1920), *The Economics of Welfare* (London: Macmillan).

Samuelson, P. A. (1941), *Foundations of Economic Analysis* (Cambridge, Mass.: Harvard U.P.).

Samuelson, P. A. (1950), 'The Evaluation of Real National Income', *Oxford Economic Papers*, N.S., **2**, Jan.

Chapter 7

Brown, C. V. and Dawson, D. A. (1969), *Personal Taxation Incentives and Tax Reform* (London: Political and Economic Planning).

Haveman, R. H. and Krutilla, J. V. (1968), *Unemployment, Idle Capacity and the Evaluation of Public Expenditures* (Baltimore: Johns Hopkins Press).

Heggie, I. G. (1976), 'Practical Problems in Implementing Accounting Prices', in *Using Shadow Prices*, eds. I. M. D. Little and M. F. G. Scott (London: Heinemann).

Little, I. M. D. (1951), 'Direct Versus Indirect Taxes', *Economic Journal*, **61**, Sep.

Little, I. M. D. and Mirrlees, J. A. (1974), *Project Appraisal and Planning for Developing Countries* (London: Heinemann).

McKean, R. (1968), 'The Use of Shadow Prices', in *Problems in Public Expenditure Analysis*, ed. S. B. Chase (Washington: Brookings Institution).

National Board for Prices and Incomes (1970), *The Price of Coal*, Cmnd 4455 (London: HMSO) Report no. 153.

Pearce, D. W. and Nash, C. A. (1973), 'The Evaluation of Urban Motorway Schemes: A Case Study – Southampton', *Urban Studies*, June.

Posner, M. V. (1973), *Fuel Policy: A Study in Applied Economics* (London: Macmillan).

Turvey, R. (1971), *Economic Analysis and Public Enterprise* (London: Allen & Unwin).

Chapter 8

Baumol, W. and Bradford, D. (1972), 'Detrimental Externalities and Non-Convexity of the Production Set', *Economica*, May.

Baumol, W. and Oates, W. (1975), *The Theory of Environmental Policy* (New Jersey: Prentice-Hall).

Bohm, P. (1971), 'An Approach to the Problem of Estimating Demand for Public Goods', *Swedish Journal of Economics*, **73**, 1.

Buchanan, J. (1965), 'An Economic Theory of Clubs', *Economica*, **32**.

Edwards, R. and Pearce, D. W. (1979), 'The Monetary Evaluation of Noise Nuisance: Implications for Noise Abatement Policy', in *Progress in Resource Management and Environmental Planning*, eds. T. O'Riordan and R. d'Arge (Chichester and New York: Wiley) vol. I.

Freeman, A. M. (1979), *The Benefits of Environmental Quality* (Baltimore: Johns Hopkins Press).

Groves, T. and Loeb, G. (1975), 'Incentives and Public Inputs', *Journal of Public Economics*, **4**.

Gwilliam, K. and Nash, C. (1972), 'Evaluation of Urban Road Investments: A Comment', *Applied Economics*, **4**, Dec.

Lindahl, E. (1958), 'Just Taxation: A Positive Solution', in *Classics in the Theory of Public Finance*, eds. R. Musgrave and A. Peacock (London: Macmillan).

Loehr, W. and Sandler, T. (1979), 'On the Public Character of Goods', in *Public Goods and Public Policy* (California: Sage).

Samuelson, P. (1954), 'Pure Theory of Public Expenditures', *Review of Economics and Statistics*, **36**.

Samuelson, P. (1955), 'Diagrammatic Exposition of a Theory of Public Expenditure', *Review of Economics and Statistics*, **37**.

Tideman, T. and Tullock, G. (1976), 'A New and Superior Process for Making Social Choices', *Journal of Political Economy*, Dec.

Chapter 9

Baumol, W. J. (1968), 'On the Social Rate of Discount', *American Economic Review*, Dec.

Dasgupta, A. and Pearce, D. W. (1972), *Cost–Benefit Analysis: Theory and Practice* (London: Macmillan).

Eckstein, O. (1961), 'A Survey of the Theory of Public Expenditure Criteria', in NBER, *Public Finances: Needs, Sources and Utilisation* (Princeton: Princeton U.P.).

Feldstein, M. (1965), 'The Derivation of Social Time Preference Rates', *Kyklos*, **18**.

Feldstein, M. (1972), 'The Inadequacy of Weighted Discount Rates', in *Cost–Benefit Analysis*, ed. R. Layard (Harmondsworth: Penguin Books).

Flemming, J. S. *et al.* (1976), 'The Cost of Capital, Finance and Investment', *Bank of England Bulletin*, **16**, 2.

Henderson, P. D. (1977), 'Two British Errors: Their Probable Size and Some Possible Lessons', *Oxford Economic Papers*, July.

Marglin, S. (1967), *Public Investment Criteria* (London: Allen & Unwin).

Page, T. (1977), *Conservation and Economic Efficiency* (Baltimore: Johns Hopkins Press).

Pearce, D. W. (1971), *Cost–Benefit Analysis* (London: Macmillan).

Scitovsky, T. (1941–2), 'A Note on Welfare Propositions in Economics', *Review of Economic Studies*, **9**.

Scott, A. (1977), 'The Test Rate of Discount and Changes in the Base-Level Income in the United Kingdom', *Economic Journal*, June.

Sen, A. K. (1967), 'Isolation, Assurance and the Social Rate of Discount', *Quarterly Journal of Economics*, Feb.

Chapter 10

Little, I. M. D. and Mirrlees, J. A. (1968), *Manual of Industrial Project Analysis for Developing Countries* (Paris: OECD).

Little, I. M. D. and Mirrlees, J. A. (1974), *Project Appraisal and Planning for Developing Countries* (London: Heinemann).

McKean, R. (1968), 'The Use of Shadow Prices', in *Problems in Public Expenditure Analysis*, ed. S. B. Chase (Washington: Brookings Institution).

Marglin, S., Sen, A. and Dasgupta, P. (1972), *Guidelines for Project Evaluation* (Vienna: United Nations).

Mazumdar, D. (1974), *The Rural–Urban Wage Gap, Migration and the Shadow Wage* (Washington: World Bank Publications).

Mishan, E. J. (1974), 'Flexibility and Consistency in Project Appraisal', *Economica*, N.S., **41**, Feb.

Sen, A. K. (1972), 'Control Areas and Accounting Prices: An Approach to Economic Evaluation', *Economic Journal*, **82**, Special Issue.

Squire, L. and Van der Tak, H. G. (1975), *Economic Analysis of Projects* (Baltimore: Johns Hopkins Press).

Chapter 11

Anand, S. (1976), 'Little–Mirrlees Appraisal of a Highway Project', *Journal of Transport Economics and Policy*, **10**.

Beesley, M. E., Coburn, T. M. and Reynolds, D. J. (1960), *The London–Birmingham Motorway – Traffic and Economics* (London: Department of Scientific and Industrial Research) Road Research Laboratory Technical Paper No. 46.

Dalvi, M. Q. and Nash, C. A. (1977), 'The Redistributive Impact of Road Investment', in *Urban Transportation Planning*, eds. P. Bonsall, M. Q. Dalvi and P. J. Hills (London: Abacus Press).

Dodgson, J. S. (1974), 'Motorway Investment, Industrial Transport Costs and Subregional Growth – A Case Study of the M 62', *Regional Studies*, **8**.

Edwards, R., Pearce, D. W. and Harris, A. (1979), *Social Incidence of Environmental Costs and Benefits* (London: Social Science Research Council) Mar.

Foster, C. D. and Beesley, M. E. (1963), 'Estimating the Social Benefit of Constructing an Underground Railway in London', *Journal of the Royal Statistical Society*, series A, **126**.

Friedlander, A. F. (1965), *The Interstate Highway System* (Amsterdam: North-Holland Publishing Co.).

Ghosh, D., Lees, D. and Seal, W. (1975), 'Optimal Motorway Speed and Some Valuations of Time and Life', *Manchester School*, **43**.

Gwilliam, K. M. (1970), 'The Indirect Effects of Highway Investment', *Regional Studies*, **4**.

Gwilliam, K. M. and Nash, C. A. (1972), 'Evaluation of Urban Road Investments: A Comment', *Applied Economics*, **4**.

Harrison, A. J. and Quarmby, D. (1969), 'The Value of Time', in *Cost—Benefit Analysis*, ed. R. Layard (Harmondsworth: Penguin Books).

Irvin, G. W. (1975), *Roads and Redistribution* (Geneva: International Labour Office).

Leitch, Sir G. (1978), (Chairman), *Report of the Advisory Committee on Trunk Road Assessment* (London: HMSO).

Little, I. M. D. and Scott, M. FG., eds. (1976), *Using Shadow Prices* (London: Heinemann).

Majumdar, J. (1973), 'Economic Choice of Railway Traction', in *First International Symposium on Transportation Research*, Bruges (Chicago: Transportation Research Forum).

Marshall, W. (1978), *Nuclear Power and the Proliferation Issue*. Graham Young Memorial Lecture, University of Glasgow, 24 February (University of Glasgow, Glasgow).

Mishan, E. J. (1971), 'Evaluation of Life and Limb: A Theoretical Approach', *Journal of Political Economy*, **72**.

Serpa, A. C. de (1971), 'A Theory of the Economics of Time', *Economic Journal*, **81**, Dec.

Stanley, J. K. and Nash, C. A. (1977), 'The Evaluation of Urban Transport Improvements', in *Urban Transport*, ed. D. A. Hensher (Cambridge: Cambridge U.P.).

Starkie, D. N. M. and Johnson, D. M. (1975), *The Economic Value of Peace and Quiet* (Farnborough: Saxon House).

Thomas, S. (1977), 'Road Investment and Pricing in Developing Countries', *Bulletin of Oxford University Institute of Economics and Statistics*, **39**, Aug.

Thomson, J. M. (1967), 'An Evaluation of Two Proposals for Traffic Restraint in Central London', *Journal of the Royal Statistical Society*, **130**.

Walters, A. A. (1961), 'The Theory and Measurement of Private and Social Cost of Highway Congestion', *Econometrica*, **29**.

Chapter 12

Bower, B. *et al.* (1971), 'Residuals Management in the Pulp and Paper Industry', *Natural Resources Journal*, Oct.

Bower, B. *et al.* (1973), 'Residuals in the Manufacture of Paper', *Journal of the Environmental Engineering Division*, ASCE, **99**.

Bower, B. (1975), 'Studies of Residuals Management in Industry', in *Economic Analysis of Environmental Problems*, ed. E. Mills (New York: National Bureau of Economic Research).

Grace, R. (1978), 'Metals Recycling: A Comparative National Analysis', *Resources Policy*, **4**, 4, Dec.

Little Inc., A. D. (1975), *Analysis of Demand and Supply for Secondary Fiber in the U.S. Paper and Paperboard Industry*, 3 vols (Cambridge, Mass.: A. D. Little Inc.).

Midwest Research Institute (1972), *Economic Studies in Support of Policy Formation on Resource Recovery*, unpublished data.

Pearce, D. W. (1979), *Waste Paper Recovery* (Paris: OECD).

Turner, R. K., Pearce, D. W. and Grace, R. (1977), 'The Economics of Waste Paper Recycling', in *Resource Conservation: Social and Economic Dimensions of Recycling*, eds. D. W. Pearce and I. Walter (New York and London: New York U.P. and Longman).

Turner, R. K. (1978), 'Local Authorities and Materials Recycling', *Journal of Environmental Management*, No. 2, May.

U.K. Advisory Group on Waste Paper Collection and Recycling (1975), *Survey of Waste Paper Salvage – England and Wales* (London: HMSO).

Wray, M. and Nation, M. (1977), *The Economics of Waste Paper Reclamation in England* (Hatfield: Hatfield Polytechnic).

Chapter 13

Deese, D. (1978), *Nuclear Power and Radioactive Waste* (Massachusetts: Heath Lexington).

Freeman, A. M. (1977), 'Why We Should Discount Intergenerational Effects', *Futures*, Oct.

Gilinsky, V. (1977), 'Nuclear Energy and Nuclear Proliferation', *Chemical and Engineering News*, 28 Nov.

Marshall, W. (1978), *Nuclear Power and the Proliferation Issue* (Graham Young Memorial Lecture, University of Glasgow, Glasgow).

Mooney, G. (1977), *The Value of Human Life* (London: Macmillan).

Nordhaus, W. and Tobin, J. (1972), 'Is Growth Obsolete?', in *50th Anniversary Colloquium of the National Bureau of Economic Research* (New York: Columbia U.P.).

Nye, J. (1978), 'Non Proliferation: A Long Term Strategy', *Foreign Affairs*, Apr.

Page, T. (1977), *Conservation and Economic Efficiency* (Baltimore: Johns Hopkins Press).

Parker, Mr Justice (1978), *Windscale Inquiry: Report* (London: HMSO).

Rawls, J. (1972), *A Theory of Justice* (Oxford: Oxford U.P.).

Roberts, L. (1979), 'Radioactive Waste – Policy and Perspective', *Atom*, Jan.

U.K. Department of Energy (1978), *Energy Policy*, Cmnd 7101 (London: HMSO).

U.K. Royal Commission on Environmental Pollution (1976), *Sixth Report: Nuclear Power and the Environment*, Cmnd 6618 (London: HMSO).

Widdicombe, D. (1978), 'Nuclear Power and Civil Liberties', in *Proceedings of Conference on Energy Requirements and the Fast Breeder Programme* (London: South Bank Polytechnic) Nov.

Index